ADVANCES IN SERVICES MARKETING AND MANAGEMENT

RESEARCH AND PRACTICE

Volume 6 • 1997

ADVANCES IN
SERVICES MARKETING
AND MANAGEMENT
RESEARCH AND PRACTICE

Editors: TERESA A. SWARTZ
College of Business
California Polytechnic State University
San Luis Obispo

DAVID E. BOWEN
School of Management
Arizona State University West

DAWN IACOBUCCI
School of Management
Northwestern University

**THIS VOLUME IS PUBLISHED IN CONJUNCTION WITH THE
FIRST INTERSTATE CENTER FOR SERVICES MARKETING
ARIZONA STATE UNIVERSITY**

VOLUME 6 • 1997

 **JAI PRESS INC.**

Greenwich, Connecticut   *London, England*

CONTENTS

LIST OF CONTRIBUTORS

Ravi S. Behara — George Mason University
Fairfax, Virginia

Deborah L. Cowles — Virginia Commonwealth University
Richmond, Virginia

Lawrence F. Cunningham — University of Colorado
Denver, Colorado

Ko de Ruyter — Maastricht University
Maastricht, The Netherlands

Richard Germain — Oklahoma State University
Stillwater, Oklahoma

Roger Hallowell — Harvard Business School
Boston, Massachusetts

Moonkyu Lee — Yonsei University
Seoul, Korea

Jos Lemmink — Maastricht University
Maastricht, The Netherlands

Sharron J. Lennon — The Ohio State University
Columbus, Ohio

Barbara Lutz — C.U.N.A. Mutual Group
Waverly, Iowa

Gian Luca Marzocchi — University of Bologna
Bologna, Italy

Jan Mattsson — Roskilde University
Roskilde, Denmark

Brian Moores   University of Manchester
                                    Manchester, United Kingdom

Michelle C. Paul   University of Maryland
                                    College Park, Maryland

Javier Reynoso   The Monterrey Institute of Technology
                                    Monterrey, Mexico

Benjamin Schneider   University of Maryland
                                    College Park, Maryland

Susan Schoenberger White   University of Maryland
                                    College Park, Maryland

Samia M. Siha   Kennesaw State University
                                    Kennesaw, Georgia

Nancy F. Stanforth   Oklahoma State University
                                    Stillwater, Oklahoma

Tracy L. Tuten   Randolph-Macon College
                                    Ashland, Virginia

Martin Wetzels   Maastricht University
                                    Maastricht, The Netherlands

Clifford E. Young   University of Colorado
                                    Denver, Colorado

PREFACE

This series exists to present the latest thinking on services marketing and management. That thinking can be found both in academic research across disciplines and in effective management practice across business functions. The uniqueness of this series, then, is that it focuses solely on services and that it emphasizes interdisciplinary and crossfunctional perspectives.

Much thought and energy went into the conception and launch of the series; however, its success would not have occurred without the support of services researchers and practitioners around the world. Papers in the series have come from authors located in 14 different countries. It should be evident that we are dedicated to presenting an international view of work on the forefront in services marketing and management.

It continues to be our hope that we can aid in breaking down the boundaries that exist across areas such as marketing, human resources and operations. These boundaries are present in academia (through disciplines such as organizational behavior and marketing) and in services organizations themselves (through functional areas such as human resources and sales). Just as leading-edge service organizations offer seamless service, we would like to offer seamless chapters. Here, more than anywhere else, there is the opportunity and encouragement to draw upon work from various fields that come to bear on services research and practice.

Advances in Services Marketing and Management: Research and Practice encourages and is committed to:

- longer, more in-depth treatment of a given topic than is accepted in traditional journals;
- empirical and/or conceptual work, both of which aid in advancing services research and practice;
- case studies that rigorously report the implementation of state-of-the-art service practice;
- interdisciplinary manuscripts that weave together research from various areas; and
- the timely presentation of thoughts and findings through an annual volume (with a shorter lag time between authorship and publication than is typical of many journals).

Our editorial policy is to provide the best and the latest in services research and practice. In that regard, we welcome query contacts as well as self-nomination of manuscripts for inclusion in the series. For more information including submission deadlines and manuscript guidelines, please contact one of the editors.

We are especially committed to encouraging more individuals to join the study of services marketing and management. It is our hope that future volumes of this series will contain the works of increasing numbers of newcomers to this challenging interdisciplinary field.

Much to Dave and Terri's delight, Dawn Iacobucci joined the team for this volume as guest editor while Steve Brown was on sabbatical. True to form, Dawn jumped in with both feet and went above and beyond the call of duty. Her energy and enthusiasm was a joy to experience and resulted in a better volume than Terri and Dave could have turned out. As for Steve, we hope he is well rested and reinvigorated as we welcome him back for the next volume.

Again, we continue to embrace the reality that services is a fun and exciting field of study. No matter where we go or what we do, we find ourselves in the midst of a live case study. For our old friends in services, we thank you for sharing this journey with us. For those new to the field, we say, "Welcome aboard!"

We encourage your support, participation and feedback.

Teresa A. Swartz
David E. Bowen
Dawn Iacobucci

ACKNOWLEDGMENTS

This book is brought to you, the reader, through the auspices of the First Interstate Center for Services Marketing (FICSM) in the College of Business at Arizona State University. The editors wish to thank the Center, as well as its charter member firms, for sponsoring this volume and for encouraging the best in services scholarship. FICSM is committed to this series and to furthering the understanding of services marketing and management issues.

Many people contributed to this volume, most notably the authors of the papers. We especially thank these individuals for the quality of their work and for being part of this volume. Our faculty colleagues at California Polytechnic State University, Arizona State University West and Northwestern University also deserve praise for encouraging this endeavor and for providing us with ideas and suggestions. This volume was produced in a timely and quality manner because of the fine support people at our respective universities and especially the staffs at ASU's First Interstate Center for Services Marketing and the Department of Marketing.

Finally, we wish to thank four people by name. Dawn Iacobucci, Professor of Marketing at Northwestern University, has effectively served as guest co-editor for this particular volume, ably assuming Steve Brown's editing role while he was on sabbatical leave. Gayle Jerman, Vice President at JAI Press, has given invaluable help in guiding this series through the production process. Gretchen Rennebaum, FICSM Associate Director, provided direction and guidance to the operations and marketing of the volume. In addition, Patti Bockbrader served as project manager for this volume. Her excellent organizational skills and attention to detail have been critical to its success.

ABOUT THE FIRST INTERSTATE CENTER FOR SERVICES MARKETING

The First Interstate Center for Services Marketing (FICSM) in the College of Business at Arizona State University is a leading university-based center for the study and research of services marketing and management. The Center's objectives include:

- expanding the frontiers of knowledge in services marketing and management via research;
- enhancing executive and student education in the field based on a solid foundation of research; and
- incorporating cross-functional, cross-industry and global perspectives.

Following are some of the major issues being investigated by the Center: service quality, customer loyalty, relationship marketing, internal marketing, the service encounter, service recovery, the physical environment as it relates to service quality perceptions, service strategy and employee empowerment. Results of many of the studies have been published in leading journals and are available as part of the Center's working paper series.

A leader in the academic services community, FICSM helped originate the "Quality in Services" (QUIS) series. The first multidisciplinary, multinational symposia on service quality, these gatherings bring together highly regarded scholars and business executives. *Service Quality: Multidisciplinary and Multinational Perspectives*, the first book to examine service quality from various disciplinary and cultural viewpoints, grew out of QUIS-1 and was co-edited by FICSM Director Stephen W. Brown.

The Center and the Arizona State University Department of Marketing were selected to host the American Marketing Association's 16th and 13th annual faculty consortiums on the topics of strategic marketing management and services marketing, respectively. Marketing and other faculty from around the world who are involved with teaching and research related to strategic marketing management and services gathered to enhance the general knowledge in the field, to provide insight and aid in the development of skills in the teaching of these topics and to cover current research trends and opportunities.

The Center is also recognized by the business community as a leader in the field. It partners with 26 charter member firms, leading service companies and firms using service and quality as a competitive advantage. These members benefit from the Center's research, executive education and MBA summer internship program.

An initiative the Center has been actively involved with is the development of the nation's first fully integrated MBA in Services Marketing and Management at ASU. Mary Jo Bitner, FICSM Research Director, helped spearhead the College of Business' efforts. A cross-functional team of faculty has created an in-depth curriculum with strong real-world infusion via internships and course projects with firms.

The FICSM offers a select number of executive education programs. Most notable is the annual fall "Activating Your Firm's Service Culture" symposium, addressing the issues firms face as they move toward a more service- and quality-oriented culture. Another annual program, the Services Marketing and Management Institute, is co-sponsored with the American Marketing Association. Senior and emerging executives attending the mini-course in the spring gain an intensive and extensive education in the latest in services marketing and management. The Center's newest annual program, "The Service Advantage," is designed for information technology professionals in services marketing and is co-sponsored by the Information Technology Services Marketing Association. In addition, the Center selectively conducts customized educational programs for firms.

Firms participate in the Center through charter membership. A board of advisors composed of distinguished executives and university leaders provides guidance to the FICSM. The Center also benefits from close ties to the ASU Department of Marketing and its faculty members, many of whom are actively engaged in FICSM research and involved in Center educational programs.

Following are the Center's charter member firms: Allegiance Corp. (formerly Baxter Healthcare Corp.), Round Lake, IL; AT&T, Basking Ridge, NJ; Blue

Cross and Blue Shield, Phoenix, AZ; Boston Scientific Corp., Natick, MA; The Co-operators, Guelph, Ontario; Cummins Engine, Columbus, IN; Elrick and Lavidge, Chicago, IL; Falcon Cable TV, Los Angeles, CA; Federal Express, Memphis, TN; Ford Motor Co., Detroit, MI; Harley-Davidson, Milwaukee, WI; IBM Canada, Ltd., Scarborough, Ontario; IBM US, White Plains, NY; Johnson & Higgins, Phoenix, AZ; Johnson & Johnson Health Care Systems, Piscataway, NJ; Lucent Technologies, Basking Ridge, NJ; Marriott Corp., Washington, DC; MicroAge, Inc., Tempe, AZ; Prudential Real Estate Affiliates, Costa Mesa, CA; Rural/Metro Corp., Scottsdale, AZ; Samaritan Health System, Phoenix, AZ; Viad Corp (formerly The Dial Corp), Phoenix, AZ; Xerox Corp., Rochester, NY; Yellow Freight Systems, Inc., Overland Park, KS.

The Center can be contacted at the following address:

First Interstate Center for Services Marketing
Department of Marketing, College of Business
Arizona State University
PO Box 874106
Tempe, AZ 85287-4106
USA
Phone: (602) 965-6201
Fax: (602) 965-2180

EXECUTIVE SUMMARIES

RELATIONSHIP MARKETING: AN ORGANIZATIONAL PERSPECTIVE

Benjamin Schneider, Susan Schoenberger White and Michelle C. Paul

In the last five years or so, an approach to marketing that emphasizes retaining customers through the establishment of long-lasting relationships with them has emerged. Relationship marketing has been defined as an attempt "to establish, maintain, and enhance relationships with customers and other partners, at a profit, so that the objectives of the parties involved are met. This is achieved by a mutual exchange and fulfillment of promises" (Grönroos 1994, p. 9).

In the current paper, we apply this relationship marketing perspective to two previous studies conducted under the heading of service quality research. These past studies showed that organizational employees' perceptions of the climate and culture of their work environment are significantly correlated with customers' perceptions of the organization's service quality. We used the ideas of relationship marketing to pursue this general finding further by dividing the components of employees' perceptions of their work environment into those connoting a "relationship-oriented" service climate and culture strategy and those connoting a "transaction-oriented" climate and culture strategy. The former are work practices and beliefs with a focus on displaying care and concern for customers, while the latter are work practices and beliefs more focused on issues such as logistics and efficiency. We then asked whether or not the relationship-oriented practices were correlated with customer perceptions of service quality, and was this correlation stronger than the correlation between the transaction-oriented practices and customer perceptions of service quality. Our results indicate that both questions can be answered in the affirmative.

Based on these findings, we present some preliminary ideas on how to conceptualize the kinds of organizational climate and culture strategies that must be in place to promote the development and maintenance of long-term relationships with customers. We offer some suggestions to managers concerning what they might do to strengthen the relationship-oriented climate and culture perceived by their employees and we also offer some suggestions for future research.

DUAL COMPETITIVE ADVANTAGE FOR SERVICE FIRMS

Roger Hallowell

An examination of the strategic positioning of four service firms presents a puzzling phenomenon. These firms are both the cost leaders in their industries and differentiated in the services they provide. Further, they have maintained this position of dual competitive advantage for some years, suggesting that it is sustained. This paper presents detailed findings on two of the four firms examined, Southwest Airlines and The Vanguard Group of Mutual Funds. Its findings may apply to other firms in industries where labor is capable of differentiating the quality of service on a day-to-day basis and is an important component of cost.

Southwest Airlines and The Vanguard Group's dual competitive advantage is derived from management initiatives described in both the organizational-strategy and competitive-strategy literatures. The organizational or resource-based literature attributes the source of a firm's competitive advantage to organizational factors, specifically capabilities of core competencies. In contrast, the competitive-strategy literature focuses on a firm's strategic positioning in its environment and argues that strategic position is the source of competitive advantage. This research integrates the two perspectives, arguing that dual competitive advantage at the firms examined requires (1) organizational factors with strategic value, (2) positioning-based initiatives and (3) the interaction of the two.

Organizational theories of competitive advantage partially explain the ability of the firms examined to deliver service quality efficiently. These firms have organizational factors enabling them to gain commitment from front-line service providers to the goals of the organization.

Strategic positioning theories of competitive advantage also partially explain these firms' dual competitive advantage. Each of these firms has achieved a strategic position that requires strategic positioning choices which focus its operations on meeting specific needs of targeted customers. For example, Southwest Airlines flies only short-haul flights. Strategic focus facilitates operational focus that delivers low cost and high service relative to the less focused operations of competitors serving more needs and/or broader customer bases.

Interactive sources of competitive advantage are also important in explaining the existence of dual competitive advantage at these firms. Interactive sources occur when firms' positioning choices are consistent with, and reinforce, their organizational capabilities.

Estimates of the contribution of organizational and positioning-choice sources of competitive advantage illustrate that both contribute to cost leadership at Vanguard and Southwest. Studies of employee turnover (a behavioral proxy for commitment) and analysis of a natural experiment suggest that commitment, or commitment combined with interactive sources of competitive advantage, may be the source of sustainability for these firms' dual competitive advantage.

CARRY-OVER EFFECTS IN THE FORMATION OF SATISFACTION: THE ROLE OF VALUE IN A HOTEL SERVICE DELIVERY PROCESS

Ko de Ruyter, Jos Lemmink, Martin Wetzels and Jan Mattsson

Research in the field of service quality has reached increased levels of sophistication both in terms of conceptualization and measurement. The relationship between service quality and customer satisfaction has been thoroughly studied by numerous authors in the field. However, more recently a third contender for the attention of researchers has emerged: customer value. It is the objective of this paper to present a value-based approach to the measurement of service quality.

We discuss the relationship between service quality, customer satisfaction and customer value. Several authors have proposed conceptual frameworks in which service quality and customer satisfaction feature as distinct constructs. Generally, it is assumed that service quality precedes customer satisfaction. Value has not played a prominent role in services research. Both a narrow and a more elaborate perspective on customer value have been suggested. In most research, it has mainly been narrowly defined as "value-for-money." In our study, we discuss a more elaborate approach first brought forward by Hartman (1967, 1973). On the basis of Hartman's model, Mattsson (1991) suggested a framework incorporating three generic value dimensions: (1) emotional, (2) practical and (3) logical.

We applied this model in hotel settings in both The Netherlands and in Sweden. In our study, we partitioned the service delivery process into five stages: (1) check-in, (2) hotel room, (3) hotel restaurant, (4) breakfast and (5) check-out. Each of these five stages was evaluated on the three generic value dimensions. Furthermore, respondents rated their satisfaction with each stage. Finally, we proposed that carry-over effects might occur among the different stages of the hotel service delivery process.

Our analysis indicates that there are considerable differences between the two hotels in our study. Additionally, we found that carry-over effects exist and significantly affect stage satisfaction and consequently overall satisfaction. On the basis of our analysis, we suggest the following managerial implications. First, management should realize that the service delivery process in hotels is a chain of interrelated service encounters. Second, the customer's perception should be used to describe the service delivery process and to distinguish its composite stages. Third, the impact of carry-over effects should be taken into account when planning service improvements. Finally, on the basis of service evaluation patterns, different customer segments might be identified.

SALESPERSON SERVICE AND CUSTOMER SATISFACTION: THE IMPACT OF STORE POLICIES

Nancy F. Stanforth and Sharron J. Lennon

When dealing with a product failure, it is important that a store makes every effort to rectify the situation for the customer. Retail stores' policies may make it difficult for salespeople to resolve the situation or comply with customer requests. This inability to meet customers' requests may result in customers attributing blame for the situation to unfriendly or unhelpful salespeople. The norms model of customer satisfaction argues that customers know what they think "ought to" or "should" happen in a given situation. Evaluations of the situation are based on a comparison of what "did" happen and what "should have" happened. There is also some indication that gender of the customer may influence the evaluation. Men are thought to be more concerned with core competencies of salespeople while women are concerned equally with core and relational competencies. The purpose of this study was to examine the effects of store policies, customer expectations and respondent gender on satisfaction with the salesperson, satisfaction with retail store service, and salesperson and store evaluations in the context of retail apparel stores' response to product failure.

Two types of stores, one that appeared to sell expensive merchandise and one that appeared to sell inexpensive merchandise, were selected to determine the impact of customer expectations on salesperson and store evaluations in the case of product failure. Two policies were used, one with a resolution that required the customer to put forth effort to resolve the problem and the other with a resolution that required the salesperson to put forth the effort.

Three-hundred-and-sixty volunteer men and women participated in a two (customer expectations) by two (policies) by two (respondent gender) between subjects laboratory experiment. Results of MANOVA and ANOVA revealed main effects for policies and customer expectations, as well as an interaction between respondent gender and customer expectations. In general, respondents tended to be more satisfied and rated the salesperson more favorably when policies required salesperson effort. In addition, they tended to be more satisfied at stores for which they had low expectations than at stores for which they had high expectations. Finally, as compared to men, women tended to prefer to shop in stores for which they had high expectations. However, women reported being likely to shop at both types of stores, while men indicated a greater likelihood of shopping at stores for which they had low expectations.

AN HISTORICAL ANALYSIS OF MARKETING BY SERVICE ORGANIZATIONS: THE CASE OF PRE-1930 BANKING IN AMERICA

Richard Germain

The purpose of the research is to examine the practice of services marketing under a historical microscope. The following research question is addressed: in the past, did managers in service organizations adopt a marketing or service orientation? To provide an in-depth description, the analysis is limited to the pre-1930 U.S. banking industry.

The findings suggest that a service orientation increasingly developed between 1800 and 1930. First, banks addressed basic service issues. They understood service properties, including intangibility, heterogeneity and perishability, and translated these traits into a debate on the similarity of service and physical product marketing. By 1930, they understood the rudiments of gap theory and found practical ways to apply them. They understood the difference between the service being performed and the manner of performance, and how the latter impacted perceptions of "service quality." Bankers thus paid much attention to service quality determinants. They adopted technological and administrative innovations to provide faster service. They adjusted operating hours to suit customer needs, including 24-hour-a-day banks in major metropolitan areas. They took great pains to instill confidence in their institutions and were concerned about and acted upon noise, courtesy, architecture and accuracy.

Second, attention to customer needs is inferred not only from bankers' attitude toward service but also from their segmentation efforts. Evidence on two demographic variables (age and gender) and on consumption status (current, potential, past customers) is presented. Concerning age, banks developed special plans to encourage thrift among children, culminating with the widespread adoption of school savings banks. Concerning gender, many major U.S. banks operated a women's department: a special room (or rooms) reserved for female customers only. By 1930, these departments were managed by females and became a bank within a bank. Banks segmented the market on the basis of consumption status by developing central information files for current customers, employee new business campaigns to attract potential customers, and special plans dealing with dormant and past customers.

Finally, banks developed organizational structures to handle marketing and promotional activities. These first appeared around 1900, and by 1930 had developed into new business departments that combined responsibility for personal selling and advertising and served to coordinate related activities throughout the firm.

"MANAGEMENT SERVICE QUALITY" IN A SERVICES MARKETING SETTING

Deborah L. Cowles and Tracy L. Tuten

Customers' impressions of satisfaction and quality are shaped by services offered by a firm, by a firm's service providers (contact persons) and by the service encounter experience. However, the potential for managerial factors (e.g., policies, procedures, actions, organizational climate) to *directly* affect customer attitudes, perceptions and evaluations of services provided has not been explored. Typically, the role of management is represented through the service provider. For example, Grönroos (1990a, p. 14) focused on organizational variables such as structure, cross-functional cooperation and internal marketing as elements of managing the "moments of truth." However, such factors are described as playing an *indirect* role in shaping customer satisfaction and perceptions of service quality. The purpose of this study is to examine empirically whether customer perceptions of a service firm's management plays a *direct* role in creating satisfied customers.

The management service quality (MSQ) perspective assumes that customers make judgments about the quality of services provided to employees, just as they assess the quality of services provided to them. Further, the quality of management services is important because contact employees represent a corporate resource integral to the creation of customer satisfaction and the delivery of quality service. In the same way that satisfaction and perceptions of quality are impacted by management's care for physical property such as tangibles (Shostack 1977) and physical evidence (Bitner 1990), customers may also be influenced by management's care for human resources, particularly contact employees.

As a result, researchers hypothesized that (1) customers use evidence available to them during the service experience to assess MSQ and that (2) customer perceptions of MSQ relate positively with customer satisfaction and perceptions of service quality.

Research findings presented here support both hypotheses. Customers appear to use both directly observable evidence (e.g., an unresponsive manager/supervisor, employee negative word-of-mouth regarding management) and cues from which they draw inferences (e.g., consistency of service during previous visits, service recovery actions) to draw conclusions about the quality of management. Moreover, customers' MSQ assessments appear to have a direct impact on customer satisfaction and perceptions of service quality, in addition to its accepted impact via the contact person and service systems.

Clearly, as the service industry becomes increasingly competitive, the role of management will become more visible and more critical to the customer.

OPERATIONALISING THE QUALITY OF INTERNAL SUPPORT OPERATIONS IN SERVICE ORGANISATIONS

Javier Reynoso and Brian Moores

Services management is a relatively young academic discipline boasting only some two decades of research. As a consequence of the marketing background of many of those working in the area, a substantial body of the research has been focused on the *customer's perspective* of the service. In associating customer service affairs with organisational matters, however, some contributions relate to what Gummesson (1993) labels the *genesis of a service*. Some researchers, including, for example, Edvardsson (1991) and Kingman-Brundage (1991, 1989), are working on aspects related to service development and service design. Other authors such as, for example, Shostack (1992, 1987, 1984), have emphasised the importance of the production system that supports the encounters with the customer, whilst others have proposed conceptual models in which the internal interactions of the service provider's organisation are clearly illustrated (e.g., Eiglier and Langeard 1987; Grönroos 1990).

Due to the internal interactions which inevitably occur between departments in any company, organisational dynamics are of particular relevance for both the service production and its delivery in service organisations. In this paper, the more significant conclusions of those various researchers, particularly as they relate to the internal customer-supplier chain, are reviewed. This is followed by a description of a research project conducted to study the nature and characteristics of interdepartmental relationships in relation to customer service. The study consisted of both qualitative and quantitative stages, with the main part of the study involving British hospitals, including one in the private sector. The project included exploratory studies, design and development, pilot testing and empirical application of two separate instruments: an *internal customers' questionnaire* and an *internal suppliers' questionnaire*. Finally, an indication of the findings which emerged from the research is presented. The statistical analysis shows, first, that it is indeed possible to capture the characteristics of internal customer service as a set of readily understood dimensions. They could also be of considerable potential to managers intent on affecting improvements on the internal dynamics of service organisations. The findings reported here also show those organisational factors which appear to be facilitating or inhibiting the successful delivery of support services to other units.

THE APPLICATION OF GROUP TECHNOLOGY PRINCIPLES TO SERVICE OPERATIONS: A CASE STUDY

Samia M. Siha and Barbara Lutz

The concepts of group technology and cellular layout have been widely applied to manufacturing. The cellular layout in an organization facilitates the implementation of Just-In-Time (JIT). Reducing product flow, minimizing work-in-process and improving customer service and quality are some of the JIT objectives that can be accomplished through the use of the cellular layout. The same concepts can be applied to service organizations. This can be established by grouping processes and employees around the natural flow of information.

This paper presents a real-life application of the cellular organization to a medium-sized life insurance company, Century Life of America (CLA). At one time, this company used the "process-oriented" layout, where employees performing the same function were grouped together in one area (station) to carry out part of the process. This process arrangement caused many problems. File tracking, bottlenecks at different stations, long turnaround time and unacceptable levels of complaints from agents are just a few to mention.

The success of other life insurance companies with the cellular organization concept spurred CLA's management to choose this path. An implementation process model is reported. It is a four-stage model that entails assessment, analysis, implementation and evaluation. The new process organization proved successful and improvements in various areas of the operation are detailed. Decreases in turnaround time, more consistency in underwriting decisions, better service to the agents and reductions in bottlenecks and idle time are some of the reported benefits. The employees, who are an important part of the company, also benefit from the change. They are empowered to make their own decisions and challenged to higher levels of responsibility and accountability. Thus, the success of the cellular organization implementation at CLA is explained by five key elements: using more generalists than specialists, utilizing effective performance measures, listening to the customers, benchmarking and explaining the benefits to everyone.

However, there are a few negative factors in the cellular organization approach. These include the need for extra training time and possible lack of cooperation between groups who may tend to get territorial.

A CUSTOMER-BASED TAXONOMY OF SERVICES: IMPLICATIONS FOR SERVICE MARKETERS

Lawrence F. Cunningham, Clifford E. Young and Moonkyu Lee

The authors report their efforts to develop a service classification scheme from a customer perspective and provide managerial insights for service marketers. In contrast to Bowen's (1990) research in developing empirically based clusters, in the current research customers were asked in a survey about their feelings and perceptions regarding services in terms of seven key dimensions. These perceptions of services were used as a basis for the development of a taxonomy. Multidimensional scaling (MDS) was used in the study to show how classifying dimensions are related to each other, how services are related to each other and how different services are located in the multidimensional classification space.

Respondents were asked to rate each of the 11 services on seven classification dimensions. They were provided with an explanation and several examples for each of the dimensions, which were developed based on the literature. Data was collected through a survey with students in an evening MBA program at a major metropolitan university.

Means aggregating over respondents were calculated for each service on each rating scale. This matrix of means was then used as input to PREFMAP, a variant of MDS (Carroll 1972), to pictorially represent the services and classification properties. First, service dimensions were described in two-dimensional space with the 11 services overlaid on the seven service dimensions. Then, the 11 services themselves were described in two-dimensional space with the service dimensions overlaid on the services.

The result of the service dimension map was a two-dimensional space described by unique versus routine in the vertical axis and generic versus customized in the horizontal axis. The services were then overlaid on the two-dimensional space and were described in terms of the labeled axes. The result of the individual services map was a two-dimensional space described by necessary versus desired in the vertical axis and low customer involvement versus high customer involvement in the horizontal axis. Service classification dimensions were then overlaid on the two-dimensional space and described. Of the two sets of perceptual maps, the map defining the perceptual space with the service classifications with services overlaid on the space seems to provide a clearer understanding of the respondent-based perceptions of the services and their classifications.

THE ROLE OF MOOD AND HEDONIC ORIENTATION ON THE PERCEPTION OF WAITING

Gian Luca Marzocchi

An increasing amount of attention has recently been given to the psychology of waiting in a service setting. The central dichotomy pointed out in these contributions is the one between *operations management* and *perception management* as separate, but not conflicting, approaches to the waiting experience.

Operations management embodies the mainstream contributions to the management of capacity-constrained service organizations. The approach focuses on accurate blueprinting and reengineering of the service delivery system in order to achieve a process as quick and smooth as possible, reducing if not eliminating the insurgence of waits. *Perceptions management* takes a different path in tackling the waiting issue: in this perspective, waiting is regarded as somehow inevitable unless one accepts a disproportionate increase in overhead costs, due to the oversizing of contact personnel, equipment and service facilities. Accordingly, the focus shifts to a better understanding of the perceptual dimensionality of waiting, trying to pinpoint and modify the most stressful psychological components of the experience.

In the retail setting, managerial degrees of freedom are further reduced: managing demand is not an easily actionable solution, given the relative insensitivity of customers' shopping time to pricing or communication strategies; moreover, typical capacity-tailoring strategies like the utilization of temporary workers, part-time labor forces and flexible work hours are much less easily implemented in the heavily unionized European countries than they are in the U.S. setting.

Given these premises, perception management becomes a fundamental issue for retailers: specifically, the attention focuses on those factors that, exerting a major influence on the queuing experience evaluation, can be exploited in the capacity planning stage, allowing a tailoring of the capacity not to the *actual* demand but instead to a sort of *tolerance-weighted* demand. This new measure can be ideally obtained by weighting the actual demand (customers' outflow) with a *sensitivity* coefficient, measuring and summarizing those factors affecting the tolerance to wait of customers standing in queue. The basic assumption under which this approach can be managerially exploitable is obvious: some of the factors affecting sensitivity to queuing must exhibit a relatively stable time pattern, on a daily or weekly basis. If this condition holds, capacity planning (i.e., check-out personnel shifts) could be accommodated to fit the forecast levels of weighted demand, capitalizing on those customers that show a higher tolerance to the waiting time.

In this study, a model representing a set of hypothesized causal relationships between evaluation of queuing and some constructs of interest are tested. Perhaps the most promising indications come from the role that hedonic shopping value plays on waiting evaluations. Analyses show a strong positive effect of hedonic orientation on different dimensions of waiting, suggesting a significantly higher tolerance of waiting for those customers scoring high on hedonic value. Moreover, a meaningful and relatively stable pattern seems to emerge in the hourly breakdown of the hedonic shopping value scores, with more positive hedonic levels in early morning and noon customers and lower levels typical of late afternoon shoppers.

If this pattern can be found in a consistent way across different locations and different time windows, an interesting opportunity opens up: store managers could reallocate capacity (i.e., redefine check-out personnel shifts) according to the expected hedonic orientation of customers, capitalizing on their higher tolerance to standing in line. In other words, a smaller number of checkouts could be opened, for example, at noon time, which would make *actual* waiting time longer on average, but the overall impact on the satisfaction with the queuing experience would be moderated by the high hedonic shopping value of customers, that in turn would make them *perceive* a still acceptably fast, short, fair, unstressing and nonirritating line.

MANAGING CREATIVITY IN SERVICES

Ravi S. Behara

As service organizations move closer to the turn of the century they find themselves in a rapidly changing competitive space. Both the sources of new challenges and the origins for possible solutions are global in scope. Many countries continue to reduce regulation and open their markets; greater freedom for the people of the world is resulting in an increased exchange of knowledge; there is dramatic innovation in information and communication technologies underway; and advanced service economies are becoming more knowledge-based. Under these circumstances, there is an urgent need to look beyond the prerequisites of effectively managing quality and processes to address competitive pressures.

The emergent emphasis on knowledge forces us to look within ourselves in search for answers, and the innate human capabilities of learning and creativity are beginning to take center stage. Service organizations are now at the threshold of the age of creation—a time when creativity is the key source of value-added and competitive advantage in an ever increasingly global market economy. The important role of creativity in economic activity is, however, not a new idea. But there appears to be an increasing emphasis on the need for *everyone* in the organization to be *more* creative. As a result, there now exists a *creativity imperative* in services.

The primary challenge that service organizations face in this new age of creativity is how to develop individual creativity and how to develop organizations that provide an environment in which individuals and groups can participate in creative work. The discussion in this paper elaborates on the various facets of creativity, its management and the implications for the management of services.

This paper identifies four sources of creativity and their breakthrough potential. These include creation—the making of something new; synthesis—the linking of previously unrelated events or entities; modification—altering something existing to perform new functions; and benchmarking—the borrowing of ideas, particularly from outside an industry. The creative ideas behind some new services such as AsiaOne of FedEx and The Disney Institute are explored to illustrate the different types of creativity at work. Many service organizations have been actively involved in attempts to increase their creativity with varying degrees of success. A variety of organizational creativity enhancers and inhibitors are identified in this paper. These include aspects of management attitude, organizational culture, organizational structure, information flow and work processes in organizations. An evaluation of these issues and a review of recent techniques and research in creativity resulted in the development of a framework to study the management of creativity in services. The results of applying this framework in a pilot study of knowledge-intensive services indicate that there is a distinct lack of emphasis on key issues regarded as important to fostering creativity in organizations.

The primary purpose of this paper is to highlight the *creativity imperative* in services today. Managers should recognize that all employees are the *thinkers* of an organization in which new ideas are a source of fundamental value. The framework developed here provides service managers with a systemic approach to addressing the management of creativity. The results of the pilot study provide an early warning that much remains to be done by service management practitioners and researchers. It appears that the greatest challenges of human creativity still lay ahead of us.

RELATIONSHIP MARKETING:
AN ORGANIZATIONAL PERSPECTIVE

Benjamin Schneider, Susan Schoenberger White
and Michelle C. Paul

ABSTRACT

In the light of recent thinking about relationship marketing, we reinterpret two earlier studies showing significant correlations between employees' perceptions of their workplace and customers' perceptions of service quality. We ask, and answer in the affirmative, the following questions of the prior studies: (1) Does an organizational focus on the maintenance and enhancement of customer relationships relate to customer perceptions of service quality? and (2) Is an organizational focus on the maintenance and enhancement of customer relationships more strongly related to customer perceptions of service quality than a transactional focus? It is important to note that, while the relationship focus was more strongly related to service quality than the transactional focus, the latter was also positively and significantly related to customer perceptions of service quality. Our findings serve as input into the beginnings of a conceptualization of the organizational climate and culture policies, practices and procedures likely to facilitate improved relationships with the customers of service organizations.

Advances in Services Marketing and Management, Volume 6, pages 1-22.
Copyright © 1997 by JAI Press Inc.
All rights of reproduction in any form reserved.
ISBN: 0-7623-0176-7

INTRODUCTION

For many businesses, the current market environment is one of increased international competition, slower growth rates and mature markets (Fornell 1992). Consequently, these businesses are competing for fewer customers who are demanding more of them. In order to survive, organizations must differentiate themselves from their competitors; service quality has been advocated as one such differentiating strategy (Barrell 1991; Berry 1995a; Buzzell and Gale 1987; Fornell 1992; Vavra 1992).

Support for an organizational emphasis on service quality derives primarily from the assumption that it leads directly to increased customer satisfaction and eventually to higher profits, typically assumed to occur through customer retention (Storbacka, Strandvik and Grönroos 1994). While the relationship between customer satisfaction and profit is not perfect, there is growing support for links between an organization's emphasis on service quality, customers' resulting satisfaction and eventual firm profitability (Deshpandé, Farley and Webster 1993; Narver and Slater 1990; Schneider 1991).

A way of thinking about the relationship between service quality and profits has emerged in an orientation toward service customers known as relationship marketing (e.g., Berry 1995b; Christopher, Payne and Ballantyne 1991; Gummesson 1994). Although the term was first introduced by Berry in 1983 (as cited in Berry 1995b), relationship marketing has moved to the forefront of marketing research and practice only in the past few years (Berry 1995b). The relationship marketing approach goes beyond ensuring that each transaction with customers be of high quality (the transactional approach to customers). Rather, it argues that establishing *relationships* with individual customers should be the goal of service delivery.

In the field of relationship marketing, the focus has largely been on the relationships that an organization establishes with individual customers (Morgan and Hunt 1994), but several authors discuss a much broader range of relationships to which relationship marketing may apply. For example, organizations are involved in relationships with other organizations such as their suppliers, the government and their own employees and business units (Christopher, Payne and Ballantyne 1991; Gummesson 1994; Morgan and Hunt 1994). In the present paper, we concern ourselves only with the relationships organizations have with individual customers (or end-user consumers).

While definitions of relationship marketing differ in their specifics, most reflect a common set of ideas. For example, as discussed by Peterson (1995), definitions proposed by both Grönroos (1990) and Shani and Chalasani (1992, p. 278) emphasize the idea that "both parties in the relationship benefit, and that the relationship is longitudinal in nature." Writings on the topic have emphasized the continuing nature of the relationship as well as the change in the relationship over time. This change in the nature of the relationship can be characterized in a variety of ways, perhaps the most succinct being in the level of loyalty or commitment the customer displays to the serving organization (Christopher, Payne and Ballantyne 1991).

Via relationship marketing, organizations try to create long-term alliances with customers by using "a combination of customized products, customized communication, and customized service and delivery—in effect, treating each customer as a unique [market] segment" (Winkleman et al. 1993, p. 29). To try to enhance relationships with customers, organizations can use relatively minor acts such as sending birthday cards to customers and addressing customers by name, or more substantial business programs such as providing current customers with advance information on new products or sales (Brierly 1994) or adding value to the credit cards of cardholders (Gill 1991). These techniques are designed to make customers feel less like "numbers" and more like valued individuals whose needs are recognized and fulfilled by the organization (Brierly 1994). The logic is that establishing relationships with customers yields long-term customer retention—and it is through customer retention that organizations are ultimately profitable.

These relationship-oriented marketing strategies (in which psychological care, concern and/or empathy predominate) as well as more transactional strategies (in which efficiency and/or price predominate) are all routes available to firms for delivering quality (Grönroos 1994; 1995). We and other researchers (e.g., Berry 1995b) regard every type of relationship marketing strategy as a synthesis of both relationship-oriented and transaction-oriented elements. These strategies can be conceptualized within a two-dimensional space, framed by relationship and transaction axes, as shown in Figure 1. These axes can be viewed as creating an umbrella of relationship marketing, encompassing a broad range of marketing approaches.

This perspective departs from the conceptualization that these strategies are arranged along a single relationship-to-transaction continuum. Rather, it illuminates the notion that relationships can be founded on elements represented by both of the axes shown in Figure 1. This perspective emphasizes the point that attempting to establish stronger relationships with customers, relationships in which customers feel a psychological bond with the organization (Storbacka, Strandvik and Grönroos 1994), may require more than just an increase in the level of a transactional marketing strategy applied to customers, no matter how good the transactional service might be. Rather, a relationship orientation toward customers is a distinct alternative requiring changes in the ways firms are managed and organized. These changes might include a stronger focus on interpersonal relationships with customers (Gummesson 1994), a consideration of customers' psychological needs for security, esteem or justice in everyday dealings with the organization (Schneider and Bowen 1995), and/or demonstrations by the organization that maintaining and enhancing the relationships with customers is a highly valued outcome.

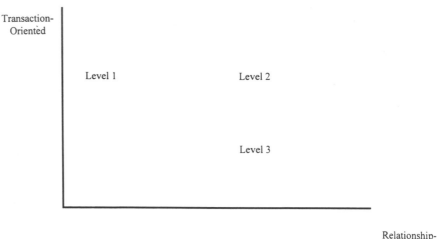

Figure 1.   Relationship Marketing Space: Berry's (1995b) Three Levels
of Relationship Marketing

One way to view the relationship between the transaction and relationship strategies and customer satisfaction is as a model analogous to Herzberg's two-factor model of employee motivation in the workplace (cf. Herzberg, Mausner and Snyderman 1959). In this model, so-called hygiene factors (pay, physical working conditions) are seen as keeping employees from being dissatisfied but contributing little to satisfaction. On the other hand, the so-called "motivators" (job design and interpersonal relationships) are said to be the major source of employee satisfaction.

By analogy, transactional approaches to service quality may yield lower levels of dissatisfaction, while relationship-oriented strategies may yield increased levels of satisfaction. This idea is reflected in Parasuraman, Berry and Zeithaml's (1991) discussion of the idea that organizations can meet the expectations of their customers by being reliable but displays of empathy and concern are necessary to exceed the expectations of customers, thus creating higher levels of service quality and increased levels of satisfaction.

The two-factor model described previously emphasizes our belief that both transaction- and relationship-oriented marketing elements are important in establishing and maintaining relationships with customers. Berry (1995b) describes how the two components may combine to form different marketing strategies; he describes three levels of relationship marketing that organizations may adopt. Level one creates repeat business primarily through financial incentives such as frequent flier programs. Level two relies more heavily on establishing a social bond between the organization and the customer, using personalization and customization of the service or good to encourage repeat business. The third level of relationship marketing focuses on providing structural solutions to customers' problems as a way of establishing a bond between the organization and customer and encouraging repeat business. Firms can adopt one or more of the approaches to serving customers, and their choices can actually serve as a basis for competitive differentiation in the marketplace.

An example of the differences that can exist between the approaches to relationship marketing emerges when one contrasts the experiences customers have at a department store such as Nordstrom with the experiences they have with the American Airlines frequent flier program. The facilities, layout, personalized attention and concern shown for customers at Nordstrom operate as multi-faceted influences on relationships and might be classified as a level two relationship marketing approach in Berry's (1995b) scheme. These influences can be compared to the more unidimensional, level one approach of frequent flier miles accrued from American Airlines. If these were the only strategies adopted by the two companies, one might ask: With which business are customers likely to experience the deeper psychological relationship and display stronger loyalty? One might hypothesize that the more multi-faceted and personal the customers' experiences, the stronger the attachment of customers to the business.

While service marketing scholars have contributed these conceptual insights and also presented some empirical work on the *customer* part of the relationship marketing equation (e.g., Grönroos 1994; Gummesson 1994; Storbacka, Strandvik and Grönroos 1994), there has been less emphasis on the kinds of practices and procedures—the kinds of internal organizational management practices—in which organizations might engage to facilitate development of a deeper and broader relationship with customers (for an exception, see George 1990). This is the focus of the present paper. We ask and attempt to provide some preliminary answers to the following questions: (1) Does an organizational focus on the maintenance and enhancement of customer relationships relate to customer perceptions of service quality? and (2) Is an organizational focus on the maintenance and enhancement of customer relationships more strongly related to customer perceptions of service quality than a more transactional focus?

In more operational terms, we are asking the following: Given that internal organizational practices are related to customer service quality perceptions, is this relationship stronger (a) when these practices emphasize service quality through care and concern for customers, or (b) when these practices focus more heavily on efficiency and transactions? It is important to note that whether customers experience excellent or poor service as a result of organizational policies is not our primary focus. Rather, we are interested in how organizational policies that differ in their emphases differ in their relationships with customer service quality perceptions.

To provide some preliminary answers to these questions, we first introduce organizational climate and culture as ways of conceptualizing how organizations can target various internal functions on specific outcomes—such as the outcome of deeper relationships with customers. We then review previously collected data from service firm employees on their firms' climate and culture for service quality and the relationship of those perceptions to customers' service quality experiences. These data on climate, culture and service quality contain employees' reports of their firms' attempts to establish deeper and broader relationships with customers as well as reports on more transaction-oriented facets of organizational practices. The presence of these kinds of data permitted a test of whether relationship-focused practices are more strongly related to customer perceptions of service quality than are the transaction-focused practices.

Rather than focusing directly on end-user customer expectations and experiences, this paper concentrates on the organizational processes that are related to those end-user customer experiences. This focus on internal practices and procedures is similar to the idea of internal marketing (Berry 1981; Bitner 1995; George 1990; Grönroos 1981; Reynoso and Moores 1995). Specifically, we explore the degree to which employee reports of their organizations' relationship orientation are related to customer reports of the service quality they receive.

Organizational Climate and Culture as Complementary Concepts

The concept of organizational climate offers one way of thinking about how the various policies and practices of an organization combine to form the organizational context employees experience. Organizational climate has been generically defined as the perceptions of employees concerning "events, practices, and procedures and the kinds of behaviors that get rewarded, supported, and expected in a setting" (Schneider 1990, p. 384). Since most organizations have multiple goals and foci, multiple climates may exist simultaneously within one organization; an organization may have a climate for safety, a climate for innovation and a climate for service quality (Schneider, Gunnarson and Niles-Jolly 1994). A service climate refers to employee perceptions of the practices, procedures and behaviors that get rewarded, supported and expected with regard to customer service and customer service quality (Schneider 1990).

Over time, research and theory have indicated that climate is multidimensional in nature; many facets of organizational functioning, in concert, yield a global perception of the organization's particular focus (Reichers and Schneider 1990). That is, it is through the perceptual *aggregation* of the experiences of many practices and procedures that members of an organization begin to share a common impression regarding the desired focus of their energies and competencies; the focus of the perceptual aggregation, service in the present case, is the climate of the organization.

Organizational culture is a more recent conceptual breakthrough than climate in understanding organizational behavior. Thus, while Kurt Lewin and his colleagues were studying climate as early as 1939 (Lewin, Lippitt and White 1939), and Argyris conceptualized the climate of banks as early as 1958 (Argyris 1958), the culture construct is relatively new to the organizational sciences, having been introduced by Pettigrew in 1979. The literature on organizational culture, rather than focusing on the practices and procedures that have been the target of climate researchers (what Schein [1992] calls "artifacts" of culture), has introduced the concepts of values, beliefs and assumptions as a way of understanding what employees experience in organizations (for an excellent review, see Martin 1992). In a culture-based view of organizations, values and beliefs of organizational members serve as the foundation for the behaviors observed there.

Schneider, Gunnarson and Niles-Jolly (1994) wrote of the link between climate and culture as an inextricable entanglement. They argued that practices and procedures (climate) emerge out of the values and beliefs of members (culture), especially out of the beliefs of founders of the organization (for a similar paradigm, see Schein 1992). In addition, they proposed that changes in climate can actually yield changes in culture—behavioral change can yield changes in values and beliefs. In summary, this perspective views climate and culture as reciprocal constructs, with culture operating at a level of beliefs and values, and climate at the operational level of practices and procedures.

Our intent in the present paper is to take a fresh look at the climate and culture research that Schneider and his colleagues (Schneider and Bowen 1985; Schneider, Parkington and Buxton 1980) have produced—from the vantage point of relationship marketing.

SERVICE CLIMATE AND CULTURE AND CUSTOMER PERCEPTIONS: THE TWO EARLY STUDIES

The data to be reexamined here emerged from two studies, the second a replication and extension of the first (Schneider and Bowen 1985; Schneider, Parkington and Buxton 1980). In both studies, questionnaires were designed to assess customer service quality experiences and the experiences of boundary workers in bank branches. Extensive focus group interviews about service quality issues with customers and boundary workers were the basis for the questionnaires. We first discuss the survey development and then examine the findings from a relationship marketing perspective.

Survey Development

The critical incident technique first proposed by Flanagan (1954) and subsequently used effectively in services marketing by Bitner, Booms and Tetreault (1990) formed the basis for the customer surveys used in the quantitative research subsequently conducted. In focus groups, customers were asked to describe experiences that made them believe the service they received was "high quality service" and/or "poor quality service." Further, they were encouraged to provide explicit details of their experiences in their bank branch rather than their general affect. The customer surveys used in the research to be described were developed prior to the creative and useful work on the measurement of service quality by Parasuraman, Zeithaml and Berry (1985; Zeithaml, Parasuraman and Berry 1991).

In the employee focus groups, boundary workers were asked to describe the "climate or culture of your branch and the role of service in it." Responses to this query (e.g., "The climate here is indifferent to customers" or "The climate of this place is pervaded by a service ethic" or "There just isn't a belief in the individuality of customers here") were followed up to illuminate the actual practices and procedures that yielded such conclusions. These reports of practices and procedures provided the basis for the boundary employee climate survey items.

In the research we are presently describing, organizational culture was also assessed using survey measures. It should be noted that the measures were not originally conceptualized as culture measures; in retrospect, however, that is what they were assessing. As will become more obvious in the following paragraphs, the culture measure asked employees to describe what their management valued in the way of serving customers. Thus, the values of interest concerned employee perceptions of what management valued, a definition of culture that has now entered the research literature (Schneider, Brief and Guzzo 1996; Schneider, Gunnarson and Niles-Jolly 1994). Due to the variety of definitions we currently have of organizational culture (cf. Martin 1992), there exists considerable debate about the appropriate operationalization of the construct (e.g., Trice and Beyer 1993). A formulation like the one used here, in which employees report what they believe management values or believes in, makes conceptual and operational sense to us.

This definition makes conceptual sense because it retains a focus on values and beliefs, as well as who actually holds those beliefs—the employees. The definition makes operational sense because it permits measurement in an attributional form—the measure asks employees to make attributions about what management believes. (For details on the employee survey design, samples studied, and so forth, see Parkington and Schneider [1979], Schneider [1980], Schneider and Bowen [1985], and Schneider, Parkington and Buxton [1980].) It should be noted here that the climate and culture measures employed in these efforts were written in the language of the employees who responded to them; the focus groups were used not only to identify constructs worthy of measurement but also to guide the phrasing of survey items. As Schneider (1990) has noted, generic surveys that tap global issues reveal less consistent relationships with outcomes of interest than do surveys tailored to the situations and the outcomes of interest.

Customer Surveys

Table 1 presents sample items from the customer scales emerging from the survey design process. These five scales are the result of factor analyses conducted by Schneider and Bowen (1985) on the 10 a priori scales used with the original sample (Schneider, Parkington and Buxton 1980). In addition to responding to these survey items, customers also responded to an item assessing overall service quality (1 = terrible; 6 = outstanding). For the two studies discussed here, a random sample of customers from each of the branches studied was obtained; typically, the sample available for analysis contained between 60 and 100 customers per branch, and analyses revealed they were representative of the sample to which the mailing was made. The items comprising each of the five scales and an overall service quality item were aggregated to provide branch level data yielding one set of scores per branch.

Table 1. Customer Scales with Sample Items

Administration (Admin)
- It is difficult to know who to call or where to write when I need specific kinds of bank-related information.
- I sometimes feel lost in the branch, not knowing where to go for a certain transaction.

Security
- My branch seems to have the most up-to-date banking equipment and machinery.
- I feel secure with my accounts being at this branch.

Courtesy/Competency (Court/Comp)
- Tellers in the branch seem well-trained and knowledgeable.
- In my branch, the tellers are generally pleasant.

Staff Adequacy (Staff)
- The lines are not too long in the branch.
- My branch seems to have enough employees to handle its customers.

Employee Morale (Morale)
- Employees seem happy about the fact that they work in the branch.

Notes: Words in parentheses appear in later tables as abbreviations for the scale name.
Sources: Partially adapted from Schneider (1990), Schneider, Parkington and Buxton (1980) and Schneider and Bowen (1985); some items presented here have not previously appeared in print.

Table 2.   Employee Climate Scales with Sample Items

Managerial Behavior (Mgr)
- My branch manager supports employees when they come up with new ideas on customer service.
- My branch manager sets definite quality standards of good customer service.
- My branch manager takes time to help new employees learn about the branch and its customers.

Customer Orientation (Cust Orient)
- When customers want to close their accounts no one really tries to keep them.
- Platform people in my branch are too busy trying to sell new customers to save old ones.

Systems Support (Sys)
- We are well-prepared by Marketing for the introduction of new products or services.
- Management makes sure that each branch is adequately staffed.

Logistics Support (Log)
- Equipment and machinery in the branch are well-serviced and rarely break.
- The branch always has adequate supplies (deposit/withdrawal tickets, plastic holders for passbooks, etc.).

Notes: Words in parentheses are used in subsequent tables as abbreviations of the scale names.
Sources: Partially adapted from Schneider (1980), Schneider et al. (1980), and Schneider and Bowen (1985); some items presented here have not previously appeared in print.

Boundary Employee Surveys

The information provided by the boundary employee focus groups resulted in the development of surveys that assessed four service climate scales; sample items for these scales are shown in Table 2. (More items than those shown in Tables 1 and 2 were used in the actual research so that the internal reliability of all scales exceeded acceptable psychometric properties.) In addition, these employees were asked to indicate, using the same six-point scale used by customers, "How do you think the customers of your branch view the general quality of the service they receive in your branch?" The items shown in Table 2 were presented as descriptions of branch policies and practices, and employees were asked to report how true each statement was of their branch. The items comprising a scale were averaged for the branch employees and then those average item responses were summed. These sums were the branch scale scores for each of the climate dimensions, resulting in one set of scores per branch.

Finally, employees were asked the degree to which they believed management wanted them to deliver service "by the book" and the degree to which they believed management wanted a more customer-focused approach to service delivery (see Parkington and Schneider [1979] for a more detailed description of this measure). In earlier papers, this has been called the Bureaucrat versus Enthusiast approach to service delivery—here, we refer to

Table 3.   Sample Bureaucrat and Enthusiast Culture
Survey Items

Bureaucrat (Bureau)
- Strictly following all rules and procedures.
- Giving customers special treatment if they have a large account.
- Doing one's job in a routine-like fashion.
- Checking identification of even well-known customers.

Enthusiast (Enthus)
- Keeping a sense of "family" among all employees.
- Showing personal concerns for any customer's banking problem.
- Having the branch involved in community affairs.
- Having cooperation among branch employees.

Notes: Employees responded to these items by describing the degree to which they
perceived the item described management beliefs about what was essential.
Words in parentheses are used as abbreviations of the scale names in subsequent
tables.

Sources: The items presented here are based on Parkington and Schneider (1979) and
Schneider (1990).

the scales as the Bureaucrat versus Enthusiast service delivery culture. The items comprising these two scales are shown in Table 3. For the items in Table 3, employees reported the degree to which management believed it was important to deliver service in each of the ways described. The items comprising a scale were averaged and for each branch the employee scale responses were summed, producing one Bureaucrat culture scale score and one Enthusiast culture scale score per branch.

The Climate and Culture Scales: A Relationship Marketing Perspective

To determine the contributions of the relationship marketing perspective to our previously collected data, we first reexamined the four climate scales presented in Table 2. Viewing the scales from a relationship marketing perspective requires a consideration of the extent to which each of the scales is relationship-oriented and transaction-oriented. In other words, these scales can be placed within the two dimensional space described earlier—remembering that here we refer to the organizational policies and practices that *employees* experience; see Figure 2.

The most transaction-oriented of the four scales are Systems Support and Logistics Support. These seem to represent policies and practices designed to provide the tangibles required to carry out efficient transactions with customers. This is not to say they are exclusively efficiency-oriented—witness the concern for staffing levels in the Systems Support scale. But a more relationship-oriented approach, stressing service quality, is found in the

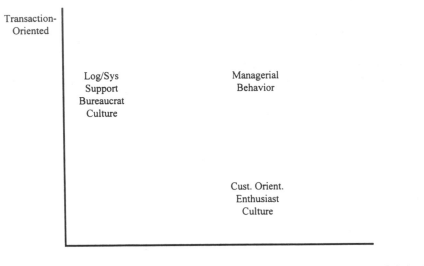

Figure 2. The Relationship Marketing Space: Climate and Culture Scales

Managerial Behavior scale. This scale connotes a managerial focus on service quality—planning for and rewarding behavior that indicates service quality as well as educating employees about the customers of the branch. The Customer Orientation scale appears to us to be the most relationship-oriented scale with its emphasis on actual maintenance of the relationship with the customers. One could argue, of course, that the scale describes a late concern for customers, with the focus on saving customers who desire to leave. We believe, however, that the items in the scale connote the essence of the relationship concept— maintaining and enhancing the relationship between employees and customers. Note that in subsequent analyses, the items for this scale were all reverse-scored such that a high score indicated a greater degree of customer orientation.

The same approach of evaluating scales to determine the extent of their focus on relationships can be taken toward the culture scales in Table 3 (the Bureaucrat and the Enthusiast scales). The Bureaucrat items reveal an approach to customers based on standardized rules and policies, clearly a more transactional or even internal efficiency orientation; little concern for the emotional content or mutuality of bank-customer relationships is evident in these items. In contrast, the Enthusiast scale is replete with items associated with relationships—items such as those dealing with the sense of family in the branch or showing personal concern for customers. It is important to recall that these items capture employee beliefs; the scale required employees to make attributions about what management valued rather than employees' direct perceptions of policies and practices they encountered.

When reviewing the items in Tables 2 and 3, it is useful to recall that the employees in the focus groups which were run early in the research process and used as a basis for survey design were not explicitly asked to report on policies and practices or management beliefs relevant to customer relationships; they were simply asked to report on issues related to climate and culture and the role of service in it. This is useful to remember because the resultant mapping of the climate and culture constructs emerged from the employees in the focus groups rather than from a priori constructs with which the researchers began. Indeed, at the time the Bureaucrat and Enthusiast constructs were first identified (Parkington and Schneider 1979), the culture construct had just begun to receive attention in the organizational sciences and the climate approach dominated this line of thinking (Katz and Kahn 1978).

Following the relationship marketing logic of the present paper, we predicted that the Customer Orientation and Managerial Behavior climate scales would be more strongly correlated with customer perceptions of service quality than would the Systems Support and Logistics Support climate scales. In addition, we predicted that the Enthusiast culture scale would be more strongly correlated with customer perceptions of quality than would the Bureaucrat culture scale.

RESULTS

The Cross-Boundary Correlations

Table 4 reveals the statistical correlations that emerged when the boundary employee and customer data were correlated across the $N = 23$ branches (Schneider, Parkington and Buxton 1980) and $N = 27$ branches (Schneider and Bowen 1985). (Table 4 presents the *average* of the two sets of correlations since analyses revealed that those two sets correlated 0.82.) There are a number of correlations that are of particular interest in the present focus on relationships.

First, we focus on the row labeled Quality, which presents correlations between customer perceptions of overall service quality and employee climate and culture reports. This row reveals statistically significant correlations with customer quality perceptions for all but the Bureaucrat culture scale. These results indicate that, in general, the climate and culture of the organization that employees experience with regard to service delivery are reflected in the overall service quality customers experience. This is perhaps most clearly shown in the correlation ($r = 0.65$, $p < 0.01$) between employee and customer perceptions of overall quality.

Table 4. Cross-Correlations of Boundary Employee and Customer Tier

Customer Variables	Boundary Employee Variables						
	Quality	Mgr	Cust Orien	Sys	Log	Enthu	Bureau
Quality	0.65**	0.54**	0.50**	0.42*	0.43*	0.54**	0.14
Court/Comp	0.39	0.29	0.29	0.27	0.20	0.44*	0.12
Security	-0.25	-0.25	-0.19	-0.10	-0.27	-0.20	-0.05
Staff	0.35	0.37	0.37	0.22	0.39	0.35	0.27
Morale	0.59**	0.48*	0.52**	0.40*	0.35	0.57**	0.17
Admin	0.54**	0.49*	0.59**	0.36	0.37	0.49*	0.18

Notes: Average correlations of two studies (Average $N = 25$ bank branches) are presented (see Schneider and
Bowen 1985 for the separate correlations).
     See Tables 1, 2 and 3 for sample items for each of the scales shown here. Also, see the same tables
for the abbreviations used in this table.
  ** indicates significance at $p < 0.01$.
   * indicates significance at $p < 0.05$.

This same row in Table 4 also reveals a hierarchy of correlations for the climate scales and customer perceptions of overall quality: Managerial Behavior ($r = 0.54$, $p < 0.01$), followed by Customer Orientation ($r = 0.50$, $p < 0.01$), Logistics Support ($r = 0.43$, $p < 0.05$), and Systems Support ($r = 0.42$, $p < 0.05$). For the culture scales, the relationships with customer perceptions of overall service quality are also in the predicted direction, with the Enthusiast scale revealing a stronger correlation ($r = 0.54$, $p < 0.01$) than the correlation for the Bureaucrat scale ($r = 0.14$, ns).

A second approach to the data in Table 4 focuses on each of the five facets of service quality experiences customers report. Here, we see that the two climate scales of Managerial Behavior and Customer Orientation are the significant correlates of the customer facets of service quality, specifically those having to do with Employee Morale and Branch Administration. The Enthusiast culture scale significantly correlated with the customer quality facets of Employee Morale, Branch Administration and Courtesy/Competency. As a group, these findings suggest that differences across branches in more transaction and efficiency-oriented climates and cultures (e.g., Systems Support and Bureaucrat Culture) are not as strongly reflected in various facets of customer experiences as are differences across branches in more relationship-oriented facets of climate and culture.

It is important to note, however, that transaction and efficiency climate and culture are consistently positively (and occasionally significantly) correlated with customer perceptions of various facets of service quality (except for Security experiences of customers, a finding we will address later). These consistent relationships indicate that efficiency and transaction orientations do not negatively affect customers' service quality experiences and are not just facets that keep customer dissatisfaction down; they just fail to contribute as much to (correlate as strongly with) service quality perceptions as do the more explicit foci on service quality and relationship maintenance.

The results shown in Table 4 also reveal two findings for which we had no prior expectations. One concerns the customer scale of Morale and the other concerns the customer scale of Security. Because of our interest in relationship issues between boundary workers and customers, we first focus on the Morale scale. This scale represents customer perceptions of the branch employees as *people* and not faceless workers (e.g., "Employees seem happy about the fact that they work in the branch"). As seen in Table 4, the Morale scale exhibits the same pattern of results that the other customer scales do: its strongest correlates are the Customer Orientation climate scale ($r = 0.52$) and the Enthusiast culture scale ($r = 0.57$). However, the Morale scale correlations lend themselves to a particularly interesting interpretation in that these correlations indicate that the customer-boundary employee relationship may run both ways. By this, we mean that not only are employees sensitive to differences in their bank branches with regard to customer relationships, *but customers are sensitive to the emotional state of those who serve them.*

The second unexpected finding in Table 4 concerns correlations between the boundary employee perceptions and the customer scale labeled Security. First, note that while the correlations are not statistically significant, they are all negative, including the correlations with the Customer Orientation and Managerial Behavior climate scales and the Enthusiast culture scale. An examination of the intercorrelations of the customer service quality facets reveals that the Security scale, as expected, is negatively correlated with the other service quality facets. Perhaps these negative correlations provide a useful note of caution against stressing any one organizational focus toward customers when customers obviously come to the service encounter with diverse and multidimensional expectations (Zeithaml, Parasuraman and Berry 1991). For example, customers may view too much of a service quality orientation as a "gimmick" rather than a genuine effort to meet their needs. An over-emphasis on quality might be associated in customer minds with laxity so far as security issues are concerned, and security is one of the main features that banks sell. These unexpected negative correlations indicate that how customers perceive the interplay of different organizational foci, such as service and security, might be usefully investigated in future research.

Post Hoc Analyses

In thinking about the results shown in Table 4, we discussed the possibility that the transaction foci in the branch might be the foundation on which the relationship focus might emerge. That is, we wondered whether the relationship focus was possible to the extent that the transaction practices and procedures were already in place. Such a conceptualization puts the relationship focus as a mediator of the relationship between the transaction climate and culture and customer perceptions of service quality.

Using data from the Schneider and Bowen study (1985; the Schneider, Parkington and Buxton 1980 data was not available for this analysis), we ran a series of multiple regressions to test this proposition. However, we found no support for a mediating relationship. Rather, the transaction- and relationship-oriented climate and culture scales both seem to be essentially independently related to customer perceptions of service quality.

SUMMARY

The results originally reported based on the data analyses summarized here indicated that employees at the boundary of organizations and the customers they serve share views about the quality of service delivered and received. In the present reexamination of the data, a more detailed conclusion can be drawn: When employees describe the climate and culture of their organization as reflecting concerns for customer relationships and quality, those reports are generally more strongly tied to customer perceptions of service quality than reports of a more transaction-oriented climate and culture; transaction and efficiency emphases have a somewhat weaker—although still significant—relationship to the service quality that customers experience.

Researchers from multiple disciplines have begun to incorporate macro-organizational management issues with more traditional marketing foci in an attempt to understand, predict and manage service organization effectiveness. While these frameworks go by such different names as service climate (e.g., Schneider 1990), organizational culture (Deshpandé, Farley and Webster 1993) and market orientation (Narver and Slater 1990), they all offer macro conceptualizations of the ways in which service organizations might be organized and managed to achieve competitiveness and profitability. Integrating these internal organization management foci with end-user consumer relationship marketing approaches could yield insights for the improved understanding of service organizations from a multi-disciplinary perspective (Reynoso and Moores 1995).

The data summarized in this paper provides one possible starting point for such an integration of internal and external perspectives. Thus, previously collected data, data not originally collected to explore the boundary employee-customer relationship issue, were reexamined through the lens of relationship marketing. Exploring these data offers a kind of "projective test" of the salience of relationship issues. That is, the data offer an opportunity to explore the degree to which relationship issues emerge in data even when such issues were not explicitly addressed in that research.

We found that the service climate scales of Managerial Behavior and Customer Orientation and the Enthusiast culture scale were the strongest correlates of customer service quality perceptions. These results reveal three key factors that appear to affect customer perceptions of service quality: (1) a managerial emphasis on quality in carrying out daily activities (planning, organizing and so forth); (2) explicit activities designed to pay attention to and preserve customers; and (3) a management that is perceived to believe in being flexible and enthusiastic about service delivery.

Also of interest in the research was the finding that the strongest correlates of customer perceptions of Employee Morale were the same scales—Managerial Behavior, Customer Orientation and Enthusiast. While the focus of the present paper is the organizational side of organization-customer relationships, this finding with regard to customer perceptions of Employee Morale indicates such relationships may be more reciprocal than has been previously discussed. For example, the item "Employees seem happy about the fact that they work in the branch" is instructive because it reveals that customers are sensitive to the experiences employees are having—as well as vice versa.

The data reviewed here clearly substantiate the *validity* of boundary worker descriptions of the policies and practices (the climate) and the management values (culture) guiding their work, in that they are consistently related to customer perceptions—a relationship empirically demonstrated in the current paper as well as in other research (*Human Resource Planning* 1991).

Cautions and Limitations

All research studies have limitations and the present effort is no exception. A problem with archival data, such as those explored here, is that it tends to be old and consequently difficult to fit into paradigms other than those that guided the original data collection. With regard to the age of the present data, the data were collected at least two years prior to the research publication dates (1980 and 1985). Furthermore, the data were collected in the banking industry, an industry that has moved quickly and made numerous changes in a relatively short period. For example, banks have been subject to numerous mergers and acquisitions, branches have been shut, ATMs have replaced teller services for many transactions and so forth.

On the other hand, the studies reviewed here were designed not to explore issues in *bank branches* but to explore relationships between employee and customer perceptions in a service industry—bank branches were a convenient sample. We hypothesize, then, that the results would generalize across industries so long as the interface of employees and customers approximates the one studied here—for example, in retail establishments where customers seek personal attention for specific problems. Evidence in other industries supports this generalization hypothesis (cf. *Human Resource Planning* 1991).

A second potential limitation of the data concerns the use of the data for purposes other than the original intention. We believe this issue is a strength, not a limitation, in the present case. As argued earlier, re-analysis of previously collected data permits a kind of projective test of the ideas presented here because, if the hypothesized relationships emerge in data not originally intended to reflect such issues, this suggests that there is some merit to these concepts. Thus, showing the stronger relationship of some facets of service climate and culture (e.g., Customer Orientation, Service Enthusiast) than others (e.g., Systems Support, Bureaucrat) to customer perceptions of service quality when the data were not collected to explore such differences lends credence to the idea that different kinds of internal organizational practices and values for service delivery have different consequences in terms of customer experiences.

Throughout this paper, we have emphasized the finding that relationship-oriented practices and policies are somewhat more strongly related to customer perceptions of service quality than are transaction-oriented practices and policies. While we have provided theoretical explanations for the finding, statistical explanations should also be considered. It is possible that the weaker (though still significant) correlations for the transaction-oriented scales are due to the restricted range of scores obtained on these scales—there was less variability among bank branches in terms of their transaction-oriented policies than in their relationship-oriented ones. Our findings, in any case, certainly deny any implications that transaction-oriented practices negatively impact service quality—all of the correlations are positive.

AN ORGANIZATIONAL PERSPECTIVE ON RELATIONSHIP MARKETING: MANAGERIAL AND RESEARCH IMPLICATIONS

In closing, we wish to suggest a series of organizational and management issues that research and theory suggest might contribute to a climate for relationships vis-à-vis service firm customers:

1. Management of the service unit must display, through its daily behaviors (planning, organizing, rewarding and so forth) deep concern for customer service quality. These behaviors are different from words; management must operationalize its concerns for service quality through its behavior.
2. Management of the service unit must create conditions for the flexible application of rules and procedures by boundary workers so that these workers can have the autonomy required to deal with the particulars of each customer's service issues. When boundary workers work in this

kind of environment, they see management as being service enthusiasts. Management can still have rules and procedures, but boundary workers should have flexibility in their application. In other words, employees must have tools that enable them to keep the service promises that the organization has made to its customers (Bitner 1995).

3. Management of the service unit must put into practice a deep concern for the retention of customers such that boundary workers actively strive to keep existing customers. The research we have summarized here indicates that this active concern for customers, through active retention, is a key to positive customer service quality perceptions. Other evidence, not summarized here, supports this issue of concern for customers. For example, Schneider, Wheeler and Cox (1992) showed that boundary workers who report their firms solicit and are responsive to customer feedback also report they work in a firm that has a positive passion for service.

4. Firms must be careful in the degree to which they may over-emphasize relationships to the exclusion of other salient customer expectations. Thus, the present results indicate that a concern for such relationships might be associated with customers feeling less secure. Other research by Sutton and Rafaeli (1988) indicates that convenience stores can overdo service quality to such an extent that high customer satisfaction is reflected in low store profits! Perhaps convenience store customers want speed, not the warm and friendly atmosphere we traditionally associate with service quality. The point is that caution must be displayed in putting into place any marketing strategy, including the relationship marketing strategy; the strategy, in all of its dimensions, should be appropriate for the various market segments in which the business competes.

5. Creating a relationship marketing orientation in organizations will require attention to many facets of organizational functioning in addition to those made explicit based on research, especially in areas of internal marketing such as training. For example, boundary workers will require training in how to show concern for customers; managers will require training in how to continuously emphasize service quality in their daily activities; operations management people will perhaps have to give up some efficiency in order to permit the more individualized attention a relationship approach may require (Schneider and Bowen 1995); and the advertising of service will have to be cautious to not "over-promise" and raise customer expectations too high (Bitner 1995).

In other words, a systems perspective will be the key to the creation of a climate and culture of relationship-orientation in a service business. We urge further research on the organizational policies, practices and procedures required to influence this kind of orientation in service firms because of the potential for customer retention inherent in such an approach. We believe, as do others (e.g., Berry 1995a; Deshpandé, Farley and Webster 1993), that a key to profitability in the long run is customer retention; a relationship orientation may be an important key to this outcome.

6. The research issues for evaluating the relative contribution of transaction and relationship approaches to service quality will be difficult indeed. Organizations that attempt interventions to establish the relationship orientation will have to assess the current situation over numerous time periods to establish base line information about the current state of the organization. Then, interventions will need to be implemented. However, if one takes the systems view on organizational functioning, then many, not few, interventions will be necessary—changes in managerial behavior, changes in active retention of customers that might require new hiring procedures, new training programs and so forth. Some control groups would be ideal for such efforts but, even if they were available, suppose the experimental groups achieve the relationship focus more than the controls. To what specific interventions would such effectiveness be attributed?

The very systems intervention approach itself, one espoused by numerous researchers and practitioners (e.g., Schneider and Bowen 1995), precludes firm establishment of what really worked. Was it the training of managers, the new selection procedures, the new training programs for boundary employees or some dynamic interaction of these?

Practitioners are concerned with effects; researchers are concerned with attributing effects to specific causes. Strategies for conducting research that can simultaneously demonstrate effects and reveal the causes of those effects presents a challenge! If the present data are taken at all seriously, however, the challenge may be worth it in improved customer perceptions of service quality.

ACKNOWLEDGMENTS

We wish to thank Len Berry, Mary Jo Bitner, Dave Bowen, Steve Brown and Terri Swartz for their helpful comments on an earlier version of the manuscript.

REFERENCES

Argyris, C. (1958), "Some Problems in Conceptualizing Organizational Climate: A Case Study of a Bank," *Administrative Science Quarterly*, 2, 501-520.
Barrell, A. (1991), "Relationship Marketing: Way Ahead for the 90s?," *Business Marketing Digest*, 17 (Summer), 49-54.

Berry, L. (1981), "The Employee as Consumer," *Journal of Retail Banking*, 3, 33-40.

_____ (1995a), *On Great Service*. New York: Free Press.

_____ (1995b), "Relationship Marketing of Services—Growing Interest, Emerging Perspectives," *Journal of the Academy of Marketing Science*, 23 (Fall), 236-245.

Bitner, M.J. (1995), "Building Service Relationships: It's All About Promises," *Journal of the Academy of Marketing Science*, 23 (Fall), 246-251.

_____, B. Booms and M.S. Tetreault (1990), "The Service Encounter: Diagnosing Favorable and Unfavorable Incidents," *Journal of Marketing*, 54 (January), 71-84.

Brierly, H. (1994), "The Art of Relationship Management," *Direct Marketing*, 57 (May), 25-26.

Buzzell, R. and B. Gale (1987), *The PIMS Principles: Linking Strategy to Performance*. New York: Free Press.

Christopher, M., A. Payne and D. Ballantyne (1991), *Relationship Marketing: Bringing Quality, Customer Service and Marketing Together*. London: Butterworth-Heinemann.

Deshpandé, R., J.U. Farley and F. Webster (1993), "Corporate Culture, Customer Orientation and Innovativeness in Japanese Firms: A Quadrad Analysis," *Journal of Marketing*, 57 (January), 23-27.

Flanagan, J.C. (1954), "The Critical Incident Technique," *Psychological Bulletin*, 51 (July), 327-358.

Fornell, C. (1992), "A National Customer Satisfaction Barometer: The Swedish Experience," *Journal of Marketing*, 56 (January), 6-21.

George, W.R. (1990), "Internal Marketing and Organizational Behavior: A Partnership in Developing Customer Conscious Employees at Every Level," *Journal of Business Research*, 20, 63-70.

Gill, P. (1991), "Added Value: Relationship Marketing Is One Way for Retailers to Build Loyalty," *Stores*, 73 (October), 39-40.

Grönroos, C. (1981), "Internal Marketing—An Integral Part of Marketing Theory," in *Marketing of Services*, J.H. Donnelly and W.R. George, eds. Chicago: American Marketing Association, 236-238.

_____ (1990), "Relationship Approach to Marketing in Service Contexts: The Marketing and Organizational Behavior Interface," *Journal of Business Research*, 20, 3-11.

_____ (1994), "From Marketing Mix to Relationship Marketing: Towards a Paradigm Shift in Marketing," *Management Decision*, 32 (2), 4-20.

_____ (1995), "Relationship Marketing: The Strategy Continuum," *Journal of the Academy of Marketing Science*, 23 (Fall), 252-254.

Gummesson, E. (1994), "Making Relationship Marketing Operational," *International Journal of Service Industry Management*, 5, 1-20.

Herzberg, F., B. Mausner and B. Snyderman (1959), *The Motivation to Work*. New York: Wiley.

Human Resource Planning (1991), 14 (2).

Katz, R. and D. Kahn (1978), *The Social Psychology of Organizations*, 2nd edition. New York: Wiley.

Lewin, K., R. Lippitt and R.K. White (1939), "Patterns of Aggressive Behavior in Experimentally Created 'Social Climates'," *Journal of Social Psychology*, 10, 271-299.

Martin, J. (1992), *Cultures in Organizations: Three Perspectives*. New York: Oxford University Press.

Morgan, R. and S. Hunt (1994), "The Commitment-Trust Theory of Relationship Marketing," *Journal of Marketing*, 58 (July), 20-38.

Narver, J.C. and S.F. Slater (1990), "The Effect of a Market Orientation on Business Profitability," *Journal of Marketing*, 54 (October), 20-35.

Parasuraman, A., L. Berry and V. Zeithaml (1991), "Understanding Customer Expectations of Service," *Sloan Management Review*, Spring, 39-48.

Parasuraman, A., V. Zeithaml and L. Berry (1985), "A Conceptual Model of Service Quality and Its Implications for Future Research," *Journal of Marketing*, 49(Fall), 41-50.

Parkington, J. and B. Schneider (1979), "Some Correlates of Experienced Job Stress: A Boundary Role Study," *Academy of Management Journal*, 22 (June), 270-281.

Peterson, R. (1995), "Relationship Marketing and the Consumer," *Journal of the Academy of Marketing Science*, 23 (Fall), 278-281.

Pettigrew, A.M. (1979), "On Studying Organizational Cultures," *Administrative Science Quarterly*, 24, 570-581.

Reichers, A. and B. Schneider (1990), "Climate and Culture: An Evolution of Constructs," in *Organizational Climate and Culture*, B. Schneider, ed. San Francisco, CA: Jossey-Bass, 5-39.

Reynoso, J. and B. Moores (1995), "Towards the Measurement of Internal Service Quality," *International Journal of Service Industry Management*, 6 (3), 64-83.

Schein, E. (1992), *Organizational Culture and Leadership*. San Francisco, CA: Jossey-Bass.

Schneider, B. (1980), "The Service Organization: Climate is Crucial," *Organizational Dynamics*, 9(Autumn), 52-65.

———— (1990), "The Climate for Service: An Application of the Climate Construct," in *Organizational Climate and Culture*, B. Schneider, ed. San Francisco: Jossey-Bass, 383-412.

———— (1991), "Service Quality and Profits: Can You Have Your Cake and Eat It, Too?," *Human Resource Planning*, 14 (2), 151-57.

———— and D.E. Bowen (1995), *Winning the Service Game*. Boston, MA: Harvard Business School Press.

———— and ———— (1985), "Employee and Customer Perceptions of Service in Banks: Replication and Extension," *Journal of Applied Psychology*, 70 (June), 423-433.

————, A.P. Breif and R.A. Guzzo (1996), "Creating a Climate and Culture for Sustainable Organizational Change," *Organizational Dynamics*, 24 (Spring), 7-19.

————, S. Gunnarson and K. Niles-Jolly (1994), "Creating the Climate and Culture of Success," *Organizational Dynamics*, 23 (Summer), 17-29.

————, J.P. Parkington and V.M. Buxton (1980), "Employee and Customer Perceptions of Service in Banks," *Administrative Science Quarterly*, 25 (June), 252-267.

————, J. Wheeler and J. Cox (1992), "A Passion for Service: Using Content Analysis to Explicate Service Climate Themes," *Journal of Applied Psychology*, 77 (October), 705-716.

Shani, D. and S. Chalasani (1992), "Exploiting Niches Using Relationship Marketing," *Journal of Services Marketing*, 6 (Fall), 43-52.

Storbacka, K., T. Strandvik and C. Grönroos (1994), "Managing Customer Relationships for Profit: The Dynamics of Relationship Quality," *International Journal of Service Industry Management*, 5, 21-38.

Sutton, R.S. and A. Rafaeli (1988), "Untangling the Relationship between Emotion, Work and Organizational Sales: The Case of Convenience Stores," *Academy of Management Journal*, 31 (September), 461-487.

Trice, H.M. and J.M. Beyer (1993), *The Cultures of Work Organizations*. Englewood Cliffs, NJ: Prentice-Hall.

Vavra, T. (1992), *Aftermarketing: How to Keep Customers for Life Through Relationship Marketing*. Homewood, IL: Business One Irwin.

Winkleman, M., D. Schultz, D. Edelman and M. Silverstein (1993), "Up Close and Personal," *Journal of Business Strategy*, 14 (July/August), 23-31.

Zeithaml, V., A. Parasuraman and L. Berry (1991), *Delivering Service Quality*. New York: Free Press.

DUAL COMPETITIVE ADVANTAGE
FOR SERVICE FIRMS

Roger Hallowell

ABSTRACT

This research attempts to (1) demonstrate that, contrary to conventional wisdom, "outlier" firms in a number of service industries have sustained competitive advantage through both cost leadership and differentiation (dual competitive advantage); and (2) suggest a framework explaining the phenomenon. The framework argues that service differentiation and cost leadership can be sustained concurrently through the support of a combination of organizational and strategic positioning-based initiatives. Specifically, organizational factors that encourage employee commitment and choices inherent to each firm's strategic positioning which focus operations on specific needs of targeted customers are both critical to the achievement of dual competitive advantage at these firms. These organizational and positioning based initiatives affect the firms examined both independently and interactively, creating formidable barriers to emulation. Analyses estimate the scale of the organizational and positioning choice benefits to cost leadership, demonstrating that these firms rely on both. Evidence presented suggests that employee commitment may be the source of these firms' ability to sustain their dual competitive advantage.

Advances in Services Marketing and Management, Volume 6, pages 23-59.
ISBN: 0-7623-0176-7

INTRODUCTION

An examination of the strategic positioning of four service firms presents a puzzling phenomenon. These four firms are both cost leaders in their industries and differentiated in the service they provide. Further, they have maintained this position of "dual competitive advantage" for some years, suggesting that it is sustained. To avoid superficiality in light of space constraints, this paper presents detailed findings on two of the four firms examined in this study, Southwest Airlines and The Vanguard Group of Mutual Funds.[1]

Southwest Airlines and The Vanguard Group's dual competitive advantage is derived from management initiatives described in both the organizational-strategy and competitive-strategy literatures. The organizational or resource-based literature (Barney 1992, 1986a, 1986b; Prahalad and Hamel 1990; Stalk, Evans and Schulman 1992; Teece and Pisano 1994; Ulrich and Lake 1990; Wernerfelt 84; among others) attributes the source of a firm's competitive advantage to organizational factors, specifically capabilities or core competencies. In contrast, the competitive-strategy literature (Caves 1984; Caves and Porter 1977; Ghemawat 1991; and Porter 1995, 1985, 1981, 1980, among others) focuses on a firm's strategic positioning in its environment and argues that strategic position is the source of competitive advantage. This research will attempt to integrate the two perspectives, arguing that dual competitive advantage at the firms examined requires (1) organizational factors with strategic value (Barney 1992); (2) positioning based initiatives; and (3) the interaction of the two. This integrative approach draws on the traditional business policy research of Learned, Christensen, Andrews and Guth (1969) and their successors.[2]

Organizational theories of competitive advantage partially explain the ability of the firms examined to manage frontline service providers in such a way that they deliver quality service efficiently. The firms examined have organizational factors enabling them to gain commitment from frontline service providers to the goals of the organization. These goals focus on the delivery of value to the customer, with customer value defined as both low price (requiring the firm to have cost leadership) and quality service (quality service being a positive service experience appropriate to the firm's particular industry segment).

Strategic-positioning theories of competitive advantage also partially explain these firms' dual competitive advantage. Each of these firms has achieved a strategic position that requires it to choose between several alternative positions, that is, to provide one type of service and not another. For example, an investment firm choosing a competitive positioning of "low risk" excludes the possibility of offering risky invetments. Porter (1995) refers to these choices as "trade-offs." (Note that these choices have no connection to choices among generic strategies as discussed by Porter [1985, 1980] and Caves [1984]). The choices made by the firms examined (described later in this paper) help them to focus their operations on specific needs of targeted customers. These focused operations (Skinner 1974) are capable of delivering higher levels of service and cost leadership than the less focused operations of competitors.

Interactive sources of competitive advantage are also important in explaining the existence of dual competitive advantage at these firms. Interactive sources occur when firms' positioning choices are consistent with, and reinforce, their organizational capabilities. As such, these sources of competitive advantage are created by factors both internal (organizational) and external (competitive-positioning based) to the firm. Interactive sources occur when positioning choices reinforce the improved operational ability created by the firms' organizational factors and vice versa. Interactions of this type are a multidisciplinary phenomenon referred to as "alignment" by Porter (1995) in the strategy literature, "complementarities" by Milgrom and Roberts (1992) in the economics literature and "congruence" by Nadler and Tushman (1992) in a sociologically based organizational context.

To date, the combinations of organizational, positioning based and interactive sources of competitive advantage at these firms have been difficult to emulate, enabling them to sustain their dual competitive advantage (see Figure 1). While each source of competitive advantage contributes to sustainability, employee commitment appears to provide a particularly difficult-to-emulate source, as suggested by Heskett, Sasser and Hart (1990), Ulrich and Lake (1990) and Pfeffer (1994). Part III of this paper presents evidence supporting this hypothesis.

This research documents these firms' dual competitive advantage and explains it with a framework that may be applicable to other services where labor is an important component of cost and capable of differentiating the

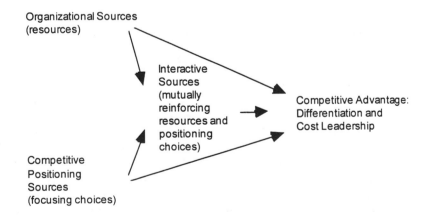

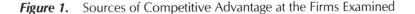

Figure 1. Sources of Competitive Advantage at the Firms Examined

quality of service on a day-to-day basis. The framework is presented as a "walking stick" (Roethlisberger 1939) for academics and managers.

METHODOLOGY AND ORGANIZATION

The study, and its methodologies, can be divided into three sections. Each is briefly highlighted.

Part I: Evidence of dual competitive advantage (cost and service leadership) is provided using publicly available cost data, and the results of surveys on service levels and (when available) behavioral evidence of service. Triangulation is used to validate service data.

Part II: Field-based clinical research is used to understand the firms' (1) organizational factors; (2) positioning choices; and (3) the alignment between them. Analyses of cost and operating data permit an estimation of the scale of organizational and positioning choice sources of cost leadership at the two firms. These analyses demonstrate that the firms rely on both sources of competitive advantage.

Part III: Quantitative studies of employee turnover rates (a behavioral proxy for commitment) support the hypothesized role of employee commitment as a factor enabling these firms to achieve dual competitive advantage. Analysis of a natural experiment occurring at Southwest Airlines confirms the role of commitment in sustaining dual competitive advantage there.

For the purposes of this paper, a firm will be considered to have dual competitive advantage when it is a leader on either cost or service differentiation dimensions and simultaneously delivers above-industry median levels on the other dimension.[3] However, note that the firms examined in this paper are industry leaders on both cost and service differentiation dimensions.

DUAL COMPETITIVE ADVANTAGE IN THEORY

Strategy theory, both competitive (Caves 1984; Porter 1980) and manufacturing (Hayes and Pisano 1996), argues that trade-offs in generic strategies are a part of the world in which firms operate. Caves argues that firms should choose between cost leadership, differentiation and focus due to limits in "managerial coordinating capacity and the need to select a system of internal organization, evaluation and reward that is designed for optimal pursuit of the chosen strategy" (Caves 1984, p. 127). Note that focus does not apply to Vanguard or Southwest using Caves' (1984) definition.[4] Hayes and Pisano argue that manufacturers should choose between cost and flexibility. Both arguments are made in terms of an industry frontier trade-off curve which illustrates possible combinations of the two options. This research does not challenge the wisdom behind such choices for the vast majority of firms.

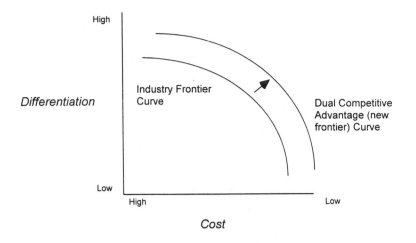

Figure 2. Frontier Trade-Off Curves for an Industry
and a Firm with Dual Competitive Advantage

However, it does illustrate that firms like Vanguard and Southwest occupy unusual positions vis-à-vis their competitors.

Southwest Airlines and The Vanguard Group believe that their purpose is to deliver both low price (necessitating cost leadership) and quality service (or differentiation),[5] which they call customer value. These firms see value as a function of price charged relative to quality of service delivered for a targeted customer.

This value perspective is reconciled with the trade-off perspective of strategy theory by considering the industry frontier trade-off curve movable, as suggested in Figure 2. In effect, these firms move the trade-off curve out, delivering both low price (necessitating low cost) and service quality to their customers, effectively creating a new frontier curve. When competitors are unable to push out the industry curve to match that of the new frontier curve, dual competitive advantage results. The forces that prevent competitors from pushing out the industry curve are the sources of sustainability for dual competitive advantage.

Another theoretical perspective useful to the analysis of dual competitive advantage is derived from Porter's (1985) discussion of value chains. Brandenburger and Stuart (1996) have developed a technique they call "value analysis," which enables a firm to view itself in contrast to its competitors from the perspective of its ability to generate value for its primary constituents.

Value analysis can be intuitively understood by considering that the firm generates value for three primary constituents: (1) buyers; (2) the firm and its shareholders; and (3) suppliers (including employees).[6] Consider Figure 3.

Source: Value chain adapted from Brandenburger and Stuart (1996).

Figure 3.   Value Analysis

Willingness to pay is what buyers are willing to pay for a good or service (how much value they attach to it). Price is what the firm charges, and cost is what the firm must pay suppliers for their goods and services.[7] Opportunity cost is the minimum amount suppliers will sell a good or service for, preferring to retain the good or not engage in the service for any less compensation. The difference between willingness to pay and price is the buyers' portion of value created. The difference between price and cost is the firm's (and its shareholders') portion. Finally, the difference between cost and opportunity cost is the suppliers' portion of value.

Figure 3 presents an abstract value analysis for a mean industry competitor and a firm with dual competitive advantage. Note that service differentiation at the firm with dual competitive advantage increases willingness to pay. Simultaneously, cost leadership enables the firm to reduce prices.[8] This increases the value delivered to customers, encouraging loyalty and increasing volume, further reducing cost and increasing the value delivered to the firm and shareholders. Finally, opportunity cost is reduced for the firm's most important suppliers, the employees. This occurs because employees receive more value in monetary and or non-monetary compensation from the firm with dual competitive advantage than from competitor firms. Because unit costs have declined but supplier value has increased, opportunity cost must decline as cost less opportunity cost is the suppliers' portion of value created.

Value analysis illustrates that at firms with dual competitive advantage, the total amount of value created (the distance from willingness to pay to opportunity cost) has increased when compared to total value created by a mean competitor. In short, dual competitive advantage firms are focused on increasing the size of the value "pie" they create, not just on its division. Further, in asking the question "How does the firm increase willingness to pay and reduce cost?" the unusually large quantity of value suppliers (employees) receive must be considered potentially related. This paper will attempt to illustrate this relationship, arguing in the abstract that Vanguard and Southwest *create* value for their employees (increasing employee commitment), *convert* some of that value to customer value through superior quantity and quality of employee effort, and ultimately *capture* value in their ability to set a price floor for their industries due to their cost leadership.

Value analysis is particularly useful in the study of dual competitive advantage because it focuses strategy on its result, the delivery of value. Strategy, whether positioning or organizational factor-based, is only useful if it enables a firm to deliver more value than its competitors to its constituents. Thus, while value analysis is somewhat abstract, it is simultaneously grounded in the fundamental purpose of strategy. That grounding is useful to this research because the delivery of value is at the heart of the dynamic picture of value creation, value conversion and value capture described in this paper.

PART I: EVIDENCE OF DUAL COMPETITIVE ADVANTAGE

Southwest Airlines: Cost Leadership

Evidence of dual competitive advantage at Southwest Airlines lies in statistics compiled by the United States Department of Transportation. Cost data show that Southwest had the lowest costs per available seat mile (ASM) of the 10 major United States airlines for at least 1989-1995. Recent cost data appear in Table 1.

Southwest Airlines: Service Differentiation

Data on quality of service appears in the Department of Transportation's monthly *Air Travel Consumer Report*, compiled by the Office of Aviation Enforcement and Proceedings. This report provides statistics on the major U.S. airlines' percentage of (1) flights delayed; (2) mishandled bags; and (3) consumer complaints. In every year since 1991, Southwest has had the lowest percentage in all of these categories. Analysis of consumer complaints indicates that mishandled bags and delayed flights are among the most frequent types of complaints received by the department, suggesting that they are highly salient dimensions of service for passengers of U.S. major airlines.

The Vanguard Group: Cost Leadership

Vanguard's low cost position is illustrated in its funds' expense ratios contrasted to those of its competitors, as suggested by the data in Table 2.

Table 1. Major U.S. Airlines' Cost Data

	Operating Expenses per ASM (in ¢)			
Airline	1992	1993	1994	1995
Southwest	6.98	7.16	7.08	7.07
America West	7.10	7.01*	7.04*	7.19
Alaska	10.49	9.88	8.27	7.71
TWA	8.74	9.08	8.45	8.28
Continental	7.56	7.90	7.86	8.36
American	8.95	8.25	8.34	8.43
Northwest	9.22	9.23	8.08	8.66
Delta	9.48	9.23	9.10	8.84
United	8.86	8.54	8.79	8.87
USAir	10.85	11.12	11.02	11.40

Note: * Note that in 1993 America West was in bankruptcy, and in 1994 the carrier emerged from bankruptcy adopting fresh-start reporting and shedding many expenses (revenues and passengers enplaned declined by over 50% in 1994), making its 1993 and 1994 figures not truly comparable to those of other airlines.
Source: Annual Reports.

Table 2 contrasts Vanguard to its median competitor, using additional data from Morningstar, Inc., and Stanford C. Bernstein & Co. Research shows that Vanguard has the lowest costs among all major firms in the mutual fund industry (see, e.g., Table 4 and Appendix B).

As Vanguard is a mutual organization, ultimately owned by its funds' shareholders, it charges its funds for services at cost, in contrast to many of its competitors that include a profit margin in their mutual fund expenses. Analysis of the difference in median costs and Vanguard's costs quickly eliminates the possibility that a profit margin could explain the difference. The

Table 2. Mutual Fund Median Expense Ratios
(in basis points)

	1994	1984
Vanguard		
All equity	35	65
All bonds	24	52
Industry Median for		
Domestic equity	117	101
International equity	160	119
Money market	52	71
Taxable bonds	96	86
Municipal bonds	68	73

Sources: Company documents; Morningstar, Inc.; and Bernstein Research (1995).

1995 expense ratios of Vanguard bond funds show taxable funds, money market funds and tax exempt funds having expense ratios of 24, 23, and 21 basis points, respectively (based on data from Morningstar, Inc.).[9] If profit alone explained the difference between Vanguard's bond expenses and those of its median industry competitor, industry median pre-tax profit margin would have to be a low of 56 percent for money market funds and a high of 75 percent for taxable bond funds. Equity profit margins would be even more extreme. Industry leaders describe a total firm (results from all operations) pre-tax profit margin of approximately 40 percent for firms performing well. Appendix A illustrates a study of pre-tax profit margins of publicly traded mutual fund companies, which suggests an industry pre-tax profit margin of 34 percent. This conclusion reinforces the contention that profit margins alone do not explain the discrepancy between Vanguard's and median industry expense ratios.

John Bogle, CEO of Vanguard, believes that up to 15 basis points of Vanguard's cost leadership may be due to savings on marketing (Vanguard's marketing expenditures are just less than one-tenth of its competitors'). Vanguard management argues that the firm has been able to grow faster than its competitors (Light and Sailer 1993) while spending dramatically less on marketing because it has earned a reputation for low costs and good service, news of which travels through the press and by word-of-mouth from satisfied clients.

The Vanguard Group: Service Differentiation

Service quality at Vanguard is illustrated in data from four independent sources. That all four sources reach similar conclusions with no common source of bias increases confidence in each source's conclusion (triangulation). Information on the four sources follows.

First, data provided by the U.S. Securities and Exchange Commission and reported in Table 3 illustrates that Vanguard received the fewest consumer complaints of any of the top five direct-marketing mutual fund providers (its direct competitors, representing over 70 percent of total direct-market mutual fund assets [see Light and Sailer 1993]).

Next, between 1989 and 1995 (excluding 1994), *Financial World* magazine conducted an annual survey asking its readers about the quality of service they received from their mutual fund providers during the previous year. In each survey, Vanguard received the highest score (in one year, Vanguard scored second behind a small, niche firm but consistently received the highest score of any major mutual fund family). Surveys were returned by large numbers of readers (1993 respondents numbered 11,000). Note that potential survey bias in favor of a respondent's particular fund organizations is mitigated by the fact that many holders of mutual funds are clients of more than one fund family

Table 3.   Complaints to the U.S. Securities and Exchange Commission

Mutual Fund Provider	Service Complaints (absolute # / per $B in assets)	Performance Complaints (absolute # / per $B in assets)
Vanguard	11 / 0.08	2 / 0.01
Fidelity	86 / 0.33	5 / 0.02
T. Rowe Price	13 / 0.33	4 / 0.10
Scudder	15 / 0.47	8 / 0.25
Dreyfus	33 / 0.49	5 / 0.07

Notes: Performance complaints involve the return (or loss) a fund has delivered to the fund holder. Service complaints concern all other dimensions of the client/fund relationship.
Source: Based on 1994 data provided by the U.S. Securities and Exchange Commission.

and can therefore judge between or among service levels provided. The 1991 survey indicated that respondents owned funds from a mean of four fund families.

Third, 1990-1994 Vanguard studies of its clients illustrate that Vanguard service is perceived by them to be superior to that of any major competitor (as noted, 79 percent of Vanguard clients hold shares in other mutual fund organizations enabling them to make an informed comparison). Service dimensions examined include overall service, helpfulness of associates, timeliness of statements, toll-free telephone service and clarity of statements. Respondents deemed related service dimensions highly salient (a rating of 4+ on a five-point scale).

Finally, Vanguard's institutional investment services were also examined for the period 1991-1995. Proprietary data from an independent financial services market research firm confirm that service provided to institutions (as opposed to individual fund holders) is ranked consistently higher than mean industry levels and often in the top 20 percent of the market.

PART II: RESULTS OF FIELD-BASED CLINICAL RESEARCH: DESCRIPTIONS AND ANALYSES OF (1) ORGANIZATIONAL FACTORS, (2) POSITIONING CHOICES, AND (3) ALIGNMENT BETWEEN THEM

A brief discussion of the framework emerging from this research is followed by more detailed descriptions of the sources of competitive advantage at the organizations examined. The framework finds its roots in the work of Heskett and colleagues (1994).

The Framework

The framework proposed next (also see Figure 4) considers the organizational, competitive-positioning and interactive sources of competitive advantage common to the firms examined, specifically the following:

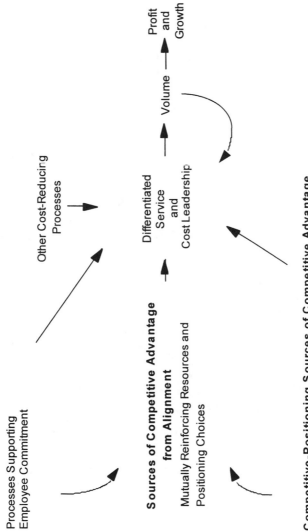

Resource-Based Sources of Competitive Advantage

Processes Supporting
Employee Commitment

Other Cost-Reducing
Processes

**Sources of Competitive Advantage
from Alignment**

Mutually Reinforcing Resources and
Positioning Choices

Differentiated
Service
and
Cost Leadership

Volume → Profit
and
Growth

Competitive-Positioning Sources of Competitive Advantage

Focusing Positioning Choices

Figure 4. Dual Competitive Advantage Framework

33

- Organizational initiatives at these firms stimulate employee commitment, resulting in employees who are motivated to serve customers well and perform efficiently.
- This motivation and efficiency, combined with tools provided by the firms designed to enable employees to provide good service efficiently (Schneider and Bowen 1993; Walton 1989), produce both quality service (differentiation) and some degree of low cost, or at least provide quality service without negating a low cost position created by other means.
- These firms' strategic positioning choices enable them to focus their operations to deliver low cost, high quality service meeting specific needs of targeted customers. For example, Vanguard's positioning as a firm offering low cost, low risk investments enables it to distinguish itself delivering index funds (essentially a commodity product) that (1) do not require expensive research and (2) enable Vanguard's organizational focus to remain on cost control and operational service quality.
- Organizational and positioning choice based initiatives also interact in a mutually reinforcing manner. Positioning choices enable the firms to focus their operations due to limited service offerings. These focused operations help motivated employees deliver service differentiation (and, in some cases, cost leadership) at these firms. This interaction is important as a source of sustainability for dual competitive advantage because it introduces (1) a self-reinforcing cycle (motivated employees able to deliver good service due to focused operations remain motivated) and (2) a new dimension of complexity in understanding and emulation for competitors to overcome.
- Other organizational factors (cost-reducing processes) and positioning choices also exist, sometimes not directly related to employees who serve customers.
- Customer satisfaction helps stimulate customer loyalty, increases volume and enables economies of scale at the operating level.
- Increased volume and economies of scale result in profit and growth.

Vanguard Organizational Factors: The Creation of Employee Commitment

Each of the firms examined has organizational factors enabling it to generate unusually high levels of employee commitment. Greater commitment exists because these firms deliver more value to their frontline employees than do their competitors. Value in these cases refers to different combinations of monetary and non-monetary exchange between the organization and the employee.

Vanguard is an organization that delivers superior levels of value to its managers and employees. Vanguard maintains a profit-sharing program that enables employees to dramatically augment (up to 30 percent of cash compensation) their already competitive salaries based on their performance and tenure at the firm (see Schlesinger and Heskett [1991] for a discussion of the role incentives can play in services). Vanguard also stresses respect and concern for individual employees as a critical part of management style, and reinforces its importance through training and evaluation of managers at all levels.

Vanguard has designed its corporate campus to be employee-friendly, windows being reserved for frontline employees. One manager commented, "It's the employees on the front line who deal with the clients—they deserve the best." Numerous services are available on campus for employees' convenience; staff can pick up their dry-cleaning, staple groceries and prepared dinners before leaving for home.

Delivering value to employees at Vanguard has an impact on service leadership and superior service quality in at least three ways. First, employees are focused on delivering quality service at a low cost because they share Vanguard's goals of (1) candid client communication; (2) speedy, accurate, friendly service; and (3) having the lowest costs possible. Second, costs are reduced through what is referred to as "constant vigilance." Employees and managers are continually aware of the need to reduce costs by eliminating waste and developing new and better ways to conduct business. Finally, individuals are willing to be flexible in order to meet the needs of the organization as a whole. Vanguard's Swiss Army is an example of this phenomenon. When call volume rises beyond levels that can be handled by the customer service representatives on duty, employees from other areas, including middle managers and executives, are called into the call centers to answer telephones.

Vanguard: Strategic Positioning Choices

The second important strategic ingredient in dual competitive advantage involves strategic positioning choices that help a firm to focus its operations to meet the needs of targeted customers.

Vanguard positions itself as the mutual fund investor's advocate. As a result, the firm is duty-bound to offer low costs and quality service, as well as funds that pose a relatively low level of risk for the average mutual fund investor. Many of Vanguard's funds have low costs and low risk because they follow a defined asset strategy, that is, they state clearly what they will invest in and then invest in only those "defined" assets. This substantially reduces the amount of research necessary to manage the funds (more passive management reduces costs) and makes the risks inherent in the fund highly visible to an investor. Index funds are the most extreme example of defined asset class investing. Of those Vanguard funds that are actively managed, none have high levels of risk, and many are less risky than those of Vanguard's competitors. The manager of a competitor's high yield bond fund recently commented, "Vanguard has almost zero tolerance for risk." Competitor firms positioned to deliver high risk, high reward investment products must conduct expensive research, requiring stables of high priced investment managers. Less risky investment vehicles with low risk tolerances do not need to be managed by superstar investment managers who command enormous salaries. Vanguard's actively-managed equity funds are managed out of house.[10] Vanguard negotiates with the managers, offering high volume in exchange for lower expense ratios.

There is also an interactive element to Vanguard's positioning choices. Vanguard's organizational factors (including those stimulating employee commitment) encourage cost control and are thus compatible with a lower cost, lower risk product profile. In this case, the interaction occurs in the consistency of the strategic positioning and operating strategies, which reinforce one another, strengthening the whole.

Vanguard: The Scale of Organizational and Positioning Choice Contributions to Cost Leadership

As illustrated, organizational factors and positioning choices contribute to cost and service leadership at Vanguard. Estimates of the scale of organizational and positioning choice contributions to cost leadership demonstrate that both contribute to Vanguard's dual competitive advantage. An estimate of the scale of benefits from organizational factors (as noted, resources) can be derived by contrasting (A) expense ratios of Vanguard funds that apply both positioning choice and organizational contributions to cost leadership to (B) expense ratios of competitors' funds with positioning choice, but no organizational benefits (after adjusting for profit).

Explanation: because this comparison contrasts (A), which has two types of benefits—organizational and positioning, to (B), which has only one of those benefits—positioning, (A) less (B) should result in an estimate of the benefit exclusive to (A). For example:

$$[organizational + positioning] - positioning = organizational$$

Table 4 illustrates such an analysis by contrasting expense ratios for Vanguard index funds to mean expense ratios for similar index funds at major competitors (such a like-kind contrast negates the benefit of indexing, the source of Vanguard's positioning choice benefit to cost leadership).

The effect of positioning choices on cost leadership at Vanguard can be estimated by comparing (1) the mean expense ratio of Vanguard funds enjoying benefits to cost leadership from both strategic positioning choices and organizational factors to (2) competitors' mean expense ratio for all similar funds not enjoying those benefits. This difference is then adjusted to remove profit and the effect of Vanguard's organizational factors, established in Table 4.

Table 4.   Scale of Organizational Factors Contribution to Cost Leadership
at Vanguard

Fund Family	Mean Index Fund Expense Ratio (in basis points)
Vanguard	21
T. Rowe Price	45
Fidelity	45
Schwab	63
Dreyfus	68
Franklin	73
Scudder	80
Janus	na
Mean (excluding Vanguard)	62
Mean weighted by individual funds (excluding Vanguard)	65
Less 34% pre-tax industry profit margin	22
Industry (excluding Vanguard) weighted mean expense ratio excluding profit	43
Less Vanguard mean expense ratio of	21
Vanguard cost reduction due to organizational factors	22

How to read this table: "Mean Index Fund Ratio" is chosen for analysis because it adjusts for product, creating a like-kind comparison of fund expenses for all funds enjoying the cost benefits of indexing (eliminating positioning choice as a source of cost leadership). "Weighted mean" gives each fund (as opposed to each fund family) an equal weighting in the calculation of the mean. "Industry (excluding Vanguard) weighted mean expense ratio excluding profit" adjusts the mean industry expense figure for profit, making it comparable to Vanguard's expense ratio (which does not include a profit component). "Vanguard cost reduction due to organizational factors" is Vanguard's expense ratio subtracted from the adjusted industry mean expense ratio, organizational factors being the only explanation for the difference (profit and positioning choices having been eliminated in the analysis).

Notes: Excludes "institutional" funds for retirement and/or institutional investors.

See Appendix I for information about the industry pre-tax margin and for a replication of this analysis for domestic equity funds.

Note that size of fund does not correlate to expense ratio except in the extreme (funds over $10 billion) when expense ratios decline approximately 10 basis points.

Source: Morningstar, Inc., 1995 data.

Calculations are provided in Appendix B. The result is a contribution to Vanguard's cost leadership from positioning choices of 30 basis points. Note that the estimates of contributions from both positioning choices and organizational factors may also include benefits from interactive sources.

Southwest Organizational Factors: The Creation of Employee Commitment

At Southwest, employees earn an industry-standard monetary wage but receive substantial non-monetary value as part of the total Southwest employee experience. Southwest actively encourages fun on the job, and its values stress concern and respect for individuals. These factors make the experience of working at Southwest highly desirable for people who are carefully selected by the firm to fit into this type of environment.

Fun coupled with respect and concern for the individual are referred to as "luv" at Southwest. Luv was Southwest's original marketing theme, designed to differentiate the airline from its competitors in the early 1970s. Flying out of Love airfield in Dallas, Southwest styled itself as "the somebody else up there who luvs you." Free drinks were referred to as "luv potions," and instant ticketing devices were called "luv machines."[11] Over the years, luv also developed an internal meaning. Southwest developed a reputation as a "family feeling" place, where employees and managers worked hard, had a good time (frequent parties are a staple of the Southwest culture) and genuinely cared for one another. Warm greetings, hugs and ever-present smiles are the norm.

Having fun on the job, a critical part of luv, takes on several dimensions. Scheduled events have included a "plane pull," in which a team from Southwest was pitted against a fire department to benefit a local charity. More frequently, gate agents hold contests to see which passenger has the biggest hole in his or her sock. Flight attendants tell jokes and sing to passengers. Employees sometimes don costumes, particularly at holidays (Elvis, the Easter Bunny, Count Dracula and other celebrities have been sighted on Southwest flights). On at least one occasion, flight attendants have hidden in the overhead luggage bins to surprise unsuspecting Customers (passengers are Customers, always spelled with an uppercase "C"). Fun at Southwest helps to develop commitment to the organization and its goals of low costs and excellent service. Employees and line managers are frequently reminded of these goals through corporate and personal communication with top management.

While Southwest has one of the highest percentages of unionized employees among the major U.S. airlines (more than 80 percent), all contracts permit employees to perform any task. Pilots have been known to carry bags to ensure on-time departures. This ability to cross-utilize, along with employees who are committed to the goals of the organization, contributes to an explanation of how Southwest, which pays industry-mean wages and benefits, has the lowest operating cost per employee of all major U.S. airlines (see Table 5).

Organizational factors sometimes include tools provided to employees to facilitate the delivery of quality service efficiently. Both Southwest and Vanguard provide tools to enable their committed employees to provide low-cost, differentiated service. These tools vary, including tangible tools such as telephony systems at Vanguard and intangible tools such as cross-utilization and procedures at Southwest. However, while some of Southwest's tools are superior to those employed by its competitors (Gittell 1995), there is no evidence suggesting that Vanguard's tools are similarly superior. In fact, Vanguard is known for staying off the "bleeding" edge of technology and, until recently,

Table 5. Major U.S. Airlines
Operating Cost per Employee

Airline	Operating Cost per Employee ($000)
Southwest	128
TWA	141
American*	145
Continental	160
America West	160
USAir	166
United	174
Northwest	182
Alaska	192
Delta	192

Note: * Excludes extraordinary loss.
Source: 1995 company annual reports.

has lagged behind some of its competitors in areas such as computer systems which create client statements. From this evidence emerges the hypothesis that *superior* tools can, but do not necessarily, play a role in the development of dual competitive advantage.

Southwest: Strategic Positioning Choices

Southwest Airlines has positioned itself as a short-haul carrier, having a mean flight time of 65 minutes. This competitive positioning choice delivers several operating advantages, including a lack of first-class cabins (unnecessary on short-haul flights, in which convenience and reliability are more important than space) and no need to serve meals, both of which increase space for seats. Southwest also positions itself as a point-to-point carrier, which does not book tickets for interline travel (travel on other carriers). As a result, the airline can fly into smaller airports near city centers which are served by fewer (if any) other airlines. Using these smaller airfields reduces total passenger travel time and cuts costs through enhanced productivity (reduced airport congestion results in shorter taxi and waiting periods).

Southwest also has interactive sources of competitive advantage. Its operational simplification from positioning choices such as similar aircraft (Southwest's fleet contains only 737s) and no meals, combined with employee commitment to organizational goals such as rapid aircraft turn, reduces the time aircraft must sit at the gate. This increases aircraft and employee utilization. In these (and other) ways, Southwest's positioning trade-offs reinforce its capabilities in cost control and the development of employee commitment, illustrating alignment.

Southwest: The Scale of Organizational and Positioning Choice Contributions
to Cost Leadership

As with Vanguard, estimates of the scale of organizational and positioning choice contributions to cost leadership demonstrate that both contribute to Southwest's dual competitive advantage.

Table 6 illustrates the results of Southwest's positioning choices, as well as the effects of Southwest's organizational factors and the interaction of the two. This data provides an "apples-to-apples" comparison of Southwest and some of its competitors by analyzing block-hour costs and daily operating statistics for virtually identical aircraft (dissimilarities in aircraft of the same model are due to airline preferences).

Examination of the data in Table 6 illustrates the role of physical and human asset utilization in increasing operating volume (capacity) and reducing operating costs at Southwest. Crew cost offers a prime example. For the 737-500, Southwest's crew costs are 21 percent below those of its mean competitor.[12] Yet (as noted) Southwest pays wages and benefits at the industry-mean level. This unlikely combination occurs due to the additional volume evident in the ASM (available seat mile) and RPM (revenue passenger mile) figures, which illustrate that Southwest has 21 percent more ASMs, or capacity, than its mean competitor flying virtually identical aircraft. More ASMs, if managed properly, lead to more RPMs, which enhance human and physical asset productivity, reducing unit costs in a high fixed-cost operation such as an airline. This reduction in unit cost is evident in the 15 percent operating cost per ASM advantage Southwest has over its mean competitor for the 737-500.

The data in Table 6 illustrates the links between physical and human asset utilization and cost advantage at Southwest. Table 7 explores this idea further. The logic behind the analysis in Table 7 (and Appendix C, which provides supporting calculations) is that Southwest has positioning choice, organizational and interactive sources of competitive advantage which act to increase its capacity (resulting in increased productivity and reducing costs). In some cases, the sources of competitive advantage can be traced directly to their effects, making it possible to estimate the scale of benefit from particular positioning choices.[13] Note that there may be additional interactive effects not identified in this analysis; for example, managers at Southwest contend that the use of less congested airports enhances commitment by sparing employees from frequent delays and disgruntled passengers.

Alignment of Strategic Positioning Choices and Organizational Factors

The preceding sections noted the alignment of Vanguard and Southwest's sources of competitive advantage. Tables 8 and 9 further illustrate the existence of this alignment, based on a persuasive argument made by Nadler and

Table 6. Major Airlines Flying 737-1/200s, 737-300s, and 737-500s: 1994 Block-Hour* Costs and Daily Utilization

	Total Operations		Departures	ASMs (000)	RPMs (000)	Operating Cost per ASM (¢)
	Crew Cost	Cost				
737-1/200						
Southwest	$323	$1,365	8.6	385	259	3.42
United	$503	$1,808	4.9	250	164	5.36
USAir	$669	$1,875	6.1	285	174	5.64
Delta	$583	$1,994	6.2	307	179	5.95
Mean excluding Southwest	$585	$1,892	5.7	281	172	5.65
% Southwest differs from mean	-45%	-28%	+51%	+37%	+51%	-39%
737-300						
Southwest	$334	$1,457	9.4	513	339	3.24
Continental	$320	$1,636	6.0	439	254	3.85
United	$492	$2,110	4.7	463	309	4.59
USAir	$596	$2,114	5.1	453	294	4.70
Mean excluding Southwest	$469	$1,953	5.3	452	286	4.38
% Southwest differs from mean	-29%	-25%	+77%	+13%	+19%	-26%
737-500						
Southwest	$327	$1,373	9.4	447	311	3.41
Continental	$338	$1,230	5.4	362	225	3.44
United	$493	$1,773	4.9	376	258	4.61
Mean excluding Southwest	$416	$1,502	5.2	369	242	4.03
% Southwest differs from mean	-21%	-9%	+81%	+21%	+29%	-15%

Note: * Block hours are from blocks under wheels out at origin (engines start and push back) to blocks in (engines cut at flight destination).

Sources: Raw data: Avitas data based on DOT form 41 filings in Lample (1996).

41

Table 7.   Southwest Airlines: Sources of Cost Leadership
through Capacity Expansion

Source of Cost Leadership	Effect	Change in Capacity
Strategic positioning choices		
Point-to-point service:		
Uncongested airports	Reduces "tarmac time"*	+8.4%
Short haul:		
No meals	Enables smaller galley permitting more seats	
No first class	Enables more seats	
	Total "seats" effect	+9.2%
Disadvantage of short haul	Requires more frequent aircraft turns	-18.8%
Operational simplification:		
No interline baggage		
No meals	Facilitates rapid	
Fleet of 737s	aircraft turns	(see below)
Organizational factors and interactions		
Employee commitment	Reduces aircraft turn time through superior effort, cross-utilization, and willingness to engage in activities such as cross-functional coordination	
Benefits from employee commitment cannot be meaningfully measured separately from benefits from operational simplification (illustrating alignment at Southwest)—total:		+22.9%

Note: * Tarmac time is block time less flight time, or time an aircraft spends after pushback, taxiing, and holding
on the runway at the departure airport (until takeoff) and taxi time (plus wait time) between runway
and gate at the arrival airport. See Appendix C for calculations.

Tushman (1992), who state that when alignment exists, there will be consistency among an organization's needs, demands, goals and structures. Tables 8 and 9 illustrate the needs and demands, goals and structures applicable to the positioning choices and organizational factors discussed for Vanguard and Southwest. These charts illustrate a high level of consistency between the needs/demands, goals and structures of these firms' (1) organizational factors and (2) positioning choices.

Other Organizational Factors and Low Cost Strategies

As suggested in Figure 4, each of these firms also has other organizational factors and positioning choices which help to reduce costs and or improve

Table 8. Alignment of Positioning Choices and Organizational Factors at Vanguard

	Needs/Demands	Goals	Structures
Competitive Positioning Choice			
"The Investor's Advocate"	Operations delivering low cost and quality service Low-risk investment strategy Candid communication with clients	Low price Quality service Low risk Informed clients	Indexing/out-of-house Highly qualified employees Constant vigilance Profit-sharing Volume Organizational values Computing/telephony
Organizational Resources			
Employee Commitment and Tools	Sources of labor Greater value delivered to employees: Monetary Non-monetary Computing/telephony	Quality service Informed clients Low cost	Recruiting and selection Profit-sharing Management style Organizational values Benefits (including campus) Volume Buy versus make technology

Table 9. Alignment of Positioning Choices and Organizational Factors at Southwest

	Needs/Demands	Goals	Structures
Competitive Positioning Choices			
Short-haul, point-to-point service, priced to compete with car travel	Adherence to schedules Low baggage non-conformance Employees who are friendly and genuinely concerned for customers Low costs	Low price Reliability Friendly service	Less congested airports No meals Fleet all 737s No interline baggage Volume Quick turns Values and "luv"
Organizational Factors			
Employee Commitment and Tools	Greater non-monetary value delivered to employees Adherence to schedules People fitting into the "Southwest spirit"	Low cost Reliability Friendly service	Selection Less congested airports Competitive pay Organizational values Quick turns Volume

44

Table 10. Vanguard Employee Productivity

Mutual Fund Family	Employees per $1 Billion in Assets under Management	Relative to Vanguard
Vanguard	19	1.0
Janus	27	1.4
T. Rowe Price	31	1.6
Franklin Templeton	34	1.8
Fidelity	48	2.5
Scudder	57	3.0
Mean (excluding Vanguard)	39	2.1

Notes: These firms are largely comparable in terms of economies of scale and scope being direct marketing mutual fund families with in-house service operations and over $10 billion in assets under management. Personal and corporate investment management services at Scudder and T. Rowe Price may slightly overstate Vanguard's employee productivity advantage in contrast to these competitors.

Sources: Company and parent company annual reports, The Investment Company Institute, company public relations offices, Dunn and Bradstreet (1996).

service. For example, Southwest does not book through all of the computerized reservation systems, which makes it less attractive to travel agents and results in significant savings on travel agent commissions. Similarly, Vanguard does not offer its mutual funds through multi-fund outlets, such as Charles Schwab's Onesource, which saves clients the hidden commission Schwab applies to such sales.

Volume

Volume at the operating level is evident in aircraft and employee utilization at Southwest (see Table 6) and in employees relative to assets under management at Vanguard (see Table 10). Volume fuels the virtuous cycle these firms enjoy, enhancing profit for Southwest and reducing costs further for Vanguard while driving growth for each. This growth and further evidence of organizational success at Southwest has been documented by Pfeffer (1994, p. 4), who reports a 1972-1992 return to Southwest shareholders of 21,775 percent. Success at Vanguard is discussed in the Harvard Business School case, "The Vanguard Group" (Light and Sailer 1993).

PART III: STUDIES OF EMPLOYEE COMMITMENT AT SOUTHWEST AIRLINES AND THE VANGUARD GROUP

The framework outlined in Figure 4 suggests that firms with dual competitive advantage should have a high level of employee commitment relative to their competitors (in firms where labor is capable of differentiating the quality of

Table 11.   Major U.S. Airlines Employee Turnover Study
(Nine of ten carriers participating)
(In percentages, 1994/1995)

Turnover Rates	Total Domestic Organization	Pilots	Flight Attendants	Agents*	Mechanics and Related Ground Crew**	Clerical
Mean	12.1/12.4	3.3/2.8	6.8/4.7	15.6/18.9	14.5/13.7	16.6/15.4
Median	10.2/10.1	2.7/1.8	4.5/3.7	12.9/16.2	10.7/10.1	12.9/14.0

Notes: * Agents are defined as non-flight customer contact personnel.
  ** Includes mechanics, fuelers, cleaners, and baggage handlers.

service and is an important component of cost). These studies, and the natural experiment occurring at Southwest (described in this section), confirm that Vanguard and Southwest do have high levels of behavioral commitment and that commitment can play an important role in sustaining dual competitive advantage.

Southwest Airlines

A survey was conducted requesting information on employee turnover from the 10 largest U.S. airlines.[14] Nine of the 10 major airlines chose to participate (Alaska, America West, American, Continental, Delta, Northwest, Southwest, TWA and USAir).[15] Results are provided in Table 11.

Survey results indicate that Southwest's employee turnover for all categories was either the lowest or second-lowest of the nine carriers participating.[16] From this data, it is reasonable to conclude that Southwest has among the lowest, if not the lowest, turnover rates in its industry. While turnover is not a perfect proxy for employee commitment, it is often a good behavioral measurement of it (Mowday, Porter and Steers 1984), particularly in an economy such as that of the United States, in which frontline service providers often switch jobs with great frequency (Schlesinger and Heskett 1991).

Employee Commitment and Service Quality

Figure 5 illustrates the relationship between employee turnover and 1994 passenger complaints to the Department of Transportation for the nine airlines participating in the turnover study.

Figure 5 illustrates that a relationship exists between complaints and employee turnover in the U.S. airline industry, validating (in part) the relationship between employee commitment and service quality hypothesized

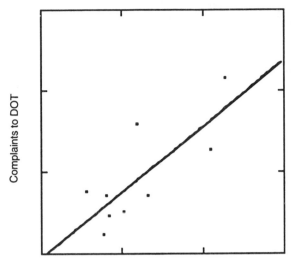

Note: Correlation = 0.79.

Figure 5. Complaints and Employee Turnover
at Major U.S. Airlines

in the framework presented in Figure 2.[17] Given that Southwest has the lowest costs of any major U.S. airline, it is also reasonable to conclude that the cost of employee commitment is not great enough to negate cost advantages derived from other sources, or that employee commitment may, at some firms, help to deliver cost leadership. Descriptive evidence suggests that for Southwest, the latter may be the case (see Hallowell 1996).

A Natural Experiment

A natural experiment occurring in the U.S. airline industry confirms the role of employee commitment in sustaining Southwest's dual competitive advantage. Both Continental and United Airlines attempted to emulate Southwest's quick turnaround strategy. In 1993, Continental introduced "Lite" flights. By late 1994, the program had been dubbed a failure and dismantled. United began its quick-turn strategy ("Shuttle by United") in 1994 as a way to regain share in the West Coast short-haul markets, of which Southwest had recently captured over 50 percent. By 1996, United had acknowledged that its shuttle had failed as an "offensive" strategy and reduced shuttle flights, often abandoning routes not integral to United's long-haul network (see Figure 6).

Sources of Competitive Advantage from Strategic Positioning Choices	Southwest	Shuttle by United	Continental Lite
No meals	Yes	Yes	Yes
No assigned seats	Yes	WILMA	No
No interline baggage	Yes	No	No
Similar aircraft	Yes	Yes	No
Uncongested airports	Mix	Mix	Mix

Sources of Competitive Advantage from Organizational Factors			
Employee commitment	Yes	No	No

Results	Continued success	Fails on operational and cost goals; CEO describes as "defensive" strategy; used to feed long-haul routes; withdraws from some markets served by SWA; losing money as of 3/96.	Ended

Sources: Company annual reports; Ziemba (1994); Bernstein (1996); *Aviation Daily* (1994); *The National Law Journal* (1994).

Figure 6. A Natural Experiment

Figure 6 illustrates the dimensions on which Continental and United successfully emulated Southwest. Because United's emulation of Southwest encompassed all of the dimensions achieved by Continental and others Continental was unable to emulate, this discussion will now turn to a comparison of Southwest and United.

Shuttle by United emulated every strategic positioning choice Southwest has made with the exception of no interline baggage transfer. Routes were short; meals were eliminated; planes were identical (also 737s) and airports were mixed in terms of degree of congestion.[18] While Southwest has a policy of no assigned seats in order to speed the passenger boarding process, United developed a system called WILMA in which passengers sitting in window seats boarded first, followed by those in middle seats, with aisle passengers boarding last. United claimed that this process reduced boarding time significantly and was designed to help make the Shuttle's turn time competitive with Southwest's (see Ziemba 1994). (United's goal, never achieved, was to turn aircraft in 20 minutes, while Southwest turns aircraft in 17.5.)

Clearly, positioning choices did not stop Shuttle by United's efforts to emulate Southwest because Shuttle by United successfully emulated almost all of Southwest's positioning choices. The only positioning choice United did not emulate, interline baggage transfer (the ability to check bags from one airline to another), is difficult to envision as the single reason for United's failure.

The variable(s) that prevented Shuttle by United from emulating Southwest's success must therefore have been organizational (or organizational and interactive). Southwest's primary organizational factor identified in this research is its employee commitment.[19] While other organizational factors at Southwest may also be involved (e.g., cross-functional coordination, as suggested by Gittell [1995], or an ingrained organizational frugality, as noted by Heskett and Hallowell [1993]), employee commitment is an integral part of these factors. Alignment of organizational factors and positioning choices may also be sources of sustainability for Southwest.

This relatively simple, natural experiment illustrates the power of employee commitment in sustaining Southwest's dual competitive advantage. The importance of employee commitment has been recognized by Southwest's management for some time. Herb Kelleher, Southwest CEO, invited Continental executives to visit Southwest and observe its operations. When asked to explain why he made this invitation to a competitor that had publicly set out to emulate his firm, he commented (paraphrased here) that his competitors could copy any aspect of his operations they wanted to, but they would never be able to copy Southwest's people's spirit.

The Vanguard Group

A survey was also conducted of large (more than $10 billion in assets) mutual fund organizations that market directly to the public and do not serve a niche market.[20] Six of the eight firms meeting the criteria for the survey elected to participate. The results of the study are presented in Table 12.

Vanguard's employee turnover rates are considerably lower than those of any of the other participating firms for the organizations as a whole. They are also considerably lower than those of the other firms for employees in

Table 12. Mutual Fund Families Employee Turnover Study
(Six of eight eligible families participating)
(In percentages, 1994/1995)

Turnover Rates	Total Domestic Organization*	Customer Service Representatives	Back Office Operations Employees
Mean	13.4/13.7	18.1/19.0	14.4/12.2
Median	14.9/13.6	17.2/21.3	13.4/11.1

Note: * Total relevant employees for vendor firm used in lieu of total organization.

particular job categories in 96 percent of the intra- and inter-company categories examined. This data suggest that Vanguard's employee commitment is higher than mean industry levels and is likely among the highest in its industry.

IMPLICATIONS: ACADEMIC SYNTHESIS AND MANAGERIAL RELEVANCE

This research identifies the interdependence of strategic positioning and organizational strategic perspectives while simultaneously acknowledging that each research stream offers independent insight into distinct aspects of competitive advantage. As such, the research is consistent with Bower's (1982, p. 631) advice that "the selection of ends [strategic positioning] turns critically on which means [organizational factors] a management is capable of pursuing." Managers on a quest for the "Holy Grail" of strategy may want to consider this interdependence and recognize that none of the strategy research streams discussed in this paper provide a panacea for all business situations if taken alone.

This research also illustrates that dual competitive advantage is possible for services. Managers of such services need to be aware that cost leadership and service differentiation can be simultaneously achieved. Reworded from the customer's perspective, managers need to recognize that customers are interested in value as they define it, which often involves both low price and quality service.

Finally, this research reinforces one of the most important themes in the service management literature: for many labor-dominant services, a firm does well by doing good. Firms with dual competitive advantage put their employees and customers first (a delicate balancing act vastly simplified by targeting appropriate employees and customers). Despite this, or perhaps because of it, their shareholders (who, as noted, are customers in Vanguard's case) have been amply rewarded. By focusing on creating value for employees and then converting it to customer value, these firms deliver more value to both employees and customers than their competitors do. Like the chicken and the egg, employee value begets customer value, enabling the creation of more employee value, and vice versa. The role of employee commitment illustrated in this research makes it possible to suggest that for labor-dominant services, both customer and employee value must be organizational foci if dual competitive advantage is to be achieved and sustained.

APPENDIX A: EXAMINATION OF MUTUAL FUND INDUSTRY PRE-TAX PROFIT MARGINS

As many mutual funds are privately held, complete data is unavailable. This study represents a gross estimation to check if 1) the industry wisdom (stating that mutual funds performing well have an approximately 40 percent pre-tax margin) is reasonable; and 2) the author's contention that profit margins do not explain the discrepancy between Vanguard's expenses and those of the median industry competitor is valid. Based on the data presented here, the author believes that these conclusions are reasonable.

Mutual Fund Provider	1994 Profit Margin Before Tax
Pioneer Corp.*	25%
Eaton Vance Corp.**	27%
Franklin Resources**	56%
T. Rowe Price**	26%
The Dreyfus Corporation***	31%
Janus Capital Corporation****	39%
Mean profit margin before tax	34%

Notes: * Investment management business only, other expenses prorated.

       ** Investment management business primarily.

       *** Investment services division of the Mellon Bank.

       **** Includes results of the Berger Funds, a Division of Kansas City Southern Corp., which contributed 15 percent of combined total revenues.

Fidelity Investments (a private company that makes some data available to the public) has been excluded from this analysis intentionally in light of its approximately 16 percent pre-tax profit margin, which is hypothesized to be caused by its practice of reducing net income through managerial compensation. The organizations included comprise all of the direct-market fund families with more than $10 billion in assets under management that release data on profitability, as well as two firms (Pioneer and Eaton Vance) that do not meet all of these criteria but do release data and are largely comparable.

APPENDIX B:
CALCULATIONS FOR POSITIONING CHOICE AND INTERACTIVE CONTRIBUTIONS TO COST LEADERSHIP AT VANGUARD

Vanguard domestic equity index funds (funds enjoying the benefits of both Vanguard's (1) strategic positioning choices and (2) organizational factors mean expenses: 22 basis pts.

Adjusted for savings due to organizational factors contributions to cost leadership (see Table 4) of: 22 basis pts.

Effectively creating Vanguard expenses for funds enjoying the benefits of positioning choices, but not organizational factors of: 44 basis pts.

Mean competitors' non-index domestic equity funds
expenses (see Appendix B, Table B.1):   112 basis pts.

   profit @ 34 percent   38 basis pts.

*Effectively creating mean competitors' expenses for funds
not enjoying Vanguard's positioning-choice or organiza-
tional benefits and not earning any profit:*   74 basis pts.

*Comparison of expenses of competitors without any of
Vanguard's sources of cost leadership or profit (74 basis
pts.) to Vanguard's expenses excluding benefit from organizational factors (44 basis points) results in benefits from
Vanguard's positioning choices (and possibly interactive
sources of cost leadership):* $74 - 44 = 30$ basis pts.

Table B.1.   Scale of Organizational Factor Contribution
to Cost Leadership at Vanguard
(Replication for Domestic Equity Funds)

Fund Family	Mean Domestic Equity Fund (non-index) Expense Ratio (in basis points)
Vanguard	45
Schwab	89
Dreyfus	100
Franklin	107
Janus	107
T. Rowe Price	109
Scudder	123
Fidelity	141
Mean (excluding Vanguard)	111
Mean weighted by individual funds (excluding Vanguard)	112
34% pre-tax industry profit margin	38
Industry (excluding Vanguard) weighted mean expense ratio excluding profit	74
Less Vanguard mean costs of	45
Vanguard cost reduction due to organizational factors	29

Notes: Excludes "institutional" funds for retirement and/or institutional investors. Weighted mean gives each fund (as opposed to each fund family) an equal weighting.
      Vanguard cost reduction due to organizational factors for domestic equity funds excludes profit of out-of-house investment advisors.
      The discrepancy between the mean Vanguard cost reduction due to organizational factors of 22 basis points for index funds and 29 basis points for domestic equity funds may be due to differences in profitability among the fund types. The publicity Vanguard has generated surrounding its low costs may have pressured its competitors to cut their profit margins for truly like-kind investment products such as index funds. Thus actual profitability of index funds may be lower than mean profitability of 34%, and profitability of domestic equity funds may be above mean profit of 34%, explaining the discrepancy found here.
Source: Morningstar, Inc. 1995 expenses.

APPENDIX C:
CALCULATIONS FOR SOURCES OF COST LEADERSHIP
AT SOUTHWEST AIRLINES

The total operating day (all hours during which operations take place) is calculated for the three types of 737s Southwest operates in order to establish a baseline for capacity enhancements and detractions caused by strategic positioning choices and organizational factors:

	Hours
Total Day = block hours + [# of departures * turn time]	
Southwest:	
737-1/200	11.85
737-300	13.75
737-500	13.45

Calculations for Increased Capacity Due to Use of Airports with Reduced Congestion

[Block hours — flight hours] / # of flights = tarmac time per flight	
Southwest 737-1/200	0.19
Mean Competitor 737-1/200	0.30
difference	0.11
* # of Southwest route segments per aircraft per day (8.6)	0.95
Portion of current capacity (% of total day)	8.0%
Southwest 737-300	0.22
Mean Competitor	0.34
difference	0.12
* # of Southwest route segments per aircraft per day (9.4)	1.13
Portion of current capacity (% of total day)	8.2%
Southwest 737-500	0.19
Mean Competitor	0.33
difference	0.14
* # of Southwest route segments per aircraft per day (9.4)	1.32
Portion of current capacity (% of total day)	9.8%
Southwest portion of current capacity due to use of uncongested airports, weighted by number of aircraft of each type in operation	8.4%

(continued)

Appendix C   (Continued)

	Hours
Calculations for Increased Capacity Due to Increased Number of Seats	
Seats:	
Southwest 737-1/200	123
Mean Competitor 737-1/200	108
Difference * [# of route segments per aircraft per day] * [average stage length]	
= seat miles of current capacity due to additional seats	47,343
Portion of current capacity	12.3%
Southwest 737-300	137
Mean Competitor 737-300	128
Difference * [# of route segments per aircraft per day] * [average stage length]	
= seat miles of current capacity due to additional seats	33,671
Portion of current capacity	6.6%
Southwest 737-500	122
Mean Competitor 737-500	107
Difference * [# of route segments per aircraft per day] * average stage length]	
= seat miles of current capacity due to additional seats	54,849
Portion of current capacity	12.3%
Southwest portion of current capacity due to increased number of seats, weighted by number of aircraft of each type in operation	9.2%
Calculations for Increased Capacity Due to Reduced Turn Time	
[Southwest turn time per aircraft less mean competitor turn time per aircraft] * [# of Southwest departures per day] = Daily time saved due to Southwest's rapid aircraft turns	
Southwest turn time (all 737s)	0.25
Mean Competitor turn time (all 737s)	0.58
Difference * mean Southwest departures per day weighted by aircraft type (9.1) = daily time saved	3.00
Southwest portion of current capacity due to reduced turn time (weighted number of aircraft of each type in operation)	22.9%
*Calculations for **Reduced** Capacity Due to Short-Haul Flights (more frequent turn time and tarmac time than mean competitor)*	
Difference in Southwest stage length versus mean competitor stage length as a percent of Southwest stage length, 737-1/200	25%
Applied to Southwest daily 737-1/200:	
Tarmac time (1.63)	0.41
Turn time (2.15)	0.54
Total	0.95
Difference in Southwest stage length versus mean competitor stage length as a percent of Southwest stage length, 737-300	71%

(continued)

Appendix C   (Continued)

	Hours
Applied to Southwest daily 737-300:	
Tarmac time (2.1)	1.49
Turn time (2.4)	<u>1.70</u>
Total	3.19
Difference in Southwest stage length vs. mean competitor stage length as a percent of Southwest stage length, 737-500	73%
Applied to Southwest daily 737-500:	
Tarmac time (1.80)	1.31
Turn time (2.4)	<u>1.72</u>
Total	3.03
Reduction in current capacity due to short-haul flights, weighted by number of aircraft of each type in operation	18.8%

Notes: USAir turn time is estimated based on USAir and other carrier performance and the knowledge of industry insiders. Turn times used are minimum turn times permitted by the airlines without penalty to the station. Southwest's actual mean turn time is 17.5 minutes (versus 15 used here). Other airlines have increased actual average turn times. Minimum turn times are used because they apply to the actual aircraft in use as opposed to the use of system-wide averages, which mix different aircraft types. The effect of the use of minimum versus actual turn times is to understate Southwest's advantage versus its competitors and to understate the contribution of reduced turn time to current capacity; both understatements are estimated to be modest.

Sources: 1994 Avitas data based on DOT form 41 filings in Lample (1996) and interviews with airline representatives conducted by Jody Hoffer Gittell in 1995 and 1996.

NOTES

1. Information on the other firms examined in the study is available from the author.

2. See Bower (1982), Heskett (1986, 1990), Bartlett and Ghoshal (1987a, 1987b), Collis and Montgomery (1995) and Grant and Schlesinger (1995), among others.

3. This definition is somewhat more stringent than Caves' (1984), which argues that a firm must produce cost leadership or differentiation superior to its median-ability competitor in order to have competitive advantage on a single dimension.

4. "Focus" is a generic strategy that is effective because a firm serves a small niche market so well that no other firm is induced to enter. Focus does not apply to Southwest Airlines or Vanguard, in light of their enormous markets and the large number of firms against which they compete. Caves (1984, p. 127) writes, "Unless the firm has the niche to itself, it still faces the same options (cost leadership or differentiation) for gaining advantage against rival occupants of that niche."

5. Zeithaml, Parasuraman and Berry (1992) suggest that service quality be considered an aspect of differentiation for service firms.

6. The firm may also generate value for competitors and substitutes, and their buyers and suppliers. This topic is discussed extensively in Brandenburger and Nalebuff (1996).

7. Excluding returns to equity capital.

8. Using cost leadership to reduce price is contrary to the general economic assumption that a cost leader prices at or slightly below market and enjoys a larger margin. It is another way in

which firms with dual competitive advantage have different assumptions about the world in which they operate and reflects the importance they place on customer value, that is, expanding the pie rather than dividing it.

9. While this data represents a modest decline in contrast to the 1994 aggregate Vanguard bond figure reported in Table 2, given the weighting that would have favored taxable bond funds in the 1994 aggregate calculation, the 1994-1995 comparison is reasonable.

10. One actively managed equity fund and two sub-portfolios of large funds are managed in-house. The decision was made to manage these in-house because they are managed in a highly quantitative style which is a potentially low-cost approach to investment management. Thus, savings from this management style are passed on to Vanguard fundholders.

11. See Harvard Business School case 575-060, "Southwest Airlines (A)."

12. The 737-500 is a good example because the two competitors flying this aircraft have pay scales above the industry mean (United) and below the industry mean (Continental), providing balance in contrast to Southwest.

13. Note that this analysis excludes some sources of cost leadership at Southwest not related to flight operations productivity (such as benefits from passengers booking a higher percent of tickets directly with Southwest in lieu of travel agents, and cost reductions due to the lower airport fees charged by smaller, less congested airports).

14. The survey was conducted in 1996. The survey instrument was developed by the author with input from executives at the Airlines Industrial Relations Conference (AIR Conference) to ensure that language was appropriate and questions about specific employee categories (e.g., flight attendants) would match the categories already in use at the majority of airlines. Surveys were mailed to the heads of human resources at each of the airlines. Respondents were informed that all responses would be kept confidential and that industry (aggregate) data would be shared with participating airlines. The heads of human resources at the participating carriers received the results as well as a recapitulation of their own turnover rates to encourage benchmarking and ensure that senior management was comfortable with the data a carrier had provided.

15. Industry observers contend that the one major carrier not participating in the survey has turnover at, or somewhat higher than, the mean rate for the other nine carriers.

16. The one carrier that sometimes had turnover lower than Southwest's is known for paying above market wages to its front line employees, and has its headquarters and most important hub in a geographic region of the United States which has relatively high unemployment. In contrast, Southwest's headquarters are in Dallas and its busiest flight centers are in the Southwest (Texas and Arizona).

17. Probability values are not provided because with nine of 10 major airlines participating in the survey, the sample represents 90 percent of the population.

18. In its West Coast operations, Southwest flies into both Los Angeles (LAX) and San Francisco airports, two of the most congested airports in the country according to the Department of Transportation.

19. Employee turnover (the behavioral proxy adopted here for commitment) at United was reported for the airline as a whole, making a direct comparison of Shuttle turnover to Southwest turnover impossible. However, commitment can also be gauged from other evidence, such as the initial resistance of United's unions to the Shuttle experiment.

20. For example, USAA was excluded because of its parent organization's focus on the military. Ten billion dollars was chosen as a cut-off point because executives at the Investment Company Institute (ICI) deemed that fund families with over $10 billion enjoyed approximately the same benefits of scale and scope. The ICI provided a list of firms meeting the criteria of the study, and their CEOs or heads of human resources were contacted by mail. Executives at the ICI were involved in the development of the survey to ensure that it was worded appropriately and that categories of employees on which data was requested would match categories in use at the firms. Because of the use of outside vendors for customer service activities at one of the fund

families contacted, the two largest providers of such activities were also solicited using a survey instrument designed to gather comparable data. Effective assets under management for the vendors solicited were over $10 billion, suggesting that they enjoy scale and scope equivalent to that of the fund families. The firms that chose to participate in the study include: Boston Financial Data Services (a vendor proxying for BankAmerica which uses an outside vendor for mutual fund servicing), Fidelity, Franklin, Janus, Schwab and Vanguard.

REFERENCES

Aviation Daily (1994), "Continental Plans More Big Changes," (September 23).

Barney, J.B. (1986a), "Types of Competition and the Theory of Strategy: Toward an Integrative Framework," *Academy of Management Review*, 11 (4), 791-800.

_____ (1986b), "Organizational Culture: Can it be a Source of Sustained Competitive Advantage," *Academy of Management Review*, 11 (3).

_____ (1992), "Integrating Organizational Behavior and Strategy Formulation Research: A Resource-Based Analysis," in *Advances in Strategic Management*, Vol. 8, P. Shrivastava, A. Huff and J. Dutton, eds. Greenwich, CT: JAI Press.

Bernstein, A. (1996), "United We Own," *Business Week* (March 18).

Bernstein Research (1995), *The Future of Money Management in America*, 1995 edition. New York: Stanford C. Bernstein & Co.

Bartlett, C.A. and S. Ghoshal (1987a), "Managing Across Borders: New Organizational Responses," *Sloan Management Review*, Fall.

_____ and _____ (1987b), "Managing Across Borders: New Strategic Requirements," *Sloan Management Review*, Summer.

Bower, J.L. (1982), "Business Policy in the 1980s," *Academy of Management Review*, 7 (4), 630-638.

Brandenburger, A.M. and B.J. Nalebuff (1996), *Co-opetition*. New York: Doubleday.

_____ and H.W. Stuart (1996), "Value Based Business Strategy," *Journal of Economics and Management Strategy*, Winter.

Caves, R.E. (1984), "Economic Analysis and the Quest for Competitive Advantage," *American Economic Review*, 74 (2), 127-132.

_____ and M.E. Porter (1977), "From Entry Barriers to Mobility Barriers: Conjectural Decisions and Contrived Deterrence to New Competition," *Quarterly Journal of Economics*, 91 (2), 241-261.

Collis, D.J. and C.A. Montgomery (1995), "Competing on Resources: Strategy in the 1990s," *Harvard Business Review*, July-August, 119-128.

Ghemawat, P. (1991), *Commitment*. New York: The Free Press.

Dunn and Bradstreet, Inc. (1996), *Dunn's Business Rankings, 1996*. Bethlehem, PA: Dunn and Bradstreet, Inc.

Gittel, J.H. (1995), "Cross-functional Coordination and Human Resource Systems: Evidence from the Airline Industry," Ph.D. Doctoral Dissertation, Cambridge, MA: Massachusetts Institute of Technology.

Grant, A.W.H. and L.A. Schlesinger (1995), "Realize Your Customers' Full Profit Potential," *Harvard Business Review*, September-October, 59-72.

Hallowell, R. (1996), "Southwest Airlines: A Case Study Linking Employee Needs Satisfaction and Organizational Capabilities to Competitive Advantage," *Human Resource Management Journal*, Fall.

Hayes, R.H. and P.G. Pisano (1996), "Manufacturing Strategy: At the Intersection of Two Paradigm Shifts," *Production and Operations Management*, 5 (1), 25-41.

Heskett, J.L. (1990), "Rethinking Strategy for Service Management," in *Service Management Effectiveness*, D.E. Bowen, R.B. Chase, T.G. Cummings and Associates, eds. San Francisco: Jossey-Bass.

———— (1986), *Managing in the Service Economy*. Boston, MA: Harvard Business School Press.

———— and R. Hallowell (1993), "Southwest Airlines: 1993," Harvard Business School Case Number 9-694-023, Boston, MA: Harvard Business School Press.

————, T.O. Jones, G.W. Loveman, W.E. Sasser, Jr. and L.A. Schlesinger (1994), "Putting the Service Profit Chain to Work," *Harvard Business Review*, March-April.

————, W.E. Sasser and C.W.L. Hart (1990), *Breakthrough Service*. New York: The Free Press.

Lample, R., ed. 1996. *Aviation and Aerospace Almanac, 1996*. New York: McGraw-Hill.

Learned, E., C.R. Christensen, K. Andrews and W. Guth (1969), *Business Policy Text and Cases*. Homewood, IL: Richard Irwin.

Light, J.O. and J.E. Sailer (1993), "The Vanguard Group (A)," Harvard Business School Case Number 9-293-064, Boston, MA: Harvard Business School Press.

Milgrom, P. and J. Roberts (1992), *Economics, Organization and Management*. Englewood Cliffs, NJ: Prentice Hall.

Mowday, R.T., L.W. Porter and R.M. Steers (1984), *Employee Organization Linkages*. New York: Academic Press.

Nadler, D.A. and M.L. Tushman (1992), "Designing Organizations that Have Good Fit," in *Organizational Architecture*, D.A. Nadler, M.C. Gerstein and R.B. Shaw, eds. San Francisco, CA: Josey-Bass.

The National Law Journal (1994), "U.S. Airlines Are Offering New Routes and Services," (August 29).

Pfeffer, J. (1994), *Competitive Advantage through People*. Boston, MA: Harvard Business School Press.

Porter, M.E. (1980), *Competitive Strategy*. New York: The Free Press.

———— (1981), "The Contributions of Industrial Organization to Strategic Management," *Academy of Management Review*, 6 (4), 609-620.

———— (1985), *Competitive Advantage*. New York: The Free Press.

———— (1995), "Positioning Trade-offs, Activity Systems, and the Theory of Competitive Strategy," Harvard Business School Working Paper, Boston, MA: Harvard University.

Prahalad, C.K. and G. Hamel (1990), "The Core Competence of the Corporation," *Harvard Business Review*, May-June, 79-91.

Roethlisberger, F.J. and W.J. Dickson (1939), *Management and the Worker*. Cambridge, MA: Harvard University Press.

Schlesinger, L.A. and J.L. Heskett (1991), "Enfranchisement of Service Workers," *California Management Review*, 33 (4).

Schneider, B. and D.E. Bowen (1993), "The Service Organization: Human Resources Management is Crucial," *Organizational Dynamics*, 21.

Skinner, W. (1974), "The Focused Factory," *Harvard Business Review*, May-June, 113-121.

Stalk, G., P. Evans and L.E. Shulman (1992), "Competing on Capabilities: The New Rules of Corporate Strategy," *Harvard Business Review*, March-April, 57-69.

Teece, D. and G. Pisano (1994), "The Dynamic Capabilities of Firms: An Introduction," *Industrial and Corporate Change*, 3 (4), 537-556.

Ulrich, D. and D. Lake (1990), *Organizational Capability: Competing from the Inside Out*. New York: John Wiley and Sons.

Walton, R. (1989), *Up and Running*. Boston, MA: Harvard Business School Press.

Wernerfelt, B. (1984), "A Resource Based View of the Firm," *Strategic Management Journal*, September-October, 171-180.

Zeithaml, V., A. Parasuraman and L.L. Berry (1992), "Strategic Positioning on the Dimensions of Service Quality," in *Advances in Services Marketing and Management*, Vol. 1, T.A. Swartz, D.E. Bowen and S.W. Brown, eds. Greenwich, CT: JAI Press.

Ziemba, S. (1994), "United Fastens Seat Belts for Shuttle Ride," *The Chicago Tribune* (September 25).

CARRY-OVER EFFECTS IN THE FORMATION OF SATISFACTION:

THE ROLE OF VALUE IN A HOTEL SERVICE DELIVERY PROCESS

Ko de Ruyter, Jos Lemmink, Martin Wetzels
and Jan Mattsson

ABSTRACT

The role of customer value has been left relatively unexplored in the field of services marketing. Generally, value has been narrowly conceptualized as "value-for-money." The authors present a value-based approach to the measurement of service quality. A conceptual framework is presented in which value is conceived as consisting of three dimensions: (1) emotional, (2) practical and (3) logical. In a hotel setting the dynamics of the service delivery process are explored using the above framework. The hotel service delivery process was divided into five distinct stages: (1) check-in, (2) hotel room, (3) hotel restaurant, (4) breakfast and (5) check-out. Each of these five stages was evaluated on the three generic value dimensions. Furthermore, respondents rated their satisfaction with each stage. Finally, we proposed that carry-over effects might occur among the

Advances in Services Marketing and Management, Volume 6, pages 61-77.
ISBN: 0-7623-0176-7

different stages of the hotel service delivery process. Results of the study indicate that carry-over effects are of a substantial magnitude. Furthermore, the hotels in our study revealed quite large differences on the effect of value dimensions of stage-wise satisfaction. Finally, managerial implications of our study are presented.

INTRODUCTION

Research in the field of service quality has gradually reached a mature stage in which new levels of sophistication, conceptualization and measurement are initiated and researchers are ready to take on the fundamental questions concerning an in-depth understanding of the concept of service quality (Grönroos 1993; Rust and Oliver 1994). In defining the key constructs in the discipline, conceptual advances and nuances have been achieved, though differences of opinion remain, for instance, as to the sequential order of the constructs of service satisfaction and service quality (Cronin and Taylor 1992; Iacobucci, Grayson and Ostrom 1994; Oliver 1993; Parasuraman, Zeithaml and Berry 1994). In the battle between these two constructs for premier attention from researchers as well as practitioners, a third candidate has recently been brought forward: customer value (Rust and Oliver 1994).

Value is often conceptualized as the combination of quality and price offerings, including, for instance, time and distance as "psychological prices" (Zeithaml 1988). In fact, it has been suggested that service quality is value-based (Garvin 1987). Others have adopted a more comprehensive perspective on value-based on writings in axiology (i.e., the formal study of values defining the logic of value [Hartman 1967, 1973]), stating that value is a multidimensional construct involving more (i.e., non-quality) dimensions than utility per dollar (Danaher and Mattsson 1994; Holbrook 1994; Holbrook and Corfman 1985). According to this perspective, value can be defined as an "interactive relativistic consumption preference experience" (Holbrook 1994, p. 27).

In the context of services, this point of view not only positions value as an evaluative customer judgement, the use of the term "experience" also entails a subject-object interaction, focusing our attention on the process of service delivery. Thus, value—by definition—is associated with the service delivery process. Relatively little is known about this service delivery process. There is some evidence that the service delivery process may be a more important determinant of customer evaluation than the actual outcome (Lehtinen and Lehtinen 1982; Brown and Swartz 1989). Moreover, it has been suggested that there may be distinct "objects" (i.e., service encounters) in the service delivery system that "subjects" (i.e., service customers) use as anchor points for their evaluative judgement (Danaher and Mattsson 1994; Singh 1991). However, not much is known about how these judgements are actually formed during the process of satisfaction.

In this paper, we address this issue in an approach to the measurement of service quality that is based on the concept of customer value. By using this approach, our aim is to gain a better understanding of the dynamics of the service delivery process. This paper is structured as follows. First, we focus on the concept of value in relation to service quality and satisfaction, and subsequently we elaborate on the role of value in the service delivery process. Secondly, we report on the result of a cross-cultural study conducted in The Netherlands and Sweden in which we focused on the hotel stay as a service delivery process. In conclusion, we address the theoretical as well as the managerial implications of a value-based approach to the service delivery process.

SERVICE QUALITY, SATISFACTION AND VALUE

In the service quality literature, the three closely related concepts of satisfaction, quality and value have been the subject of much conceptual and empirical attention. Recently, much emphasis has been placed on conceptualizing and contrasting service quality and satisfaction (Cronin and Taylor 1992; Oliver 1993; Rust and Oliver 1994). In general, service satisfaction is viewed as a cognitive and affective judgement resulting from the (dis)confirmation of expectations, while service quality is considered predominantly as a performance-based concept. However, it should be noted that in their early work, Parasuraman and his colleagues used a similarly relativistic formulation of service quality (Parasuraman, Zeithaml and Berry 1985). There is a tendency to treat satisfaction as a construct subsequent to service quality. Some evidence with regard to this sequential order has been accumulated. Cronin and Taylor (1992) undertook an empirical test of the reciprocity between satisfaction and quality across several service industries. Using structural equation modeling, they found that service quality can be seen as a determinant of satisfaction, which in turn influences purchase intentions, although it must be noted that this study suffers from important imperfections, particularly in the area of operationalization. Oliver (1993) and Rust and Oliver (1994) also adhere to this service quality-precedes-satisfaction order, because the latter is viewed as a summarized cognitive and emotional reaction to the service delivery process. Parasuraman, Zeithaml and Berry (1994) have argued that transaction (or episode) satisfaction is based on customer evaluations of service quality, product quality and price. Inclusion of price in the satisfaction formation process has led to the introduction of value as a third type of customer evaluative judgement.

Value is often viewed as a proxy for the relationship between price and quality. It has been argued that service providers that maximize quality minus the disutility from prices are favoured by customers (Zeithaml 1988); a service may be perceived to be of good quality but still be experienced as poor value if the price of that service is too high (Liljander and Strandvik 1994). Accordingly, quality is perceived to be an antecedent to value in combination with price. This conceptualization of value may be termed the value-for-money approach. Value-for-money can be viewed as a cognitive type of antecedent to satisfaction. However, if we acknowledge affect as an essential component of postpurchase responses (Oliver 1994), we must also take the role of affect into account in conceptualizing value. A comprehensive approach to the concept of value that takes both cognitive and affective components into account has been proposed by Hartman (1967). Hartman argues that value is essentially a three-dimensional construct. This typology is based on a distinction commonly used in axiology, the difference between extrinsic and intrinsic value. Intrinsic value represents the affective appreciation of the process of a service episode, regardless of the actual outcome, and it reflects the emotional aspects of a service episode. Extrinsic value, by contrast, depicts the notion that a service episode is a useful means to a certain end, and it can best be described as practical or functional. To these, a third dimension of systemic value is added. Central to this approach is the notion that value is created during the (service) experience or process, not by its consequential object, the service output. Lewis (1946, p. 539) states that "value is some potentiality of the object for realizations of satisfaction in experience." Systemic value reflects on the relationships between concepts in their systematic interaction, for example, the relationship between quality and financial sacrifice. It points to rational or logical aspects of a service episode.

Mattsson (1991) translated Hartman's formal model into three generic value dimensions, emotional (E), practical (P) and logical (L), with $E > P > L$ in terms of richness of content. The three value dimensions were used as underlying service value dimensions in a study of customer satisfaction during the service delivery process in the hotel business by Danaher and Mattsson (1994). In their operationalization, emotional items focused on the consumers' affective evaluation related to the "Gestalt" experience of the service episode. Practical items reflected the functional aspects of the service episode such as good and easy-to-order meals. Finally, the logical items concentrated on rational aspects of the hotel episode such as a good selection of food. This largely corresponds to the value-for-money approach discussed previously. The three value dimensions were treated as antecedents of satisfaction; satisfaction was treated as a synopsis of cognitive and affective response to the value dimensions pertaining to a service episode.

Hence, service satisfaction is treated as the penultimate construct in this model. Satisfaction is determined by three antecedent value dimensions, one of which is service quality. Service quality together with price constitutes the logical dimension. The conceptual framework of our value-based approach to the dynamics of the service delivery process is rendered in Figure 1. In the

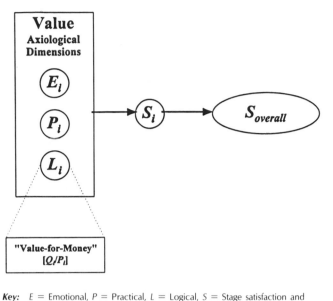

Key: *E* = Emotional, *P* = Practical, *L* = Logical, *S* = Stage satisfaction and
     i = stage.

Figure 1. A Conceptual Framework

figure, the letters E_i, P_i, L_i and S_i refer to the emotional, practical and logical quality dimension and the satisfaction score of the ith service stage.

THE DYNAMICS OF SERVICE DELIVERY

By characterizing value as experiential, Holbrook (1994) argues that it is by definition linked to the service delivery process. If the service delivery process is modeled as a system, it can be broken down into a number of objects depending on the type of service that is being provided (Armstrong 1992; Singh 1991). Modeling the service delivery process according to this micro-perspective, each stage represents a service encounter in itself. Some of the stages are characterized by personal interaction (checking into a hotel), others are described in non-interactive terms (e.g., a hotel room). A customer goes through a number of stages during the service delivery process. The hotel service delivery process per se would begin by checking in and end with checking out. In the interim, the customer would evaluate the room, the hotel bar, the breakfast service and so forth. Each specific stage in the service delivery process can be evaluated according to the three dimensions of value (emotional, practical and logical). For instance, a hotel guest expects his or her room to be cosy (emotional) and equipped with comfortable furniture (practical), and she or he wants to obtain value-for-money (logical). Moreover, at each stage a customer's cumulative satisfaction is affected by the most recent stage and the stages that preceded it. The level of satisfaction at the ith stage (S_i) denotes satisfaction with the service delivery up until the point of measurement. S_i is thus determined by the joint value dimensions E_i, P_i and L_i. In addition, S_i is determined also by E_{i-1}, P_{i-1} and L_{i-1}, and so forth. This means that satisfaction with the service delivery up till the point of measurement is determined by the cumulation of all preceding value dimensions. Our way to model dynamics into this recursive relationship is to let S_i be determined by both E_i, P_i and L_i and satisfaction with the preceding encounter, S_{i-1}. We denote the S_{i-1} corresponding effects as carry-over effects.

By monitoring the service delivery process in terms of its individual stages, one may obtain a detailed insight into the dynamics of the formation of satisfaction during the service delivery process. The service delivery process can be broken down into a number of context-specific attributes rather than the commonly used standard service quality dimensions. The overall service delivery process as well as each individual stage can be profiled in terms of the three value dimensions. Moreover, it can be determined which stage contributes significantly to the formation of overall satisfaction during the service delivery process. Stages that have a negative impact on overall satisfaction must be evaluated in the light of quality improvement efforts. Profiling these items in terms of their underlying value dimensions may pinpoint how quality improvement should take place.

In this study, we first explore the dimensionality of the service delivery process. Then, we test the hypothesis that the formation of satisfaction is determined directly by the value dimensions of the most recent encounter and indirectly by the satisfaction with preceding encounters by carry-over effects. In the next section, we report on a study designed to demonstrate our value-based approach to the service delivery process and the impact of these carry-over effects.

AN EMPIRICAL STUDY

We tested our approach in the service delivery process in the context of hotels. Two hotels (one in The Netherlands and one in Sweden) were selected for our research. The Swedish hotel has a customer base of business travelers, whereas the Dutch hotel attracts a more general public. Hence, practical and logical considerations might play a more important role in the Swedish than in the Dutch data sample.

The service delivery process was partitioned into five distinct service stages: (1) check-in, (2) room, (3) restaurant, (4) breakfast and (5) check-out. The questionnaire that was designed for this study consisted of a booklet containing different parts, each of which measured value in one stage in the hotel service delivery process. Each part was printed on a separate slip of paper in a different color to distinguish them from each other. Each part contained four items. Hotel guests were asked to fill out each part immediately after they experienced the corresponding service stage.

The first three items on each part of the questionnaire comprised the three generic value dimensions as defined by Hartman (1967). The first dimension concerned an emotional aspect (E_i) focusing on the feelings a guest could get from experiencing a stage. The second item corresponded to the practical dimension (P_i) concerning the physical and functional aspects of the service stage. The third item reflected the logical aspect (L_i) of the service centering on the rational and abstract characteristics of the stage, that is, right or wrong, correct or incorrect, and so forth. The fourth item on each part of the questionnaire asked how satisfied the visitor was until the stage he or she had just passed (S_i). Hence, this satisfaction score is determined jointly by the components of the most recently experienced stage and all of the components of the previous stages the guest already experienced. The items were formulated to be as short as possible in order to obtain clear and easy-to-read questions, because the questionnaire had to be filled out while experiencing the service. For the purpose of clarification and illustration, part of the questionnaire has been included as Table 1.

In addition to the satisfaction scores relating to the individual stages, each respondent was asked his or her overall satisfaction with the hotel at the end of the visit ($S_{overall}$). Two descriptive items (age and gender) were included.

For the purpose of collecting data from foreign visitors, the questionnaire was back-translated into English. Finally, during the data collection it appeared that it was necessary to adapt the questionnaire as a result of context-specific circumstances in this cross-cultural study. This resulted in slightly different Swedish and Dutch rating scales. In the Dutch questionnaire, an 11-point Likert-type scale was used. On the basis of the Dutch experience, we learned that a number of respondents had difficulty using this type of scale; as a result, we decided to use a different scale for the data collection in Sweden. Instead of the Likert-type scale, we employed an 11-point scale using smiling and sad faces.

Data collection took place on weekdays as well as weekends. A systematic pseudo-random sample of each third guest was used. Completed questionnaires were collected at the end of the stay at the hotel. The data collection resulted in 174 usable responses: 107 respondents in The Netherlands and 67 respondents in Sweden.

Table 1. List of Items in Questionnaire

CHECK-IN

☹   ☺

1. Nice treatment?	1	2	3	4	5	6	7	8	9	10	11
2. Quick check-in?	1	2	3	4	5	6	7	8	9	10	11
3. Correct booking?	1	2	3	4	5	6	7	8	9	10	11
4. How satisfied are you now?	1	2	3	4	5	6	7	8	9	10	11

ROOM

☹   ☺

1. Cosy room?	1	2	3	4	5	6	7	8	9	10	11
2. Are furniture and equipment useful?	1	2	3	4	5	6	7	8	9	10	11
3. Value for money?	1	2	3	4	5	6	7	8	9	10	11
4. How satisfied are you now?	1	2	3	4	5	6	7	8	9	10	11

RESTAURANT

☹   ☺

1. Fine atmosphere?	1	2	3	4	5	6	7	8	9	10	11
2. Good food?	1	2	3	4	5	6	7	8	9	10	11
3. Value for money?	1	2	3	4	5	6	7	8	9	10	11
4. How satisfied are you now?	1	2	3	4	5	6	7	8	9	10	11

BREAKFAST

☹   ☺

1. Calm atmosphere?	1	2	3	4	5	6	7	8	9	10	11
2. Abundant and easy to get food?	1	2	3	4	5	6	7	8	9	10	11
3. Good selection of food?	1	2	3	4	5	6	7	8	9	10	11
4. How satisfied are you now?	1	2	3	4	5	6	7	8	9	10	11

CHECK-OUT

☹   ☺

1. Nice treatment?	1	2	3	4	5	6	7	8	9	10	11
2. Quick check-out?	1	2	3	4	5	6	7	8	9	10	11
3. Correct bill?	1	2	3	4	5	6	7	8	9	10	11
4. How satisfied are you now?	1	2	3	4	5	6	7	8	9	10	11

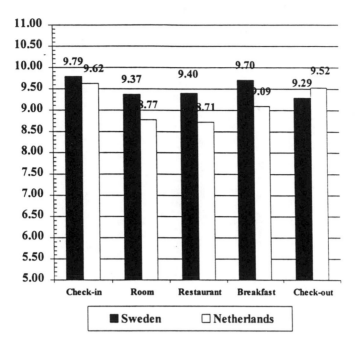

Figure 2. Mean Satisfaction Scores per Stage

RESULTS

Descriptives

No differences in gender and age distribution were found between the Swedish and Dutch data sample. Twenty-eight percent of the respondents were female. Seventeen percent of the respondents were younger than 30 years old, and six percent were over age 55. Figure 2 gives the mean satisfaction scores for each of the stages of the hotel stays per country.

It can be observed that the mean satisfaction scores per stage are generally higher for the Swedish hotel, except for the check-out stage. The results of the one-tailed t-tests reveal that significant differences between mean satisfaction scores occur with respect to the breakfast ($t = 2.45$; $p < 0.016$) and the restaurant ($t = 2.57$; $p < 0.011$) stages. In both cases, the satisfaction with the Swedish hotel is higher. Furthermore, a U-shaped curve can be discerned on the basis of the mean satisfaction scores in Figure 2, again except for the Swedish check-out stage. The check-in resulted on average in the highest satisfaction scores; the room and restaurant had somewhat lower scores.

Table 2.   Factor Analysis of Value Items (Sweden)[a]

Stage	Value Dimensions	Factor Loadings[b]				
		Factor 1	Factor 2	Factor 3	Factor 4	Factor 5
Check-in	E_1	0.74				
	P_1	0.79				
	L_1	0.55				
Room	E_2		0.88			
	P_2		0.81			
	L_2		0.76			
Restaurant	E_3			0.71		
	P_3			0.80		
	L_3			0.90		
Breakfast	E_4				0.68	
	P_4				0.89	
	L_4				0.89	
Check-out	E_5					0.93
	P_5					0.93
	L_5					0.92
Total explained variance				82.3%		

Notes: [a] Principal axis factoring with varimax rotation.
              [b] Factor loadings > 0.3.

Factor Analysis and Reliability Analysis

Factor analyses and reliability analyses were conducted to check the dimensionality of the value construct across the stages. We hypothesized a five-factor solution. Both Bartlett's test of sphericity (646.86, $p < 0.00001$ for the Swedish sample; and 815.09, $p < 0.00001$ for the Dutch sample) and the Kaiser-Meyer-Olkin measure of sampling adequacy (0.76 for the Swedish sample and 0.88 for the Dutch sample) suggest the multidimensional nature of the service delivery process. The result of principal axis factoring with varimax rotation for the two countries are provided in Tables 2 and 3. In addition to the orthogonal solution, we also explored the possibility of interrelated factors using an oblique rotation. Using the factor pattern matrix, we found a similar solution for the Swedish and the Dutch data sample (factor intercorrelations ranged from −0.42 to 0.46 for the Swedish data sample and from −0.44 to 0.29 for the Dutch sample).

For the Swedish sample, the five-factor solution explains 82.3 percent of the total variance, while for the Dutch sample, 80.5 percent of the total variance can be explained. The results of the factor analyses clearly support our value-based approach to the hotel service process consisting of a number of separate

Table 3. Factor Analysis of Value Items (The Netherlands)[a]

Stage	Value Dimensions	Factor Loadings[b]				
		Factor 1	Factor 2	Factor 3	Factor 4	Factor 5
Check-in	E_1	0.72				
	P_1	0.73				
	L_1	0.85				
Room	E_2		0.69			
	P_2		0.54			
	L_2		0.75			
Restaurant	E_3			0.84		
	P_3			0.63		
	L_3			0.83		
Breakfast	E_4				0.77	
	P_4				0.85	
	L_4				0.83	
Check-out	E_5					0.77
	P_5					0.73
	L_5					0.61
Total explained variance				80.5%		

Notes: [a] Principal axis factoring with varimax rotation.
[b] Factor loadings > 0.3.

Table 4. Reliability Analysis

Stage	Items	Coefficient Alpha	
		Sweden	The Netherlands
Check-in	E_1, P_1, L_1	0.67	0.88
Room	E_2, P_2, L_2	0.87	0.82
Restaurant	E_3, P_3, L_3	0.85	0.89
Breakfast	E_4, P_4, L_4	0.88	0.92
Check-out	E_5, P_5, L_5	0.93	0.83

stages; all stages load highly and collectively on one factor, respectively. In addition, we examined the reliability of the measures using Cronbach's coefficient alpha. Table 4 shows that the coefficient alpha for each stage in the Swedish and Dutch samples with the exception of one exceeds the cut-off value suggested by Nunnally and Bernstein (1994).

Regression Analysis

The objective of our research was to measure how overall satisfaction with a service is formed during the service delivery process. For this reason, we

Table 5.   Regression Analysis of Value Dimensions on S_i

Stage	Value Dimensions	Sweden			The Netherlands		
		Beta	F-test	Adj. R^2	Beta	F-test	Adj. R^2
Check-in	E_1	0.20**	47.48***	0.69	n.s.*	51.48***	0.59
	P_1	0.27**			0.43***		
	L_1	0.54***			n.s.*		
Room	E_2	0.41***	115.46***	0.85	0.23***	68.14***	0.67
	P_2	0.42***			n.s.*		
	L_2	0.20***			0.57***		
Restaurant	E_3	0.26***	57.68***	0.74	0.39***	112.93***	0.80
	P_3	0.44***			n.s.*		
	L_3	0.28***			0.49***		
Breakfast	E_4	0.23**	36.30***	0.62	0.41***	244.44***	0.88
	P_4	0.50***			0.18**		
	L_4	n.s.*			0.43***		
Check-out	E_5	0.41***	128.23***	0.86	n.s.*	167.49***	0.84
	P_5	0.31**			0.58***		
	L_5	0.28***			0.34***		

Notes: * n.s. = not significant at $\alpha = 0.05$.
          ** $p < 0.05$.
        *** $p < 0.01$.

conducted a two-step approach to monitor the dynamics of the service delivery process. The first step examines the influence of the ith service stage's value dimensions (E_i, P_i and L_i) on the satisfaction level (S_i) per stage. The second step incorporates the influence of the satisfaction with the preceding stage (S_{i-1}) on satisfaction per stage (S_i). Ordinary least-squares (OLS) regression was used. In the first step, five regression analyses were conducted for each sample in order to assess the impact of value dimensions (E_i, P_i and L_i) of each service stage on the satisfaction score of that particular service stage (S_i). The results of the first step regression analysis are presented in Table 5.

On a general level, the results show that the adjusted R^2 is high for both samples and differs significantly from zero for all stages of the service delivery process. This means that there is a high degree of explanatory power of the three value dimensions on service stage satisfaction. On a more specific level, the results of the regression analysis can be used to profile each stage, pointing to parts of the process that contribute significantly to the formation of satisfaction and elements with respect to which there is room for improvement of quality. There are considerable differences in beta-weights of value dimensions between the hotels. This means that there are hotel specific factors involved. Probably the type of visitor (tourist or business), atmosphere and

Table 6. Regression Analysis of Value Dimensions on S_i
with Cumulative Effects

Stage	Value Dimensions	Sweden			The Netherlands		
		Beta	F-test	Adj. R^2	Beta	F-test	Adj. R^2
Check-in	E_1	0.20**	47.48***	0.69	n.s.*	51.48***	0.59
	P_1	0.27**			0.43***		
	L_1	0.54***			n.s.*		
Room	E_2	0.30***	101.43***	0.86	0.25***	59.57***	0.70
	P_2	0.37***			n.s.*		
	L_2	0.18***			0.47***		
	S_1	0.22***			0.27***		
Restaurant	E_3	0.26***	57.68***	0.80	0.33***	101.44***	0.83
	P_3	0.40***			n.s.*		
	L_3	0.24**			0.39***		
	S_2	0.20***			0.25***		
Breakfast	E_4	n.s.*	44.93***	0.74	0.37***	228.16***	0.91
	P_4	0.43***			0.21***		
	L_4	n.s.*			0.34***		
	S_3	0.42***			0.17***		
Check-out	E_5	0.45***	101.25***	0.86	n.s.*	159.21***	0.87
	P_5	n.s.*			0.51***		
	L_5	0.30***			0.29***		
	S_4	0.11**			0.24***		

Notes: * n.s. = not significant at $\alpha = 0.05$.
** $p < 0.05$.
*** $p < 0.01$.

character of the hotel play an important role in shaping guest expectations; for example, the practical value dimension (waiting time) is a more important determinant of satisfaction with the check-in stage in the Swedish sample than in the Dutch sample. The Swedish hotel is more of a business traveler's hotel, perhaps corresponding with guests' expectations of fast service when entering the hotel. In contrast, the effect of the logical dimension (correct handling of payment) on check-in satisfaction is relatively stronger in The Netherlands. Tourists are generally less experienced with hotel payment arrangements because they less frequently make use of hotel facilities. While we make these statements as a function of our knowledge of the two hotels, clearly in future research, we would ask additional questions of the respondents, including their purpose of travel and their expectations on these attributes. Again, analysing beta-weights in such a way can be of great help for management in deciding which quality improvements are necessary.

In the second step of the regression analysis, we examined the carry-over effect of satisfaction with the preceding stage (S_{i-1}) on S_i. It can be concluded that incorporating S_{i-1} contributes significantly to R^2, without changing the direct effect of the value dimensions in terms of their beta-weights. Seven out of eight incremental changes in the F-value by introducing lagged satisfaction are statistically significant with $\alpha = 0.05$. The changes in F-values with the corresponding p-values are as follows: Sweden: $F_{change} = 9.61$, $p = 0.003$ for room, $F_{change} = 10.05$, $p = 0.0025$ for restaurant, $F_{change} = 28.86$, $p < 0.0001$ for breakfast, $F_{change} = 3.60$, $p = 0.0525$ for check-out; and for The Netherlands: $F_{change} = 11.65$, $p = 0.0009$ for room, $F_{change} = 15.08$, $p = 0.0002$ for restaurant, $F_{change} = 17.97$, $p < 0.0001$ for breakfast, $F_{change} = 27.58$, $p < 0.0001$ for check-out. Table 6 shows that effects of lagged satisfaction are statistically significant. This means that carry-over effects exist, and consequently cumulative satisfaction with the stages of hotel service experiences does contribute to the final satisfaction with the hotel service.

CONCLUSIONS AND DISCUSSION

The results of our study reveal that the hotel service delivery process can be broken down into distinct stages. Some of the stages involve personal interaction with contact personnel (e.g., check-in, restaurant) while others do not (room). The results of factor analyses show a close relationship between the emotional, practical and logical value dimensions of the consecutive service stages. Since the three value dimensions explain a large part of the variance per service stage, we have found additional evidence for the support of the multifaceted perspective on customer value.

The relationship between the value dimensions per stage is stronger than that between all emotional items, all practical items or all logical items across all service stages. For this, two explanations are plausible. First, respondents rated their satisfaction score immediately after experiencing a service stage. This could have resulted in high correlations between the scores on questions concerning one service stage. In terms of the multi-trait, multi-method matrix proposed by Campbell and Fiske (1959), we are confronted with shared method bias in our study because the value dimensions ("traits") are measured using quite similar items ("methods"). The second explanation concerns the content of the questions: it could be that some of the questions do not cover their underlying quality factor, in particular, the items with somewhat lower reliability coefficients. Holbrook (1994, p. 56) argues that "any one consumption experience is likely to involve more than one type of value simultaneously." Moreover, value distinctions have a tendency to intermingle. In services, this will be the case as usually more than one stage is involved, in combination with a number of underlying dimensions. This problem also appears in measuring service quality with the SERVQUAL model. Apart from problems with contextuality (Paulin and Perrien 1996), services with multiple stages may have less clear identification of underlying quality dimensions.

Descriptive analyses of the mean satisfaction scores per service stage reveal a U-shaped profile of the dynamics of the hotel service delivery process. Similar findings were by Danaher and Mattsson (1994). Check-in into the hotel resulted in high satisfaction; the room was not so satisfying; the restaurant rated the worst; the satisfaction scores rose again after the breakfast experience and rose once more after check-out. Other findings show that there are substantial differences between the importance of value dimensions between hotels. It very much depends on the type, atmosphere and character of the hotel and implicitly upon the intentions and motivations people have for visiting the hotel.

Another observation is the importance of carry-over effects, which can be substantial and provide evidence for treating satisfaction during the service delivery process as a cumulative concept. Satisfaction with earlier stages do have an impact on final satisfaction with the whole hotel service.

In general, we can conclude that if managers understand the process dynamics of their service operations, they are in a position to concentrate on the most effective quality improvements from the perspective of the dynamics of the service delivery process. Because there are substantial carry-over effects, it is important to devote attention to all stages in the service delivery process from the guest's perspective, even if one of the service stages does not appear to directly contribute substantially to satisfaction.

Finally, a number of managerial implications arise. First, it is important for management to consider that customers are experiencing a sequence of "moments of truth" which are interrelated. The way a hotel service is usually organized, with functional and quite independent reponsibilities for managers, hardly acknowledges this interdependence. Second, the use of service mapping to describe the service delivery process from a customers' point of view (cf. Gummesson and Kingman-Brundage 1992) and subsequently the use of questionnaires for each of the stages in the service process identified contributes to a better understanding of the way service encounters are experienced by customers. Third, the results of such studies explicitly taking into account carry-over effects would typically reveal areas in the service delivery process that might have a substantial impact (albeit negative or positive) on subsequent stages of the service delivery process and consequently on overall customer satisfaction. These stages have to be identified and might provide a useful starting point for service improvements. Moreover, it follows from our results that more research is needed in which groups of customers can be identified with similar service perceptions and service evaluation patterns across stages. Individual differences are likely to exist with respect to intentions regarding the hotel visit and subsequently, the intensity of the carry-over effects and the importance of the contribution of individual service stages to overall satisfaction. Realizing that there are different groups of customers with different intentions regarding the hotel visit can be very rewarding for management. It allows for stressing and improving the quality of the right service stages. In general, identifying service stages and collecting such information about individual or customer group differences opens up opportunities for management trying to locate and serve niche markets.

REFERENCES

Armstrong, P.K. (1992), "A Systems Approach for Analyzing Quality in High Contact Services," Ph.D. dissertation, Philadelphia, PA: The Wharton School, University of Pennsylvania.

Brown, S.W. and T.A. Swartz (1989), "A Gap Analysis of Professional Service Quality," *Journal of Marketing*, 53, 92-98.

Campbell, D.T. and D.W. Fiske (1959), "Convergent and Discriminant Validation by the Multitrait-Multimethod Matrix," *Psychological Bulletin*, 56, 81-105.

Cronin, J.J., Jr., and S.A. Taylor (1992), "Measuring Service Quality: A Reexamination and Extension," *Journal of Marketing*, 56, 55-68.

Danaher, P.J. and J. Mattsson (1994), "Customer Satisfaction During the Service Delivery Process," *European Journal of Marketing*, 28, 5-16.

Garvin, D.A. (1987), "Competing on the Eight Dimensions of Quality," *Harvard Business Review*, 65 (November-December), 101-109.

Grönroos, C. (1993), "Toward a Third Phase in Service Quality Research: Challenges and Future Directions," in *Advances in Services Marketing and Management*, Vol. 3, T.A. Swartz, D.E. Bowen and S.W. Brown, eds. Greenwich, CT: JAI Press, 49-64.

Gummesson, E. and J. Kingman-Brundage (1992), "Service Design and Quality: Applying Service Blueprinting and Service Maping to Railroad Services," in *Quality Management in Services*, P. Kunst and J. Lemmink, eds. Assen, The Netherlands: Van Gorcum, 101-114.

Hartman, R.S. (1967), *The Structure of Value: Foundations of a Scientific Axiology*. Carbondale, IL: Southern Illinois Press.

———— (1973), *The Hartman Value Profile [HVP]: Manual of Interpretation*. Muskegon, MI: Research Concepts.

Holbrook, M.B. (1994), "The Nature of Customer Value: An Axiology of Service in the Consumption Experience," in *Service Quality: New Directions in Theory and Practice*, R.T. Rust and R.L. Oliver, eds. London: Sage, 21-71.

———— and K.P. Corfman (1985), "Quality and Value in the Consumption Experience: Phaedrus Rides Again," in *Perceived Quality: How Consumers View Stores and Merchandise*, J. Jacoby and J.C. Olson, eds. Lexington, MA: D.C. Heath, 31-57.

Iacobucci, D., K.A. Grayson and A.L. Ostrom (1994), "The Calculus of Service Quality and Customer Satisfaction: Theoretical and Empirical Differentiation and Integration," *Advances in Services Marketing and Management*, Vol. 3, T.A. Swartz, D.A. Bowen and S.W. Brown, eds. Greenwich, CT: JAI Press, 1-67.

Lehtinen, U. and J.R. Lehtinen (1982), *Service Quality: A Study of Quality Dimensions*. Helsinki, Finland: Helsinki School of Economics.

Lewis, C.I. (1946), *An Analysis of Knowledge and Valuation*. La Salle, IL: Open Court.

Liljander, V. and T. Strandvik (1994), "Estimating Zones of Tolerances in Perceived Service Quality," *International Journal of Service Industry Management*, 4 (2), 6-28.

Mattsson, J. (1991), *Better Business by the ABC of Values*. Chartwell-Bratt, UK: Lund.

Nunnally, J.C. and I.H. Bernstein (1994), *Psychometric Theory*. New York: McGraw-Hill.

Oliver, R.L. (1993), "A Conceptual Model of Service Quality and Service Satisfaction: Compatible Goals, Different Concepts," in *Advances in Services Marketing and Management*, Vol. 2, T.A. Swartz, D.E. Bowen and S.W. Brown, eds. Greenwich, CT: JAI Press, 65-85.

_____ (1994), "Conceptual Issues in the Structural Analysis of Consumption Emotion, Satisfaction and Quality: Evidence in a Service Setting," in *Advances in Consumer Research*, Vol. 21, C.T. Allen and D. Roedder John, eds. Provo, UT: Association for Consumer Research, 16-22.

Parasuraman, A., V.A. Zeithaml and L.L. Berry (1994), "Reassessment of Expectations as a Comparison Standard in Measuring Service Quality: Implications for Further Research," *Journal of Marketing*, 58, 111-124.

_____, _____, and _____ (1985), "A Conceptual Model of Service Quality," *Journal of Marketing*, 49 (4), 41-50.

Paulin, M. and J. Perrien (Forthcoming), "Measurement of Service Quality: The Effect of Contextuality," in *Managing Service Quality, QMS*, P. Kunst and J. Lemmink, eds. London: Paul Chapman Publishing.

Rust, R.T. and R.L. Oliver (1994), "Service Quality: Insights and Managerial Implications from the Frontier," in *Service Quality: New Directions in Theory and Practice*, R.T. Rust and R.L. Oliver, eds. London: Sage, 1-19.

Singh, J. (1991), "Understanding the Structure of Consumers' Satisfaction Evaluations of Service Delivery," *Journal of the Academy of Marketing Science*, 20, 223-244.

Zeithaml, V.A. (1988), "Consumer Perceptions of Price, Quality and Value: A Means-End Model and Synthesis of Evidence," *Journal of Marketing*, 52, 2-22.

SALESPERSON SERVICE AND CUSTOMER SATISFACTION:
THE IMPACT OF STORE POLICIES

Nancy F. Stanforth and Sharron J. Lennon

ABSTRACT

The purpose of this study was to examine the effects of store policies, customer expectations and respondent gender on satisfaction with the salesperson, satisfaction with retail store service, and salesperson and store evaluations when in service failure situations in a retail store. Three hundred and sixty volunteers participated in a two (expectations) by two (policies) by two (gender of respondent) between subjects experiment. Results of MANOVA and ANOVA revealed main effects for policies and customer expectations, as well as an interaction between respondent gender and customer expectations.

INTRODUCTION

The level of customer service to be offered in a retail apparel store is of concern to store management. Defining which services are important to customers and

Advances in Services Marketing and Management, Volume 6, pages 79-99.
Copyright © 1997 by JAI Press Inc.
All rights of reproduction in any form reserved.
ISBN: 0-7623-0176-7

lead to increased patronage and improved sales is critical to stores' profitability. Customer service is a broad term, encompassing a wide variety of activities and presenting management with a bewildering array of options. Offering expensive services that are not desired by customers and do not lead to satisfaction or patronage can erode profit margins.

Customer service can be classified into two parts, a relational component and a core component (e.g., Iacobucci and Ostrom 1993). The relational component refers to the way that service is delivered and generally is a function of salespeople and customer service representatives in the store: in other words, the people. In contrast, the core component refers to the service being delivered. Services that may be offered in a retail store include special orders, availability of gift boxes and wrapping, home delivery and salesperson assistance. Core components are developed by management as part of the overall merchandising mix and can be added and deleted as management chooses. In retail apparel stores, core aspects of customer service are typically regulated by store policies.

Salesperson service seems to be particularly troublesome to many customers and store managers. Once hired, management has a substantial investment in salespeople. Expensive training may be required to establish core competencies: that is, how to operate the point-of-sale terminal or complete paperwork for special orders.

Relational aspects of salesperson service are even more difficult to manage. Employing friendly, outgoing people with skills in core activities is a formidable task for management. Salespeople come with their own personalities, and training them to respond as management wishes is a challenge. Many retail situations are stressful to salespeople and each person responds differently to these situations. Dealing with complaining and dissatisfied customers may produce anxiety and erratic responses from salespeople, making it difficult for management to predict and control the interaction of customer and salespeople. Managing the relational component of salesperson service is somewhat uncertain.

In addition, the need for salespeople to comply with core components or store policies limits their ability to respond to customer requests. For example, store policies may mandate that salespeople remain in their assigned areas, whereas a customer might prefer the salesperson to accompany him or her to other areas of the store when seeking additional merchandise. Thus, it is important for management to balance critical core activities with customers' demands for improved relational aspects of salesperson service.

Some core activities, as defined by management policies, irritate customers and give rise to complaints concerning customer service in retail stores. While it seems intuitively reasonable that management would eliminate or modify these irritating policies, experience tells us this is not so. Policies which cause customers to be dissatisfied are in place in many stores; some are in place for legal reasons; others are designed to prevent fraud. However, many others exist simply because management has not evaluated policies to determine their impact on customer-salesperson relations. While policies may be the source of customer irritation, customers often attribute poor customer service to salespeople and employees choosing not to be helpful (Becker and Wellins 1990; Bitner, Booms and Mohr 1994). Indeed, some service employees report an inability to satisfy customer needs because of "constraints placed on them by laws or their own organization's rules and procedures" (Bitner, Booms and Mohr 1994, p. 99). In this way, irritating policies or core components may make it impossible to provide salesperson service that delights customers. The purpose of this research was to examine the effects of store policies, customers' expectations for service and respondent gender on evaluations of and satisfaction with salesperson service in retail apparel stores in problematic situations.

LITERATURE REVIEW

We now discuss the norms model of customer satisfaction, the schema construct and gender differences as related to salesperson service in a retail environment. We then proceed to test our hypotheses.

Customer Satisfaction

Customer (dis)satisfaction may be based on the "norms" models of consumer satisfaction (Erevelles and Leavitt 1992), which suggest that goods and services are compared to a standard, or norm. Accordingly, satisfaction results from comparing an actual good or service to a comparison standard (Woodruff et al. 1991). Customer's normative expectations for salesperson service are what the customer thinks "should" happen when interacting with a salesperson. The difference between what the customer thinks "will" happen and what the customer thinks "should" happen is an important component of these models. If a customer shopped at a store and waited in line five minutes, for example, the next time this customer shopped, she or he may expect that he or she "will" wait in line again. However, the customer may actually think that he or she "should" wait no more than a minute. A third concept is the customer's "ideal" expectations, that is, what would be expected if the service encounter were ideal. Ideal expectations are not related to what is reasonable or feasible for a store to provide. For example, ideally, customers may want very high levels of service from salespeople but also very low prices on apparel (Boulding et al. 1993).

Comparison of these elements to normative expectations is an evaluation of the experience and is thought to lead to positive disconfirmation when salesperson service is better than expected (creating satisfaction), and negative disconfirmation when salesperson service is worse than expected (creating dissatisfaction). Confirmation occurs when normative expectations are met; this state is also thought to result in satisfaction (Woodruff et al. 1991). In general, consumers' perceptions and expectations for what should occur serve as the foundation for most consumer satisfaction models.

Consumer satisfaction researchers have focused primarily on the *process* of satisfaction (i.e., antecedents and consequences [Singh 1991]). However, the *structure* (i.e., content and dimensions) of satisfaction may be equally important. Singh (1991) studied the structure of satisfaction in a health care setting. While it may seem that health care and retail store service are very different, they have many elements in common. Just as a patient may be satisfied with the outcome of surgery but dissatisfied with the nursing staff, satisfaction with a store and satisfaction with merchandise purchased in that store may have no relationship. A customer may be pleased with the merchandise but be very displeased with the salesperson who sold it.

Customer structural evaluations are of two major types: attribute-based and object-based (Singh 1991). Singh (1991) found that attribute-based evaluations are composed of three dimensions: (a) expressive, (b) instrumental and (c) access or cost. For example, in a retail setting, an expressive feature might be the overall ambiance of the store and how that makes a shopper feel; an instrumental feature might be the ease with which one can locate desired merchandise when shopping; access or cost refers to the effort required of the customer to consummate the purchase. Object-based evaluations are concerned with the focus of customer satisfaction, for example, toward salespeople, merchandise or management. Evaluations of the various objects may vary from one encounter to another within a store, for example, a customer may be very satisfied with the salesperson but not with the person in alterations. Thus, global evaluations of retail apparel stores will include individual evaluations of many objects, with individual customers weighting objects differently, so clearly it is important to study isolated component objects that may account for the variation in satisfaction evaluations by customers. In particular, this study seeks to isolate the salesperson as an object of evaluation in a disconfirming service encounter to determine the impact of store policies on that evaluation.

The Schema Construct

The concept of schema (Wyer 1980) can help us understand the way in which store policies, customer expectations and respondent gender might affect satisfaction with retail salesperson service. According to Fiske and Taylor (1991, p. 98), a schema is a "cognitive structure that represents knowledge about a concept or type of stimulus including its attributes." Schemata are thought to contain information abstracted from experience (Wyer 1980) and may structure expectations. One particular type of schema research focuses on event schema (Taylor and Crocker 1981). Event schemata or scripts are a subtype of schemata that describe typical activities in everyday situations (Abelson 1981), such as shopping for apparel.

Store policies establish the appropriate sequence of events for salesperson-customer interactions, given that they are specified by store management, and as such are a type of *management event schema*. Such event schemata specify core components of service as mandated by store management and include policies that prescribe merchandise returns, merchandise delivery, acceptable forms of payment and sales floor staffing. Retail apparel stores often have standardized service policies requiring that salespeople treat all customers in the same manner. In a common situation such as shopping in an apparel store, the scripts are well-defined and both salespeople and customers know what to expect from one another. In a more customized encounter, the salesperson would adapt to the customer's desires. For example, customized apparel shopping might include a personal shopper, who would accommodate the customer as much as possible. However, when the situation is not routine, there are interferences (Schank and Abelson 1977) which interrupt the expected script. These interferences may require less routine behaviors, which may cause a discrepancy between the customer's and the salesperson's scripts. Some interference is caused by management-mandated policies which force the salesperson to perform complex subscripts to complete a transaction. In case of service failures, management interference may be a source of conflict. Therefore, store policies examined in this research are the mandated service responses to failure situations (i.e., service worse than expected). Although these types of service responses are established by store management, customers may evaluate the store policy as a function of their expectations for service in that context.

In a retail store setting, the store's mandated policy for a salesperson-customer interaction may not be in congruence with customers' normative expectations, and consequently customers may experience disconfirmation. Salesperson service is an intangible, making it difficult to measure or test. Intangibility makes it difficult for the store management to understand customers' perceptions of the salesperson encounter (Parasuraman, Zeithaml and Berry 1985). The physical distance between customers and store executives exacerbates the problem. Executives may rarely meet a customer and so may not be aware that customer expectations for service are different from store policies. For example, customers may not only expect to receive assistance when selecting merchandise, customers may also expect salespeople to arrange to have alterations completed and the merchandise sent to their homes. In other words, being able to purchase an item may be only part of what customers expect from salesperson service. They may also expect the salesperson to expedite this process through effort on his/her part. Therefore, we suggest the following hypotheses:

Hypothesis 1. Store policies which require customer effort will negatively affect perceived customer satisfaction, as compared to store policies which require salesperson effort.

Hypothesis 2. Store policies which require customer effort will negatively affect salesperson evaluations, as compared to store policies which require salesperson effort.

Gender Differences

Another well-researched type of schema is role schema, and one type of role schema focuses on gender roles. Gender roles are culturally defined expectations for men's and women's behavior in certain situations (Ruble and Ruble 1982). Recently, researchers have found that gender may have an impact on salesperson evaluations (Eagly and Johnson 1990; Iacobucci and Ostrom 1993). It is believed that men and women employ different information processing styles (Coughlin and O'Connor 1985; Deaux 1984; Meyers-Levy 1989; Meyers-Levy and Maheswaran 1991; Meyers-Levy and Sternthal 1991). According to the selectivity model, women are comprehensive information processors, considering both objective and subjective elements, and using subtle cues. Men tend to be more selective information processors, employing heuristics more often and missing subtle cues (Eagly and Johnson 1990). Consequently, men may be more influenced by core aspects of service while women are influenced by both core and relational aspects of service (Iacobucci and Ostrom 1993). While both men and women expect that the salesperson can competently carry out the core aspects of service, women also are thought to expect more friendly salesperson service. Thus women may be more influenced by relational components of customer service than men.

Women are typically believed by both men and women to be more emotional, gentle and sensitive to others (Antill 1987; Briton and Hall 1995; Rosenkrantz et al. 1968). Given that many salespeople are women, this stereotypical view of women's communication styles may be an important element in the evaluation of salespeople in a retail apparel store. In addition, many of the relational components of the salesperson's job are tasks at which women are stereotypically thought to excel.

This gender-based stereotype may be most important for "one-shot" encounters when customers must make instant satisfaction judgments than for longer term relationships. Since many retail apparel store service encounters are one-shot encounters, it is likely that customers might expect female salespeople to be skilled in the relational component of service. Iacobucci and Ostrom (1993) predicted that men would be more attentive to the quality of the core component of a service interaction and women would be more attentive to the relationship component for short-term interactions, such as salesperson or restaurant service. Their study used printed descriptions of initial encounters with service providers, varying occupation to further investigate the effects of gender on evaluations. Findings suggest that the expected duration of the service provider/customer interaction had an effect. While the results of this series of studies were somewhat unclear, some intriguing trends were found. When respondents expected to have short-term interactions with the service provider and there was little time for the relational component to be developed, there was little difference between respondent genders on overall evaluation of service providers. They also found that the gender of both rater and service provider impacted evaluations such that women tended to rate women providers more favorably. Given that most salespeople in the apparel industry are women and women's apparel comprises the largest share of the family's apparel expenditures (*American Demographics* 1993), female-female interactions are particularly important to study. However, initial encounters are often routine experiences which are highly scripted activities. Encounters to resolve service failures are not as scripted and should cause customers to be more attentive to the service providers' attributes. These considerations suggest the following hypotheses:

Hypothesis 3. As compared to women, men will rate the salesperson lower on core variables.

Hypothesis 4. As compared to women, men will be more sensitive to variations in the core components of service; for example, they will be more affected by policies varying core components than will women.

Expectations

Customers use physical cues in the retail environment to categorize stores (Means 1981) and make inferences about probable services (Ward, Bitner and Barnes 1992). Indeed, research shows that the physical environment of a business may generate a set of expectations in the customer (Bitner 1990). Thus, the physical appearance of discount stores may initiate one set of customer expectations for service, and the appearance of fine specialty stores may initiate another. For example, a store that is very neat, with wide aisles and subdued lighting, may cause customers to categorize the store as expensive and to expect prompt individualized service. Customers are likely to be dissatisfied with the service response if it does not meet these higher expectations. It follows from the relativism posited by satisfaction theory that if a customer expects less from the shopping experience, he or she will be satisfied with less. Based on these considerations the following hypotheses were formulated:

Hypothesis 5. Customer expectations will affect perceived customer satisfaction with customer service.

Hypothesis 6. Customer expectations will affect salesperson evaluations.

Patronage

Retailers are service businesses, and it is believed that those who consistently provide value to their customers through good quality service will gain a long-term competitive advantage (Berry 1986) which presumably will lead to increased patronage. Exceeding customers' expectations for service is thought to generate customer loyalty and support. While this premise seems reasonable, there are times when other factors may be important to patronage. Consumers may patronize stores that do not provide quality service or satisfaction due to customer time constraints, convenience of location or other factors. Therefore, the importance of satisfaction with salesperson service is also of interest to retailers. However, there has been little empirical investigation of the link between consumer satisfaction and patronage intent (Bitner 1990; Oliva, Oliver and MacMillan 1992; Oliver 1980). Thus, we hypothesize the following:

Hypothesis 7. As compared to policies which require salesperson effort, policies which require customer effort will have a negative effect on patronage intentions in disconfirming situations.

As men are thought to be more influenced by core aspects of service, when relational aspects of service are held constant, men might be expected to be less satisfied and more likely to refuse to patronize a store. We hypothesize that:

Hypothesis 8. Patronage intentions of men will be more negatively affected by policies that require customer effort than will patronage intentions of women.

Finally, it is often assumed that customers prefer to shop where service is expected to be superior. Therefore, the following hypothesis was formulated:

Hypothesis 9. Customer expectations will affect patronage intentions.

Apparel Retail Purchasing

The retail apparel store was selected as the context for this research for several reasons. Previous research has explored satisfaction in the contexts of restaurants (Swan and Trawick 1981), banks (Surprenant and Solomon 1987) and travel agencies (Bitner 1990). However, the results of these studies may not be directly applicable to apparel purchasing. Apparel is a special good. It is visible when in use and is often chosen by consumers as a means of self-expression (Davis and Lennon 1985; Harrison et al. 1986; Horowitz 1982; Schlick and Rowold 1991) and for appearance management purposes (e.g., Cash 1985; Cash and Kilcullen 1985; Thurston, Lennon and Clayton 1990). Because clothing is a symbol which communicates nonverbally (e.g., Damhorst 1990), its purchase may be very ego-involving and therefore may be different from other types of purchases.

METHOD

Development of Stimulus Materials

Problematic retail store policies were identified within the context of a focus group interview with six retail store salespersons. Policies identified as management-mandated were isolated and two of them involving apparel purchasing were selected to be used in this research: (1) an advertised garment which was unavailable, and (2) the return of a defective garment which was guaranteed by the manufacturer. Alternative policies were formulated to operationalize two levels of store policies, that is, the unavailable advertised garment could be sent from another store to the customer's home in one condition, or it had to be picked up by the customer at another store in the other condition. The difference between the two levels of store policies was that in one condition the solution required salesperson effort and in the other condition the solution required customer effort to solve.

In accord with previous research (Surprenant and Solomon 1987), we developed one-sided scripts of a salesperson politely handling a customer-salesperson interaction. Four scripts reflecting each of the policies and their alternatives were pretested and found to be believable, unambiguous and intelligible. Finally, the scripts were audio-taped in a professional sound studio by a female actor.

Because physical aspects of retail stores have been found to affect customers' inferences (Means 1981; Ward, Bitner and Barnes 1992), we decided to use visual merchandising to manipulate customers' expectations. Twenty-six undergraduates viewed and categorized 80 colored slides of store interiors. Five slides were classified by all 26 respondents as representing stores that sold expensive merchandise and five slides were classified by all 26 respondents as representing stores that sold inexpensive merchandise, and these exemplar stimuli were selected for the research.

Multiple stimuli (two policies, and two levels of visual merchandising each operationalized using five slides) were employed for stimulus sampling purposes (Fontenelle, Phillips and Lane 1985). Stimulus sampling is used so that the results can be generalized over more than one stimulus (Fontenelle, Phillips and Lane 1985), that is, for purposes of external validity. In the present research, stimulus sampling required that more than one policy and more than one level of visual merchandising be used to ensure that possible significant effects were not caused by idiosyncratic properties of an individual stimulus.

Manipulation Check

Seventeen undergraduates viewed the 10 slides and indicated their expectations for customer service in the stores represented in the slides. Six five-point agree-disagree items were completed for each slide, for example, "I expect prompt service in this store." Data were summed for a composite expectation score and analyzed using a matched groups t-test. A main effect was found for visual merchandising on expectations, $t(16) = 8.47, p < 0.00001$. Respondents had lower expectations for the inexpensively merchandised store ($\bar{x} = 13.9$) than for the expensively merchandised store ($\bar{x} = 25.7$). Thus, the slides selected by pretest respondents as representing stores which sold inexpensive or expensive merchandise could be used to manipulate low and high levels of customers' expectations, respectively.

Instrument Development

The dependent measure was based on previous research (Surprenant and Solomon 1987) and consisted of a series of seven-point rating scales. Four scales addressed satisfaction (with salesperson treatment, with the alternatives offered, with store policy and overall satisfaction) and four addressed patronage intent (likelihood of refusing to shop in that store, likelihood of looking in another store for the garment, likelihood of walking out without making a purchase and likelihood of shopping in the store again). In addition, 19 items were included to evaluate the salesperson, focusing on both core and relational aspects. Six items were used to evaluate the store, focusing on both core and relational qualities. Finally, respondents indicated an overall rating of the salesperson and of the store using items anchored by poor and excellent.

Respondents

Three hundred and sixty volunteers (200 females and 160 males) were recruited to participate. Participants were undergraduates enrolled in two Midwestern universities. They were members of the "baby-bust" generation, born between the mid-1960s and the mid-1970s and considered to be a distinct and lucrative market segment (Dunn 1992). Busters are the "second-largest group of young adults in U.S. history," spending nearly $17 billion on clothing and related items in 1991 (Zinn 1992, p. 74). These savvy consumers represent approximately 17 percent of the U.S. population and are more likely to spend their earnings than save them (*Stores* 1989). Thus, this is an important consumer group to study within an apparel retail context.

Procedure

Groups of two to 15 respondents were randomly assigned to treatment conditions. To establish a context for customer service, the students viewed slides depicting a retail store in which a customer-salesperson interaction was purported to have occurred. The respondents then listened to a one-sided audio recording of a customer-salesperson interaction and were asked to consider what their reactions would be if they were the customer in that situation. After exposure to the stimuli, the participants were asked to complete the dependent measures, which took approximately 20 minutes. They were then debriefed.

RESULTS

Principal components were used for data reduction of the salesperson rating scale. An oblique rotation was used, and the data were analyzed separately for men and women. For the men, four factors were generated, but for the women only three factors were generated and the items loading on the factors were dissimilar for men and women. Therefore, for simplicity, individual items were treated as separate dependent variables. Core variables were defined as ratings on those adjectives which referred to the service being offered: capable, efficient, businesslike, organized, practical, slow, reliable, conscientious, thorough and responsible. The relational variables were defined as ratings on adjectives which referred to the way the service was delivered: helpful, formal, sincere, sociable, caring, talkative, not rude, considerate and friendly.

The same procedure was applied for data reduction of the store rating scale. These analyses revealed similar factor structures (only one factor) when analyzing the men's and women's data separately, so the data were combined and refactored. A single factor was generated, and the resultant single scale consisted of four items (Cronbach's alpha = 0.91) and accounted for 57 percent of the variance. The ratings for each of the items loading on this factor were summed and used as the dependent variable of store trustworthiness (see Table 1).

Data were entered into a two (policies) by two (expectations) by two (gender of respondent) between subjects' multivariate analysis of variance. For data analysis, data from both scenarios was combined to minimize possible

Table 1.   Factor Analysis and Reliability of the Store Rating Scale

Factors/Factor Items	Factor Loadings	Percent of Variance	Cronbach's Alpha
Factor 1: Trustworthiness			
Friendly	0.66	59.2%	0.91
Reliable	0.80		
Caring	0.80		
Responsible	0.78		

idiosyncratic effects of any one policy on responses. There were 33 dependent variables: overall satisfaction, satisfaction with alternatives, satisfaction with salesperson, satisfaction with store policy, liking to shop in the store, likelihood of shopping in the store again, likelihood of telling the salesperson about the policy, likelihood of complaining about the policy to management, likelihood of looking in another store for the garment, likelihood of refusing to shop in the store again, likelihood of walking out of the store, overall rating of the store, overall rating of the salesperson, the 19 salesperson rating scales and the store's trustworthiness.

Multivariate Analyses

A single multivariate MANOVA test was run to alleviate concerns regarding possible Type I errors, considering the relatively large number of dependent variables. The MANOVA significance tests are described here, and then the univariate follow-up tests are described in order to communicate a parsimonious sense of the results. There was a significant multivariate main effect for store policies, multivariate $F(33, 320) = 8.83, p < 0.0001$. There was also a significant multivariate main effect for customer expectations, $F(33, 320) = 2.30, p < 0.0001$. The two-way multivariate interaction between customer expectations and gender of respondent was significant, $F(33, 320) = 1.75, p < 0.008$. Neither the multivariate main effect for gender of respondent, the three-way multivariate interaction, nor any of the other two-way multivariate interactions were significant. Only those effects which were significant at the multivariate level were probed further by means of univariate analyses.

Univariate Analyses

Store Policies

There were main effects for store policies on overall satisfaction [$F(1, 352) = 116.68, p < 0.0001$], satisfaction with alternatives [$F(1, 352) = 151.16$,

$p < 0.0001$], satisfaction with salesperson treatment [F (1, 352) $=$ 84.14, $p<0.0001$], and on satisfaction with the policy [$F(1, 352) = 217.70, p<0.0001$]. As expected, overall satisfaction was lower when the policy required the customer to exert effort to solve the problem ($\bar{x}$= 4.07) rather than requiring the salesperson to exert the effort ($\bar{x}$ = 5.96). Likewise, satisfaction with alternatives was lower when the policy required customer effort to resolve the problem ($\bar{x}$ = 3.78) rather than requiring salesperson effort ($\bar{x}$ = 5.87). In addition, satisfaction with salesperson treatment was lower when the policy required the customer to exert effort to resolve the problem ($\bar{x}$ = 4.62) rather than requiring the salesperson to exert effort to resolve the problem ($\bar{x}$ = 6.12). Finally, satisfaction with the policy was lower when the policy required customer effort to resolve the problem ($\bar{x}$ = 3.46) rather than requiring salesperson effort ($\bar{x}$ = 5.99). Therefore, Hypothesis was supported.

There were main effects for store policies on 17 of the 19 salesperson rating scale items (see Table 2). In each case, the salesperson was rated higher when the policy required salesperson effort rather than when the policy required customer effort. In addition, there was a main effect for policy on the overall salesperson rating, [F (1, 352) $=$ 61.00, $p < 0.0001$]. The overall rating of the salesperson was lower when the policy required the customer to exert effort to resolve ($\bar{x}$ = 4.59) rather than requiring the salesperson to exert effort to resolve ($\bar{x}$ = 5.88), thus supporting Hypothesis 2.

Additionally, there were main effects for policies on the store's trustworthiness [$F(1, 352) = 78.71, p<0.0001$] and on the store's overall rating [$F(1, 352) = 93.50, p<0.0001$]. The store was rated as more trustworthy when the policy required salesperson effort to resolve the problem ($\bar{x}$ = 21.62) rather than when the policy required customer effort to resolve the problem ($\bar{x}$ = 16.3). Finally, the store's overall rating was higher when the policy required salesperson effort to resolve the problem ($\bar{x}$ = 5.51) rather than requiring customer effort ($\bar{x}$ = 3.89).

There were main effects for store policies on the likelihood of looking in another store [F (1, 352) $=$ 37.24, $p < 0.0001$], the likelihood of refusing to shop in the store again [$F(1, 352) = 80.49, p<0.0001$], the likelihood of walking out of the store [$F(1, 352) = 67.14, p<0.0001$] and the likelihood of shopping in the store again [F (1, 352) $=$ 93.76, $p < 0.0001$]. As expected, participants reported being more likely to look in another store when the policy required the customer to exert effort to solve the problem ($\bar{x}$ = 4.99) rather than requiring the salesperson to exert the effort ($\bar{x}$ = 3.61). Likewise, they reported being more likely to refuse to shop in the store in which the policy required customer effort to resolve the problem ($\bar{x}$ = 3.63) rather than requiring salesperson effort ($\bar{x}$ = 1.94). In addition, respondents reported being more likely to walk out of the store when the policy required the customer to exert effort to resolve the problem ($\bar{x}$ = 4.92) rather than requiring the salesperson to exert effort ($\bar{x}$ = 3.17). Finally, they reported that they were less likely to

Table 2.   Cell Means for Store Policies on the Salesperson Rating Scale

Dependent Variables	Customer Effort	Salesperson Effort	F	p
Businesslike	5.38	5.83	8.20	0.004
Capable	5.37	6.24	41.36	0.000
Caring	4.43	5.66	51.74	0.000
Conscientious	4.52	5.64	46.25	0.000
Considerate	4.78	5.89	49.20	0.000
Efficient	4.81	5.96	49.15	0.000
Formal	5.07	5.16	0.38	0.536
Friendly	5.32	6.12	32.56	0.000
Helpful	5.26	6.33	54.42	0.000
Not rude	5.33	6.08	22.04	0.000
Organized	4.97	6.16	60.50	0.000
Practical	4.68	5.83	52.85	0.000
Reliable	4.59	5.82	61.61	0.000
Responsible	4.81	6.00	53.37	0.000
Sincere	4.44	5.35	22.87	0.000
Not slow	5.42	5.84	7.86	0.005
Sociable	5.23	5.76	11.16	0.001
Talkative	5.59	5.84	2.85	0.092
Thorough	4.81	5.99	52.80	0.000

shop again in the store in which the policy required customer effort to resolve the problem ($\bar{x} = 3.91$) rather than requiring salesperson effort ($\bar{x} = 5.78$). Thus, as compared to policies which required salesperson effort, policies which required customer effort had a negative effect on patronage intent in disconfirming situations and Hypothesis 7 was deemed plausible.

Customer Expectations

There were main effects for customer expectations on overall satisfaction [$F(1, 352) = 4.72, p < 0.03$], on satisfaction with alternatives [$F(1, 352) = 6.49, p < 0.01$], on satisfaction with salesperson treatment [$F(1, 352) = 9.53, p < 0.002$] and on satisfaction with the policy [$F(1, 352) = 4.62, p < 0.03$]. As expected, overall satisfaction was lower in stores for which customers had high expectations ($\bar{x} = 4.82$) than in stores for which customers had low expectations ($\bar{x} = 5.20$). Likewise, satisfaction with alternatives was lower in stores in which customers' expectations were high ($\bar{x} = 4.62$) than in stores in which customers' expectations were low ($\bar{x} = 5.03$). In addition, satisfaction with salesperson treatment was lower in stores in which customers had high expectations ($\bar{x} = 5.11$) as compared to stores in which customers had low expectations ($\bar{x} = 5.63$). Finally, satisfaction with the policy was lower in stores in which customers' expectations were high ($\bar{x} = 4.54$) than in stores in which

Table 3. Cell Means for Customer Expectations on the Salesperson Rating Scale

	Expectations			
	High	Low		
Dependent Variables	$\bar{x}$	$\bar{x}$	F	p
Businesslike	5.63	5.57	0.41	0.525
Capable	5.64	5.97	6.46	0.011
Caring	4.74	5.35	12.19	0.001
Conscientious	4.85	5.31	7.40	0.007
Considerate	5.16	5.52	4.90	0.028
Efficient	5.22	5.54	3.44	0.064
Formal	5.14	5.09	0.12	0.734
Friendly	5.53	5.90	6.60	0.011
Helpful	5.59	6.00	7.59	0.006
Not rude	5.47	5.94	7.97	0.005
Organized	5.39	5.73	4.41	0.036
Practical	5.02	5.49	7.70	0.006
Reliable	4.98	5.42	7.41	0.007
Responsible	5.12	5.66	12.97	0.000
Sincere	4.71	5.08	3.46	0.064
Not slow	5.39	5.86	8.38	0.004
Sociable	5.27	5.72	8.81	0.003
Talkative	5.59	5.85	3.36	0.068
Thorough	5.15	5.65	10.36	0.001

customers' expectations were low ($\bar{x} = 4.91$). Therefore, Hypothesis 5 was supported.

There were main effects for customer expectations on 14 of the 19 salesperson rating scale items. In each case, with the exception of formality, the salesperson was rated higher when customer expectations were low than when customer expectations were high (see Table 3). In addition, there was a main effect for customer expectations on the overall salesperson rating, $[F (1, 352) = 7.77, p < 0.006]$. The overall rating of the salesperson was higher when customer expectations were low ($\bar{x} = 5.46$) as compared to when customer expectations were high ($\bar{x} = 5.01$), and Hypothesis 6 was accepted.

Gender of Respondent

None of the main effects for gender of respondent was significant. However, there were customer expectations by gender of respondent interactions on liking to shop in the store $[F (1, 352) = 6.60, p < 0.01]$, likelihood of shopping in the store again $[F (1, 352) = 4.46, p < 0.04]$ and store trustworthiness $[F (1, 352) = 4.08, p < 0.04]$. Inspection of the interaction cell means revealed that although men ($\bar{x} = 4.80$) and women ($\bar{x} = 4.75$) were similar in terms

Table 4.   Cell Means for Interaction of Gender and Customer Expectations

| Dependent Variables | Customer Expectations | Gender | | F | p |
		Men $\bar{x}$	Women $\bar{x}$		
Liking to shop in store	High	4.35	5.25	6.60	0.010
	Low	4.80	4.75		
Likelihood of shopping in store again	High	4.50	4.95	4.46	0.040
	Low	5.25	4.85		
Store trustworthiness	High	17.70	19.74	4.08	0.040
	Low	19.30	18.92		

of liking to shop at the store for which customer expectations were low, women liked shopping at the store for which customer expectations were high ($\bar{x} = 5.25$) to a greater extent than did men ($\bar{x} = 4.35$). Additionally, women reported similar likelihoods of shopping at the store for which customer expectations were high ($\bar{x} = 4.95$) and at the store for which customer expectations were low ($\bar{x} = 4.85$), while men reported a higher likelihood of shopping at the store for which customer expectations were low ($\bar{x} = 5.25$) as compared to the store for which customer expectations were high ($\bar{x} = 4.50$). Finally, although ratings of the store's trustworthiness by men ($\bar{x} = 19.30$) and women ($\bar{x} = 18.92$) were similar when customer expectations were low, men rated the store's trustworthiness lower when customer expectations were high ($\bar{x} = 17.70$) as compared to women ($\bar{x} = 19.74$). None of the other univariate interactions with gender of respondent were significant (see Table 4).

DISCUSSION

The purpose of this study was to examine the effects of store policies, customer expectations and respondent gender on satisfaction with the salesperson, satisfaction with retail store service, and salesperson and store evaluations in the context of a retail apparel store. Store policies requiring customer effort were expected to negatively affect perceived customer satisfaction, as compared to store policies requiring salesperson effort (Hypothesis 1). Results of multivariate and univariate analyses of variance supported this hypothesis. Store policies had a significant effect on 31 of the 33 dependent variables. In general, satisfaction (with alternatives, with salesperson treatment, with the policy and overall satisfaction) was lower when the policy required the customer to exert effort to solve the problem, rather than requiring the salesperson to exert the effort. Thus, Hypothesis 1 was supported.

Store policies requiring customer effort were also expected to negatively affect salesperson evaluations as compared to store policies requiring salesperson effort (Hypothesis 2). There were main effects for store policies on 17 of the 19 salesperson rating scale items, as well as on the overall salesperson rating. In each case, the salesperson was rated higher when the policy required salesperson effort as compared to when the policy required customer effort. Thus, Hypothesis 2 was supported. In addition, store policies affected ratings of the store's trustworthiness and the store's overall rating. Both the store's overall rating and rating of trustworthiness were higher when the policy required salesperson effort to resolve the problem, rather than requiring customer effort.

We also predicted and found main effects for store policies on patronage intentions (Hypothesis 7). Policies affected the likelihood of looking in another store, of refusing to shop in the store again, of walking out of the store and of shopping in the store again. As expected, respondents reported being more likely to look in another store (to refuse to shop in the store, to walk out of the store and not to shop in the store again) when the policy required customer effort to resolve the problem rather than requiring salesperson effort. Thus, as compared to policies which required salesperson effort, policies which required customer effort had a negative effect on patronage intent in disconfirming situations, and Hypothesis 7 was accepted.

We predicted that customer expectations would affect satisfaction (Hypothesis 5). In fact, overall satisfaction and satisfaction with alternatives, with salesperson treatment and with the policy were all affected by customer expectations. In each instance, satisfaction was higher in stores for which customers had low expectations as compared to stores for which customers had high expectations. Thus, Hypothesis 5 was supported. In addition, we predicted and found that customer expectations affected ratings of the salesperson (Hypothesis 6). On 13 of 19 salesperson rating items, in addition to the overall salesperson rating, the salesperson was rated higher when customer expectations were low than when customer expectations were high. Therefore, Hypothesis 6 was supported. Although customer expectations were expected to affect patronage intentions (Hypothesis 9), no relationships were found.

We predicted that compared to women, men would rate the salesperson lower on core variables (Hypothesis 3). No such effects were found. We also predicted a respondent gender by policy interaction (Hypothesis 4), that is, that men would be more sensitive to variations in the core components of service than women. However, no such effects were found. Finally, we predicted that, compared to women, men's patronage intentions would be more negatively affected by policies that required customer effort (Hypothesis 8), but again, the analysis did not support the hypothesis.

However, there were unexpected gender of respondent by customer expectations interactions on three dependent variables (liking to shop in the store, likelihood of shopping in the store again and store's trustworthiness). When customer expectations were low, men and women agreed in terms of the extent to which they liked to shop in the store. Compared to men, women preferred shopping at the store for which expectations were high, but they did not distinguish between the stores in terms of where they were likely to shop again. Men, however, reported a greater likelihood of shopping at the store again when customer expectations were low compared to when they were high. Finally, ratings of the store's trustworthiness did not differ by customer expectations, but men rated the store's trustworthiness lower when customer expectations were high than when customer expectations were low. These interactions suggest that men and women differ in terms of which type of store they prefer, which type of store they are likely to shop in again and which they rate as trustworthy.

CONCLUSIONS

MANOVA and ANOVAs revealed that policies affect satisfaction with the salesperson, satisfaction with service and salesperson evaluations. In general, participants tended to be more satisfied and to rate the salesperson more favorably when policies required salesperson effort to resolve the problem. Store policies that require the customer to participate in the resolution of the problem are not as satisfying as those which require the salesperson to exert the effort. Given that the term "service" implies that something is going to be done "for" someone, it seems intuitive that customers would be less satisfied with resolutions that require them to exert effort. However, many retail stores have policies that require just that, and as this study illustrates, those policies will influence the evaluation of several factors, including the salesperson. The salesperson was rated lower when enforcing a policy that required customer effort, although the relationship component of the interaction was held constant. Thus, some of the dissatisfaction with salesperson service in retail apparel stores may be the consequence of policies instituted by management and independent of salesperson behavior. Evaluation of policies to determine which are dissatisfying to customers should be undertaken by retail management. While all policies cannot be changed to meet customer expectations, recognition that the policy is dissatisfying might reduce some misplaced blame.

Finally, there were interactions between respondent gender and customer expectations on liking to shop in the store, likelihood of shopping in the store again and the store's trustworthiness. Men reported being more willing to shop again in the inexpensively merchandised store than in the expensively merchandised store, while women were equally willing to shop again in both types of stores, which might suggest greater willingness on the part of women to shop around rather than patronize one type of store.

Compared to men, women respondents preferred to shop at the more expensive-looking store, that is, a well-merchandised, neat environment. This study also suggests that women use subtle cues in the visual environment to determine the store's trustworthiness. Given that women are frequently the predominant shoppers for families, the difference in men's and women's responses to salesperson service and store trustworthiness is important. Furthermore, recognizing that a dissatisfied woman shopper may have no aversion to shopping elsewhere has important implications for retailers. New technologies, such as television and on-line computer shopping, provide alternatives to store shopping (Salomon and Koppelman 1992). These alternatives may be less expensive and more convenient for shoppers. The marketers' adage that the cost of attracting a new customer is many times the cost of retaining a current customer is more important today than ever. It is critical to retain current customers, as attracting new customers is often difficult and expensive.

Future research should study perceptions of customer service in conjunction with the purpose of the shopping trip. In this study, the customer was in the store to resolve a problem and consequently expected to interact with a salesperson. However, those who are in the store for information gathering (e.g., Wilson and Woodside 1991) or entertainment (e.g., Holbrook and Hirschman 1982) may have different expectations. Expectations for salesperson service may vary greatly depending on the reason for the shopping trip. As most shopping trips are not undertaken to resolve a problem, it is important to investigate those expectations as well.

REFERENCES

Abelson, R.P. (1981), "The Psychological Status of the Script Concept," *American Psychologist*, 36, 715-729.

American Demographics (1993), "Hot Clothes," *American Demographics*, July, 10-11.

Antill, J.K. (1987), "Parents' Beliefs and Values About Sex Roles, Sex Differences, and Sexuality: Their Sources and Implications," *Review of Personality and Social Psychology*, 7, 294-328.

Becker, W.S. and R.S. Wellins (1990), "Customer-Service Perceptions and Reality," *Training and Development Journal*, 44 (3), 49-51.

Berry, L.L. (1986), "Retail Businesses Are Services Businesses," *Journal of Retailing*, 62 (1), 3-6.

Bitner, M.J. (1990), "Evaluating Service Encounters: The Effects of Physical Surroundings and Employee Responses," *Journal of Marketing*, 54, 69-82.

_____, B.H. Booms and L.A. Mohr (1994), "Critical Service Encounters: The Employee's Viewpoint," *Journal of Marketing*, 58, 95-106.

Boulding, W., A. Kalra, R. Staelin and V.A. Zeithaml (1993), "A Dynamic Process Model of Service Quality: From Expectations to Behavioral Intentions," *Journal of Marketing Research*, 30 (February), 7-27.

Briton, N.J. and J.A. Hall (1995), "Beliefs about Female and Male Nonverbal Communication," *Sex Roles*, 32, 79-90.

Cash, T.F. (1985), "The Impact of Grooming Style on the Evaluation of Women in Management," in *The Psychology of Fashion,* M.R. Solomon, ed. Lexington, MA: Lexington Books, 343-355.

_____ and R. Kilcullen (1985), "The Aye of the Beholder: Susceptibility To Sexism and Beautyism in the Evaluation of Managerial Applicants," *Journal of Applied Social Psychology*, 15, 591-605.

Coughlin, M. and P.J. O'Connor (1985), "Gender Role Portrayals in Advertising: An Individual Differences Analysis," in *Advances in Consumer Research,* Vol. 12, E.C. Hirschman and M.B. Holbrook, eds. Provo, UT: Association for Consumer Research, 238-244.

Damhorst, M.L. (1990), "In Search of a Common Thread: Classification of Information Communicated Through Dress," *Clothing and Textiles Research Journal*, 8 (2), 1-12.

Davis, L.L. and S.J. Lennon (1985), "Self-Monitoring, Fashion Opinion Leadership, and Attitudes Toward Clothing," in *The Psychology of Fashion,* M.R. Solomon, ed. Lexington, MA: Lexington Books/ D.C. Heath, 177-182.

Deaux, K. (1984), "From Individual Differences to Social Categories: Analysis of a Decade's Research on Gender," *American Psychologist*, 39 (February), 105-116.

Dunn, W. (1992), "Hanging Out with American Youth," *American Demographics*, (February), 24-27, 30-35.

Eagly, A.H. and B.T. Johnson (1990), "Gender and Leadership Style: A Meta-Analysis," *Psychological Bulletin*, 108, 233-256.

Erevelles, S. and C. Leavitt (1992), "A Comparison of Current Models of Consumer Satisfaction/ Dissatisfaction," *Journal of Consumer Satisfaction, Dissatisfaction and Complaining Behavior*, 5, 104-114.

Fiske, S.T. and S.E. Taylor (1991), *Social Cognition.* New York: McGraw-Hill.

Fontenelle, G., A. Phillips and D. Lane (1985), "Generalizing Across Stimuli as well as Subjects: A Neglected Aspect of External Validity," *Journal of Applied Psychology*, 70, 101-107.

Harrison, A., R. Sommer, M. Rucker and M. Moore (1986), "Standing Out from the Crowd: Personalization of Graduation Attire," *Adolescence*, 21 (84), 863-874.

Holbrook, M.B. and E.C. Hirschman (1982), "The Experiential Aspects of Consumption: Consumer Fantasies, Feelings, and Fun," *Journal of Consumer Research*, 9, 132-140.

Horowitz, T. (1982), "Excitement vs. Economy: Fashion and Youth Culture in Britain," *Adolescence*, 17 (67), 227-236.

Iacobucci, D. and A. Ostrom (1993), "Gender Differences in the Impact of Core and Relational Aspects of Services on the Evaluation of Service Encounters," *Journal of Consumer Psychology*, 2 (3), 257-286.

Means, B. (1981), "Clothing Store Windows: Communication Through Style," *Visual Communication*, 7, 64-71.

Meyers-Levy, J. (1989), "Gender Differences in Information Processing," in *Cognitive and Affective Responses to Advertising,* P. Cafferata and A. Tybout, eds. Boston, MA: Lexington Books, 219-260.

_____ and D. Maheswaran (1991), "Exploring Differences in Males' and Females' Processing Strategies," *Journal of Consumer Research*, 18, 63-70.

_____ and B. Sternthal (1991), "Gender Differences in the Use of Message Cues and Judgments," *Journal of Marketing Research*, 28 (1), 84-96.

Oliva, T.A., R.L. Oliver and I.C. MacMillan (1992), "A Catastrophe Model for Developing Service Satisfaction Strategies," *Journal of Marketing*, 56, 83-95.

Oliver, R.L. (1980), "Theoretical Bases of Consumer Satisfaction Research: Review, Critique, and Future Direction," in *Theoretical Developments in Marketing,* C.W. Lamb, Jr. and P.M. Dunne, eds. Chicago, IL: American Marketing Association Proceedings Series, 206-210.

Parasuraman, A., V.A. Zeithaml and L.L. Berry (1985), "A Conceptual Model of Service Quality and Its Implications for Future Research," *Journal of Marketing*, 49 (4), 41-50.

Rosenkrantz, P., S. Vogel, H. Bee, L. Broverman and D.M. Broverman (1968), "Sex-Role Stereotypes and Self-Concepts in College Students," *Journal of Consulting and Clinical Psychology*, 32, 287-295.

Ruble, D. and T. Ruble (1982), "Sex Stereotypes," in *In the Eye of the Beholder: Contemporary Issues in Stereotyping,* A. Miller, ed. New York: Praeger, 188-251.

Salomon, I. and F.S. Koppelman (1992), "Teleshopping or Going Shopping? An Information Acquisition Perspective," *Behaviour and Information Technology*, 11 (4), 189-198.

Schank, R. and R. Abelson (1977), *Scripts, Plans, Goals and Understanding: An Inquiry into Human Knowledge Structures.* Hillsdale, NJ: Erlbaum.

Schlick, P.J. and K.L. Rowold (1991), "Senior Cords: A Rite of Passage," in *Dress and Popular Culture*, P.A. Cunningham and S.V. Lab, eds. Bowling Green, OH: Bowling Green State University Popular Press, 106-124.

Singh, J. (1991), "Understanding the Structure of Consumers' Satisfaction Evaluations of Service Delivery," *Journal of the Academy of Marketing Science,* 19 (3), 223-244.

Stores (1989), "Cohorts' Study: Age Matters," *Stores*, 71 (11), 36-37.

Surprenant, C.F. and M.R. Solomon (1987), "Predictability and Personalization in the Service Encounter," *Journal of Marketing*, 51 (2), 86-96.

Swan, J.E. and I.F. Trawick (1981), "Disconfirmation of Expectations and Satisfaction With a Retail Service," *Journal of Retailing*, 57 (3), 49-67.

Taylor, S.E. and J. Crocker (1981), "Schematic Bases of Social Information Processing," in *Social Cognition: The Ontario Symposium,* Vol. 1, E.T. Higgins, C.P. Herman and M.P. Zanna, eds. Hillsdale, NJ: Erlbaum, 89-134.

Thurston, J.L., S.J. Lennon and R.V. Clayton (1990), "Influence of Age, Body Type, Currency of Fashion Detail, and Type of Garment on the Professional Image of Women," *Home Economics Research Journal*, 19 (2), 139-150.

Ward, J.C., M.J. Bitner and J. Barnes (1992), "Measuring the Prototypicality and Meaning of Retail Environments," *Journal of Retailing*, 68 (2), 194-220.

Wilson, E.J. and A.G. Woodside (1991), "A Comment on Patterns of Store Choice and Customer Gain/Loss Analysis," *Journal of the Academy of Marketing Science*, 19 (4), 377-382.

Woodruff, R.B., D.S. Clemons, D.W. Schumann, S.F. Gardial and M.J. Burns (1991), "The Standards Issue In Cs/D Research: A Historical Perspective," *Journal of Consumer Satisfaction, Dissatisfaction and Complaining Behavior*, 4, 103-109.

Wyer, R.S. (1980), "The Acquisition and Use of Social Knowledge: Basic Postulates and Representative Research," *Personality and Social Psychology Bulletin*, 6 (4), 558-573.

Zinn, L. (1992), "Move Over, Boomers," *Business Week*, (December 14), 74-79, 82.

AN HISTORICAL ANALYSIS OF MARKETING BY SERVICE ORGANIZATIONS:

THE CASE OF PRE-1930 BANKING IN AMERICA

Richard Germain

ABSTRACT

This research addresses the question of whether managers in service organizations were marketing their businesses prior to 1960. The analysis, limited to the pre-1930 U.S. banking industry, demonstrates that bankers had adopted a marketing orientation through attention to needs (service and segmentation) and through a coordinated business effort.

INTRODUCTION

A common sentiment among marketing educators is that during the 1960s, something called "services marketing" was initially recognized as a distinct academic discipline. Few doubt the dearth of services marketing examples in

Advances in Services Marketing and Management, Volume 6, pages 101-123.
Copyright © 1997 by JAI Press Inc.
All rights of reproduction in any form reserved.
ISBN: 0-7623-0176-7

the classic marketing textbooks of the 1920s through the 1950s. During the 1970s, calls for integrating services with goods marketing further spurred interest in the topic (e.g., Shostack 1977). Since that time, research by the academic community has been substantial, assisted by services marketing conferences and start-up journals, culminating with an explosive increase in output after 1985, a period in services marketing evolution that Fisk, Brown and Bitner (1993) labeled "walking erect."

This is contrasted with ambiguity concerning the practice of marketing by service organizations. For example, Berry and Parasuraman (1993, p. 14) argued, "Both academicians and practitioners were interested in applying marketing to services long before 1970." Yet, Lovelock (1984, p. xiii), in the first textbook devoted exclusively to services marketing, wrote, "Until now, few managers of service businesses have accorded the marketing function as much importance as have their counterparts in manufacturing." Thus, while a consensus exists on the history of services marketing academic thought concerning the post-1960 period as one of emergence and then refinement, there exists some doubt about the history of services marketing practice. Indeed, we assert that services marketing practice has not been put to rigorous historical analysis.

The purpose of this research is to examine services marketing practice under a historical microscope to address the following question: in the past, did managers in service organizations adopt a marketing orientation? Obviously, it would be physically impossible to examine all service industries in all geographic regions across all time periods and we are thus forced to balance breadth against depth. We opt for the latter to provide a "thick" description of a single service industry (banking), within, for the most part, one geographic region (the United States), and for a limited time period (1800-1930). These limits are, however, not as severe as one might suspect at first glance. The banking industry has a long tradition of documenting its efforts in individual bank retrospectives, in banking and economic histories and, in particular, in the banking trade press. For example, *The Bankers' Magazine* provides a trail of evidence extending back to 1843 on what bankers were doing and thinking. Thus, ample evidence exists for a determination of the extent of a marketing orientation within banking prior to 1930. Indeed, we present only a fraction of the available documentation.

We organize the analysis around three themes. First, we examine the historical evidence in relation to "service" and address whether bankers discussed or acted upon: (1) service "thought," that is, service traits (e.g., intangibility), the (dis)similarity of services versus and goods marketing, and gap theory; and (2) service quality determinants (e.g., transaction velocity). But marketing by service firms involves more than a service-orientation. The second theme concerns whether service firms addressed the needs of consumers. This involves an analysis of whether bankers crafted their products to meet the needs of consumers through segmentation. As examples, we discuss special banking efforts to serve children and women. In addition, because banks form member relationships with customers, one would expect them, if they had adopted a marketing-like orientation, to segment the market on the basis of consumption status: that is, splitting the market into current, potential and past customers and devising special plans for each. The third and last theme concerns organization: namely, that a marketing orientation requires, especially among large institutions, the presence of marketing-like occupational specialties. A marketing-like department conceivably would coordinate activities across functions such as marketing-related training, cross-selling and so forth. The remainder of this paper is organized around the themes of service, segmentation and organization.

THE SERVICE EVIDENCE

Service Thought

Service Properties

Economists have long grappled with traits that distinguish services from goods. Jean-Baptiste Say (1767-1832) stated that services are activities consumed at the time of production (i.e., inseparability) and coined the term immaterial product (i.e., intangibility) (1821). Bankers readily adopted the concept of intangibility during the 1910s and 1920s: "He [a banker] is selling something which is intangible" (Dean 1914, p. 514); and "Financial advertisers have a particularly hard and impregnable problem in the intangibility of the goods which they offer" (Handerson 1923a, p. 97). At the same time, bankers recognized heterogeneity as a service trait: "But it [bank service] is not like a commodity that is fixed in nature and quality when it leaves the factory. It is, on the contrary, dependent from day to day and week to week on the continuous support of the operating personnel" (Douglas 1922, p. 23); and "[a bank] ... is not offering a standardized, machine-made article, but a highly personalized, confidential service" (Knapp 1925, p. 12). Bankers were apparently little concerned with inseparability since consumption and production of many bank services occur separately and with perishability for the much same reason. But railroad service is perishable, and thus a railroad executive proclaimed: "When a service is ready for delivery, it at once begins to depreciate. Service cannot be stored. Neither can it be salvaged. Service is perishable—sell it quickly" (Downs 1929, p. 15).

Services Versus Goods Marketing

While we are unable to state whether a debate on the similarity of services versus goods marketing occurred among practitioners of all service industries, we assert that one took place in banking during the 1920s. On the side of similarity, bankers argued, "Bank advertising is subject to the same laws as any other advertising, because it is intended to react upon the same objects—namely, people" (Handerson 1923b, p. 97); and "The same fundamental rules of marketing apply with equal force to selling trust accounts as to selling any product no matter what it is" (Neibel 1930, p. 9). These comments contrast with those made on the dissimilarity of services and goods marketing: "Bank advertisers have a specialized problem. They have nothing physical to sell" (Currier 1920, p. 25); and "Methods employed in commercial advertising cannot be adapted bodily to financial institutions because of the intangibility of the 'product'" (O'Reilly 1924, p. 40).

Gap Theory

Gap theory states that a difference between expected performance and realized performance impacts perceptions of quality. Although other gaps have been identified in a services marketing context, it is on this one that bankers focused. In particular, they were concerned with whether expectations engendered by promotions were fulfilled during service encounters: "The men of the working staff should know just what advertising their institution is doing ... and then prepare themselves to work in harmony with the advertising for the good of the institution" (*The Bankers' Magazine* 1908c, p. 594). This sentiment was repeated many times by 1930: for example, "Good advertising backed up by poor service will lose practically all of its effects" (Vincent 1913, p. 49). Advertisements were posted in the bank to expose employees to promises made (De Bebian 1921, p. 244). Some banks' presidents even distributed a letter to all employees on the subject. For instance, in 1915 on the eve of a major advertising campaign, the president of Security Trust & Savings Bank, the largest bank in Los Angeles and Southern California, wrote to employees that: "You are asked to read in the newspapers all the advertising of the bank and keep yourselves 'in tune' with it" (*The Bankers' Magazine* 1915, p. 822).

Service Quality

To fully address service quality, bankers must have acknowledged: (1) the distinction between a service being performed and the process underlying its performance; (2) the existence of service quality itself; and (3) the existence of some set of "determinants" capable of affecting consumers' perception of quality. In all three cases, bankers were cognizant: (1) "Under the term 'service,' he [a banker] ... also has in mind the way in which these various functions, banking and others, are performed" (Clarke 1922, p. 136); (2) "The external house organ seeks to sell not only the many definite services your bank has to offer, but the quality of its services" (Kittredge 1923, p. 455); and (3) "To them [customers] time is almost everything, and they determine the quality of the service upon the length of time it takes for them to transact their business with the bank" (Morehouse 1918, p. 32). Building upon such knowledge, bankers addressed many of the service quality determinants identified by contemporary authors.

Service Velocity

Bankers were very concerned with the speed with which transactions could be accomplished, and throughout the 1850-1930 time period, many examples exist of administrative innovations being used to improve service speed. Around 1900, banks experiencing rapid growth replaced multiple paying and receiving tellers with multiple "unit tellers." A unit teller handled many types of transactions (e.g., deposits, withdrawals, check cashing) and, in larger banks, a unit teller consisted of several tellers who shifted work between them to create a fast moving line for customers with a small number of simple transactions and a slow moving line for those with more complex transactions. The benefits were faster, more personable service and greater efficiency from the workforce (Jess 1907). Banks responded to transaction bulges: The First National Bank of Chicago in 1904 created a "Flying squadron, consisting of a dozen to fifteen higher clerks, who are sent all over the bank as the need arises" (Payne 1905, p. 5872). A 1923 promotional booklet of the Continental & Commercial National Bank (Chicago) said, "Trained men and an elastic system by which capacity may be instantly doubled, or tripled, are very necessary" (Welton 1923, p. 12). Slack resources of the sort able to triple capacity would have been very inefficient and we thus suspect that it was capacity at the departmental and not the overall level that was elastic.

Banks also adopted an incredible number of technological innovations to improve transaction velocity. In 1869, the first telegraph exchange system operating in the United States was installed for the benefit of New York City banks. The TelAutograph, invented during the 1890s by Elisha Gray (co-founder of what later became Western Electric Company), reproduced handwritten messages at remote locations and sped communication between tellers and bookkeepers (Ekrich 1910). Banks had long adopted manually powered coin counters, and electric ones became popular during the early 1900s. Electric coin-counting machines were stressed in promotions as an innovation allowing the bank to better serve its merchant customers. Automatic cashiers were machines that deposited coins in a tray in response to a teller pressing a set of keys indicating the value desired. These machines were much faster than manually counting and proofing coins and were adopted as they became available early during the 1900s (*The Review* 1909). Check listing machines, perforators, sorters, check writers, page printing telegraph technology, mechanized filing cabinets, adding-subtracting machines and comptometers (to calculate interest), among others, were not only adopted for transaction velocity, efficiency, security and accuracy purposes but were also interjected into newspaper advertising, direct mail campaigns and window displays to indicate modernity (Davis 1919).

Accessibility

Defined as the ability to enter, approach or communicate with, accessibility was of significant concern to bankers. Savings banks, from their inception in the United States in the 1810s, for the most part tailored their operating hours to suit the needs of their customers by operating at least one evening every week or late during Saturday afternoon. Furthermore, their hours of operation were given high visibility on passbooks and in classified-type newspaper advertising throughout the mid- to late-nineteenth century (e.g., Holdsworth 1928; Shoyer 1955). Commercial banks between 1850 and 1900 followed bankers' hours, or a close variant thereof, demand permitting. Given that many clearinghouses enforced bankers' hours as a membership requirement prior to 1900 (e.g., James 1938), these hours were derived in part from a desire to manage competition. But in 1905, an innovative institution was begun in New York City. The Night & Day Bank was open 24 hours per day, six days per week. The following year, it became the first bank in the city to offer armored courier service for its customers (Hill 1907). Both innovations spread relatively quickly to major and in some cases minor metropolitan areas in the United States. By 1910, the Night & Day Bank (Oklahoma City), the Franklin Trust Company (Philadelphia), the German National Bank (Little Rock), the All Night & Day Bank (Los Angeles) and the Greenwich Bank (New York) were open until midnight or later. Promotion of operating hours was aggressive (e.g., Cross 1927; *New York Times* 1910).

On another level, personal accessibility was a concern to bankers: "If National City Bank of New York ... has its officers quarters out in plain sight from the lobby ... we think any other bank can profitably do so" (MacGregor 1914, p. 496). A.P. Giannini, founder and president of the Bank of Italy [now called Bank of America (San Francisco)], maintained his desk beside the head office's main entrance (James and James 1954). And accessibility of this sort was often the focal point of newspaper and direct mail appeals. Canadian and European bankers tended to be more formal: concerning London offices of American banks, English bankers were apparently "impressed by the openness and ... accessibility of their personnel" (Mottram 1930, p. 97).

Accessibility refers to location as well. Major metropolitan banks often stressed location convenience in their promotions, and a number of banks regardless of location adopted slogans illustrating location convenience (Densch 1920). But U.S. banking laws that severely restricted geographic dispersion retarded the ability of bankers to manipulate the place component of the marketing mix. California was an exception, and the Bank of Italy's growth was in measure due to taking aggressive advantage of location legislation loopholes. In Canada, where coast-to-coast banking was allowed, during the 1900s and more so during the 1910s, banks used specially designed prefabricated structures, the fronts of which resembled miniature Greek temples, to establish a "first mover" advantage in newly emerging towns on the Western prairies (Mills and Holdsworth 1975).

Courtesy

Prior to 1930, bank tellers were highly respected and trained; unlike today, these positions were not entry-level jobs and were only obtained after a considerable amount of experience. The importance of courtesy rose as banks' markets became more inclusive between 1870 and 1930. One of the earliest admonishments appeared in 1885: a cashier said, "I would earnestly urge, then, that true courtesy, which has no taint of servility, be cultivated by every one [sic] connected with a bank, and as a first step toward reaching so desirable a point, that every thought of superiority be dismissed from the mind" (An Old Cashier 1885, p. 736). Between 1900 and 1920, an incredible number of articles appeared in the trade press and in banks' employee magazines on the importance, role and purpose of courtesy in enlarging the scale of a bank (e.g., *The Bankers' Magazine* 1899a; Griffith 1907; Rose 1922).

Confidence

Prior to the establishment of deposit insurance in 1933, the importance of developing and maintaining an aura of confidence in the institution was incalculably important. The First Bank of the United States, completed in 1797, was a Grecian temple that followed Thomas Jefferson's design for the Virginia State Capital building; the latter was completed in 1789 and was the first application of the temple style to a building in modern times. The Greek or Roman temple design for a bank, so popular prior to 1930, symbolized longevity, permanence and a democratic ideal. So popular was the design that the first several floors of some early bank skyscrapers were fronted with Greek columns: for example, the Continental & Commercial National Bank of Chicago (McGraw-Hill 1990).

But inspiring confidence went well beyond that engendered by the physical structure. Slogans often stressed reliability or longevity (Densch 1920). By 1910, a variety of tangibles such as animals, mountains and vaults appeared on stationary and in promotions for their symbolic meaning: "The Rock of Gibraltar, used as a trade mark [sic] by Prudential, connotes strength, of course, and the dog emblems used by some institutions stand for fidelity, and so on" (*The Bankers' Magazine* 1908b, p. 90). Well-recognized antiquities such as the pyramids and Tower of Babel were used: that is, the bank was "as permanent as the pyramids."

There were, in addition, confidence themes used with regularity. Recent growth in deposits (with the information explicitly presented) was often used in promotions to demonstrate the public's confidence as were absolute or relative size. Banks emphasized age: "The argument of age is one of the very strongest that any bank can use to prove that it is worthy of the confidence of prospective customers" (*The Bankers' Magazine* 1908d, p. 90). "Old National..." and "First National ..." bank names were selected to convey age and, hence, reliability. Anniversaries were often the cause of full-page newspaper campaigns and elaborate promotions celebrated in the bank's lobby (*The Bankers' Monthly* 1928). Management quality and integrity was another theme in several pre-1930 bank promotions.

Finally, during financial crises and panics, bankers required but did not always possess a keen understanding of consumer and mob psychology. Isaiis W. Hellman responded to the 1893 crisis by displaying piles of gold behind the tellers' cages at the Farmers & Merchants Bank, Los Angeles, and instructed his staff to transact withdrawals at a methodical pace. Customers responded positively and the bank never closed its doors during the crisis. Meanwhile, just a few doors down, the new president of the First National Bank stood on the bank's steps and "harangued the crowd," paid out deposits as fast as possible and threatened staff with dismissal if caught among those waiting outside. A more deliberate policy, it has been said, would have allowed the bank to remain open during the crisis; as it was the bank survived the run but was badly shaken and was forced to close for an entire month (Cleland and Putnam 1965).

Other Determinants of Service Quality

Transaction velocity, accessibility, courtesy and confidence, the dimensions of service quality discussed thus far, are by no means collectively exhaustive. Some banks handed out clean money to female customers, and thus some of the country's largest banks operated currency washing machines (*The Review* 1914). The internal atmosphere of the bank was of concern to bankers. Staff were lectured on the importance of speaking softly both to ensure confidentiality and to control overall noise. Employees were to crank the telephone in a dignified manner and in "complete silence" (Tymeson 1955). Structures designed before 1900, however, were ill-equipped to handle modern bank machinery. Bankers in these institutions installed special sound absorbing materials to walls and ceilings to control noise levels. Rubber floor tiles were also popular to control noise. Security concerns spawned a whole range of check-punching machinery. Indeed, microfilm was developed during the mid-1920s by a banker, George L. McCarthy, who wanted to retain a record for his bank of checks that were written. Unsuccessful at marketing his own product, in 1928 he accepted Eastman Kodak's offer and, as head of the newly formed Recordak Corporation, established the first market for microfilm in the United States. The company's target market in its initial year consisted of banks: more than 100 of the machines were leased to New York City banks in the first year alone (*The Kodak Magazine* 1929). Accuracy as well was tremendously important to bankers and a number of the technologies mentioned earlier were adopted to increase it. During the 1890s, New York City and Chicago banks developed "efficiency marking systems" that tracked who made and detected errors. They were used to identify deadweight personnel and those suitable for promotion and pay increases. By 1920, many banks in the United States used such systems to improve accuracy. We could go on, but we believe that our point has been made: namely, that banks prior to 1930 were highly sensitive to the performance of what we currently call service quality determinants.

THE SEGMENTATION EVIDENCE

Age Segmentation

By age segmentation, we mean avowed efforts to reach children and youth. These efforts can be traced back to school savings banks developed by German communities during the 1820s, the objective of which was to cultivate thrift, a morally proper trait, among children. By 1890, these programs were widespread throughout Europe: for example, in 1886 in France there were 24,000 school savings banks with $2.4 million in deposits; and in 1893 in Belgium there were 5,282 of them with 240,000 depositors. These programs were introduced to the United States in 1885 by a retired Long Island businessman. In Europe, educators deposited savings into state-operated postal savings banks. In the United States, no such institution existed until 1910, and thus American educators were forced to deal with private sector banks to generate interest on accounts (*Report of the Commissioner of Education* 1898). These programs spread rapidly throughout the entire nation. By 1930, there were about 4.5 million school savings depositors, representing about 13 percent of the total U.S. population between the ages of five and 19 (American Bankers Association 1935).

Between 1885 and 1930, educators and bankers cooperated closely in encouraging thrift among young people. Initial systems were based upon the educator selling stamps to children; a child was allowed to open a bank account once one dollar had been accumulated. During the mid-1910s, stamp vending machines appeared in New York City and elsewhere, alleviating the burden upon educators. At the same time, some high school seniors received credit for operating a school bank at their institution and for collecting deposits from neighboring primary schools (Du Four 1921). However, some bankers were wary of school savings banks because they were not perceived as profitable in the short run, and some elements of the public were concerned with defalcation. This led to some unusual institutions being created. For instance, in 1919 in Louisville (Kentucky), concerned bankers, educators and socially minded civic associations formed the School Savings Bank. The bank was a nonprofit institution that was virtually defalcation-free by virtue of security bonds. The bank was exclusively devoted to servicing children's accounts (Harrington 1926).

Marketing to children, however, went beyond school savings banks. Banks sponsored essay-writing contests (during the 1900s) and gave away passbooks containing one dollar to Sunday schools to give away as prizes and to children who presented the bank's advertisement to the bank (during the 1910s). In rural areas during the 1910s, banks sponsored farm clubs on sheep, baby cattle, bees, dairy animals and poultry (A.W. Shaw Company 1918). They awarded prizes to children who secured new accounts, distributed house organs with such titles as *The Busy Bee* and the *School Savings Journal* to high schools, advertised in high school newspapers and provided tours of facilities to school-aged children (MacGregor 1913). To better facilitate transactions at the bank itself, special "Children's Tellers" were created. These ranged from a box with a rail and a special sign to special banking rooms. In the case of the latter, for instance, a branch of the Boston Savings Bank (in 1930) created for children a miniature banking room "separated from the main banking room by eight Roman arches and their accompanying columns" (*The Bankers' Magazine* 1930).

Efforts to reach high school students illustrate that bankers sought out youths as well as children. Some major metropolitan banks designed special promotional campaigns to attract young entrepreneurs (during the 1900s). "June appeals" appeared regularly every year to attract young newlyweds. Banks advertised in university newspapers (e.g., Stillwater State Bank advertised in the initial 1895 issue of a paper published by Oklahoma State University students). It was, however, students attending prestigious institutions who were particularly attractive. During the 1900s, the City Trust Company made special efforts to reach Harvard students through direct mail (*The Bankers' Magazine* 1908a).

Gender Segmentation

The development of banking to women consists of three periods. The first period lasted from the 1830s until the 1870s. During these decades, some banks reserved some operating hours for female customers. Women were welcome at any time, but at those banks with a gender-based policy, they alone were welcome during special periods. One of the earliest to adopt the policy was the Greenwich Bank, New York, in 1833. The bank was open two hours a day, two days a week, and the Friday hours were reserved just for women (Husband 1933). Other banks in New York City adopted the policy and advertised the policy in classified-like advertisements during the 1850s. The policy was not limited to the Northeast. In 1847, the Boatman's National Bank, St. Louis, in 1,000 handbills announcing the opening of the bank, declared Fridays as the day when only women were welcome (Rule 1947).

During the second period, extending from the 1870s to the 1900s, banks began to provide a banking room reserved for females. This new policy may have been the result of an inability or lack of desire to enforce the prior policy. Apparently, the first bank in the United States to provide a special room (with direct access to its own teller) was the Second National Bank of New York (sometime during the 1870s). This was accomplished despite the bank having only five female customers, but the fact that the bank was located where fashionable shops and wealthy residences met suggests that they targeted upper-class, possibly widowed, women (*The Bankers Magazine* 1911). The success of the policy was evident to other bankers and by 1930, many of the best-known banks in America had imitated it. The list includes The First National Bank of Chicago, the Columbia Trust Company (New York), the Guaranty Trust Company of New York, the Bank of Italy (San Francisco), the Continental & Commercial National Bank of Chicago, the Cleveland Trust Company and the First National Bank of Los Angeles. Many of these banks, too, were successful. The Bank of Italy's department by 1925 had $5 million in deposits, this being over twice the size of the bank's average branch (James and James 1954). Regardless of whether the department served upper-class customers, most were elaborately furnished and provided free writing desks and paper. Those in upper-class neighborhoods had maid service, provided refreshments and telephone and social secretary service, interviewed servants at employment agencies and chaperoned children when necessary (Baley 1922).

The last stage in the development of gender segmentation began during the 1900s and extends beyond 1930. What marks this period is that banks began employing women to staff and manage women's departments. This was a radical departure for banks, but in the long run it proved a successful segmentation-based policy. It is impossible to state which bank first hired a female to manage its women's department, but some of the earlier instances were the Mercantile Trust Company, St. Louis (by 1905), the Crown Bank of Canada, Toronto (in 1906), the Columbia Trust Company, New York (in 1907), and the Portland Trust Company, Oregon (in 1907). One reason given for employing women was the insensitivity of male employees to the special needs and information requirements of women: "Each [woman] needs a place where she can go over her business matters in confidence and in an informal way with one of her own sex; where she can be frank; where she can display her ignorance ... without embarrassment" (Moorehouse 1909, p. 511). As female managers increasingly demonstrated an aptitude for cultivating customers, they were increasingly given operations and marketing responsibilities. Women's departments opened and closed their own accounts, hired and released employees on their own accord, conducted their own bookkeeping, planned and operationalized their own advertising and promotions and developed their own special products and ancillary services. The success of the Bank of Italy during the 1920s was a replication of what other banks had accomplished once women were given managerial authority and responsibility. For instance, under female guidance, customers and deposits of the First and Security National Bank, Minneapolis, women's department respectively grew from 1,500 to 5,500 and from $400,000 to $1.5 million between 1911 and 1915 (*The Bankers' Magazine* 1917). So widespread was female management of these departments that the 1920s policy of The First National Bank of Chicago to employ men only in its women's department was seen as a novelty (Baley 1922).

A flurry of special promotions and products coincided with the appointment of women to manage women's departments. Perhaps the most important was that banks developed campaigns whose selling point was the appointment of a female to manage the women's department. Checkbooks appeared in multiple colors and sizes. Elaborate home-financing booklets were distributed and, in some instances, banks hired university-trained home economists to work in the women's department. In newspapers, direct mail and brochures they promoted checking accounts and safety box deposits and trust account services. And they engaged in general advertising, promoting the acceptability and welcome of women to the bank; for example, the Northern Trust Company, Chicago, in 1909 said: "It might surprise you to know how many of our depositors are women" (*The Bankers' Magazine* 1909, p. 1006).

Consumption Status Segmentation

Current Customers

Early in the 20th century, bankers, acknowledging a debt to manufacturers, expressed concern over marketing to current versus potential customers: "Do we want more depositors or do we want our present depositors to transact more business and carry larger balances?" (Ingraham 1912, p. 227). Implementing a strategy of concentration upon current customers requires a detailed understanding of who current customers are and what services are being consumed. Toward this end, central information files were developed during the 1900s and 1910s. They were centralized, manually maintained listings of customers (along with demographic information and services used). These files were repeatedly referred to as critical to the firm: for example, "[they] may rightly be termed one of the most important cogs in the bank's operating machinery" (Heitzman 1926, p. 17). These files became even more important as the scale of the bank and its product scope increased; they were more commonly found in large banks. By 1930, the Security Trust & Savings Bank (Los Angeles), the Hibernia Bank & Trust Company (New Orleans), the Equitable Trust Company of New York, the Guaranty Trust Company of New York and the Chase National Bank (New York), among others, had adopted such files. The Equitable Trust Company of New York, for instance, created a central information in 1918. The cards of its 1928 Findex system contained a series of holes at the bottom, each corresponding to a particular customer characteristic. The hole was elongated if the customer possessed any given trait. By inserting rods through the cards (which were contained in what resembled now-defunct library card catalogues) and swiveling the files upside down (which the system was designed to do), the bank was able to generate a list of, say, female customers banking to the east and above 59th Street West, with an account size above $1,000 but without safety box deposit service. But the files also served other purposes: for example, those passing on overdrafts could ascertain the standing of the customer. Equitable's central information file contained the names of 55,000 individuals and was operated by six full-time employees, and the department received about 1,400 inquiries per day (*The Equitable Envoy* 1929).

But banks did much more than operate central information files in relation to current customers. The distribution of house organs to current customers and of trade and business books and booklets to commercial customers became increasingly popular during the 1910s. For example, between 1916 and 1920, the Guaranty Trust Company of New York distributed around 100 publications with such titles as *The Argentine Republic* (4) and *The War Tax Law* (132). In 1919, the National City Bank of New York distributed 2.5 million items, including weekly and monthly finance periodicals (e.g., *Blue Sheet, The Americas*). During World War I, banks developed plans to cross-sell services to those entering a bank to purchase Liberty Bonds (Gail 1919). Concerning research, they measured deposit and service usage increases of customers who were mailed booklets on services offered and compared the returns to those who did not receive the booklets; the results were quite positive (Ecklund 1925).

One facet of how banks dealt with current customers must be kept in mind. The fact that most banks possessed a minimum deposit policy (one dollar being the minimum for some, and hundreds of dollars for some banks in New York City) suggests a concern for profitability and not just volume. In checking accounts, individual customer profitability was a serious problem. It was suggested that banks specializing in demand deposit accounts and commercial credit employed about two and a half times the number of clerks and officers as comparably sized savings banks (using deposits as a barometer for scale). The labor intensity of operating demand deposit accounts led bankers to develop financial methods for ascertaining the profitability of individual customers. Serious efforts to weed out less profitable customers were begun during the mid-1900s. The number of trade press articles on the topic, a trickle in 1900, escalated thereafter such that by 1930, hundreds had appeared. The articles illustrated the many mathematical models that could be used, repeatedly commented upon the need to be mindful of profitability and not volume, reported on the positive financial effect on banks that had culled demand deposit customers thought to be unprofitable and admonished bankers to be respectful of customers in the process used to cull the demand deposit customer base and to be mindful of customers who utilized multiple services (e.g., Reihl 1906; Wilson 1906).

Potential Customers

The second leg of consumption status segmentation consists of special efforts devised to attract potential customers. Obviously, much of what was discussed under the age- and gender-based segmentation headings overlaps with that discussed here. But there were some activities and products directed to the mass market with the intent of generating new customers. One was personal solicitation. The banking industry had long frowned upon soliciting for new customers. The standard (and "gentlemanly") approach was to let customers come to the bank, a practice of European origin. For instance, in 1839, Belfast's three largest banks banned solicitation in a written agreement (Ollerenshaw 1987). In the United States, clearinghouses enforced the ban, but bankers could not help but notice the success of mass marketers that had moved forward by absorbing personal selling functions. Thus, between 1900 and 1910, banks increasingly turned to personal solicitation to attract consumers, and these efforts culminated with the appearance of employee new-business campaigns. These campaigns were built upon awarding cash and other prizes to bank employees who secured new accounts during a fixed time period. These campaigns were one of the most cost-effective methods of attracting new customers (i.e., contest prize and administration cost against contest new account value). They appeared early during the 1910s (e.g., the German-American Trust & Savings Bank, Los Angeles, 1912) and were relatively widespread by 1930. By this date, the list of banks having adopted employee new-business campaigns included the Cleveland Trust Company, the Exchange National Bank (Tulsa), the National City Bank of New York, the Union Trust Company (Chicago), and the Mississippi Valley Trust Company (St. Louis). As a rule, with the exception of the most senior executives, all bank employees, including janitors, participated. Individual-based contests eventually displaced team contests, and continual contests eventually displaced contests of a fixed time length (Kerman and Griffin 1926; Morehouse 1913b).

Between 1890 and 1930, banks developed several new products to attract potential customers. Home safes were introduced during the mid-1890s. They were rust-resistant, long-lived, metal safes that customers added to at home until one dollar was accumulated. Banks named them Fortune Builder, Receiving Teller, and so on (Mann 1908). Christmas Clubs, introduced during the mid-1900s, required customers to follow a schedule of deposits (at the bank) during the year. Payouts were made two weeks before Christmas (hence the name). Banks usually offered several standardized plans to fit various pocketbooks. From the bankers' perspective, there were several advantages to Christmas Clubs over home safes: banks had access to the funds when deposits were made; back office operations were reduced since interest calculations were limited to the number of standard plans offered; the minimum value of the account, if it was rolled over, was normally greater than the one dollar generated by a home safe; and rolling over the account into a savings account required the customer to visit the bank (which contrasted with home safes, which could be rolled over into any bank). Christmas Clubs were popular; the number of banks offering them grew at an annual rate of 34 percent between 1913 (904 banks) and 1923 (17,400 banks). In 1920, banks reported that more than one million people in the United States had Christmas Club accounts, and in the same year, it was reported that more than 20 Christmas Club promotional material suppliers existed (Woodworth 1921). At the same time, banks sought the assistance of employers to have blue and white collar employees directly deposit part of their wages into interest-bearing savings accounts. These plans were initially offered during the 1900s, and by the 1920s they were routinely called Industrial Savings Plans (Tinsley 1921).

Other less specific promotions were used to generate potential customers. Banks began taking advantage of window displays during the 1910s (Morehouse 1919). During the same decade, cooperative community campaigns were developed whereby a bank would organize a campaign involving civic and business associations (e.g., chambers of commerce, unions, manufacturers' associations) to increase a community's savings rate (Harlow 1916).

Past Customers

The length of time for an active account to become an inactive one and then to become a dormant one is a matter of bank policy and regulation. The purpose of this section is not to quibble over definitional issues but to illustrate that bankers took active efforts to manage relations with customers whose accounts became inactive or dormant, and with customers who flat out closed their accounts. Three pieces of evidence suggest that banks did such. First, banks developed a set of standard letters along with a policy of using them in connection with the central information file. In the mid-1910s, the German-

American Trust & Savings Bank, Los Angeles, kept track through its central information file of customer account activity and letters mailed. Standard letters (each individually typed) were used when customers were first secured and again six months later. A set of standard letters existed for inactive accounts; if activity resumed, then one letter was sent out, but if no activity ensued, then another was sent out. Standard letters were mailed when a customer closed an account. All the letters accounted for the services used by the customer (Morehouse 1913a, 1914). Second, banks employed specially trained account close-out tellers whose job it was to retain the customer should the account be deemed worthwhile. Finally, banks experimented with different appeals while blocking for length of account inactivity and account size in an effort to determine which appeals worked best, if any at all, under which circumstances (e.g., James and James 1954; Robinson 1924).

THE ORGANIZATION EVIDENCE

Throughout the nineteenth century, banks regularly advertised their services and existence in classified-like newspaper advertisements. Some placed advertisements directly with publishers. Others used advertising agencies such as John Hooper & Co., which promoted itself as suitable to bankers in New York City dailies during the 1860s, and Albert Frank Guenther Law, another New York City advertising agency that specialized in financial advertising and could trace its existence back to 1872.

But prior to 1900, few if any banks in the United States utilized a marketing- or advertising-like department. In 1900, the Royal Bank, one of Canada's coast-to-coast banks, established one of the earliest bank advertising departments in North America. One of its major responsibilities was managing and coordinating advertising efforts across the bank's approximately 900 domestic and international branches (Bourne 1928). The largest banks in the United States had yet to follow suit. In 1903, advertising by The First National Bank of Chicago was the part-time responsibility of one of two vice presidents. It was around 1905 that bank titles of advertising or publicity manager first appeared, and in that year, The First National Bank of Chicago created an advertising-like department that it called the "new-business department." Early writings on its functions indicate little in the way of difference between it and an advertising department. But as time progressed, the term "new-business" came to mean much more than advertising or promotion. By 1930, the difference was noticeable, and many of the larger banks in the United States had created a "new-business department" and presumably had adopted a new-business orientation. The list of banks utilizing a new-business department by 1930 includes the Bankers Trust Company (New York), the Guaranty Trust Company of New York, the Hibernia Bank & Trust Company (New Orleans), the Marine Trust Company (Buffalo), the Guaranty Trust & Savings Bank (Los Angeles) and the Shawmut National Bank (Boston).

What exactly did new-business departments do? The responsibilities varied from bank to bank, but various sources included the following. The department operated the new account and account close-out tellers. It managed employee new-business contests. It planned and implemented mass media and direct mail campaigns (along with management over the mailing lists). It may have been responsible for window and lobby displays. The department may have operated the central information and prospect files. Many published daily officer bulletins. New-business departments provided solicitation training to clerks and tellers and administered exams to them. The department may have conducted research for commercial account solicitors. In some instances, they tracked competitors, collected suggestions on how to improve bank operations and operated the bank's in-house printing and engraving machinery (MacGregor 1917, 1918; *The Bankers' Magazine* 1920; Ellsworth 1920; Knapp 1925).

As important as the range of activities undertaken by new-business departments was the philosophy that the department should fulfill a coordinative function. The department was described as "a 'clearing house' for the work of all departments in the work of trying to obtain new customers" (MacGregor 1917, p. 10) and as a "connecting link between the various departments and branches of the bank" (Flint 1927, p. 25). Furthermore, the department "must cooperate with other departments in increasing their efficiency" (*The Bankers' Magazine* 1922, p. 710). In larger banks, the new-business and advertising departments were often distinct. Yet, the fact that "these two departments operate to best advantage under the supervision of the same executive officer" (Flint 1927, p. 25) suggests an understanding of the need to coordinate marketing activities when they were split into multiple departments. We thus feel entirely justified in stating that the typical new-business department transcended a mere advertising orientation and appears to have adopted a marketing-like orientation.

CONCLUSION

The purpose of this research was to investigate whether managers in service firms adopted a marketing orientation prior to 1960. We limited the analysis to the pre-1930 banking industry in the United States. The evidence presented supports the historical thesis that managers in a service industry were behaving in a manner consistent with the adoption of a marketing orientation. Bankers understood service properties (e.g., intangibility) and translated them into a debate over the similarity of service versus product marketing. Bankers utilized the fundamentals of gap theory, understood the difference between service quality and functional service, realized that how a service was performed (e.g., transaction velocity) impacted perceptions of service quality and acted upon improving the delivery of service (e.g., accessibility). By 1930, they had crafted special marketing mixes for different market segments based upon age (e.g., children), gender (e.g., women) and consumption status (e.g., current customers), indicating a concern with meeting differentiated needs. Finally, bankers coordinated various promotional and advertising activities. This was accomplished through the creation of new-business departments that blended personal selling and advertising functions.

Support for the research thesis that services marketing is not a new phenomenon has several implications. First, the research suggests that the marketing concept, formally articulated during the 1950s, may have been operationalized, if only informally, much earlier. Bankers took an integrative approach through new-business departments to meeting needs and wants through a service-orientation and segmentation. Not presented was evidence to the effect that marketing should increase profit and not volume. A hint of a profit orientation is found in bankers' willingness to cull unprofitable demand deposit customers. A more succinct statement of a profit objective was provided by *The Bankers' Magazine* (1899b, p. 183): "The value of advertising as a means of increasing profits is becoming more generally recognized by progressive bank managers." But no amount of evidence will convince the skeptic. To paraphrase Stanley C. Hollander (1984, p. 262), no psychogalvanometer is available to tell us whether marketers of 50 or more years ago were somewhat less, just about as much or somewhat more interested in their customers than contemporary marketers.

Second, why is services marketing perceived to be new when it is old? The answer to the question depends upon whether one asks practitioners or academicians. When the question is directed to practitioners, the key explanatory factors are the 1930s Depression and World War II, events that had profound effects on the banking industry. During the 1930s, commercial credit, the main source of bank revenue, declined precipitously. To offset the decline, bankers invested in government securities, but interest rates on these instruments were low. This led bankers to discourage rather than promote savings: that is, many banks engaged in demarketing and actively sought to remove what would have been otherwise profitable savings and demand deposit customers from their books. When commercial and government demand for credit increased during World War II, it was the government that led the way in encouraging savings. After World War II, unlike the period prior to 1930, a surplus of capital existed and demand for commercial and personal consumptive credit was strong. Banks did not need to promote thrift to meet the demand for credit. It was only during the 1960s that a service-orientation began to reappear. The three-decade period between 1930 to 1960 when customer orientation was at a nadir was of sufficient length to erase much institutional memory, especially when much of that memory resided in a male-dominated workforce that was siphoned off in the defense of the nation and when that memory was of fostering thrift rather than consumption. In addition, the passage of federal deposit insurance during the 1930s reduced the need for banks to actively promote confidence in their institutions. Thus, the first explanation for why services marketing, at least within banking, is perceived to be new when indeed it is old, is that environment dynamics reduced the need for a service-orientation for a 30-year period. It is the job of the historian to discover underlying trends, and the trend here is one of: (1) a gradual increase in customer orientation between 1800 and 1930; (2) a steep decline in customer-orientation resulting from the 1930s Depression; (3) a prolonged period characterized by a low level of customer-orientation through the 1950s; and (4) the reappearance of a customer orientation during the late 1950s and 1960s. When bankers began to adopt a customer-orientation during the 1960s, they assumed a straight-line increase in its level, and they drew the conclusion that it was new. Whether a similar mechanism operated in other service industries remains to be seen.

The answer to why services marketing is perceived by academicians to be new when it is old is quite different and may be a simple matter of not looking in the right places. The trade magazines, institutional histories, and original archival material reported in this research are not readily accessible. These sources do not form the foundation of general marketing theory history texts (e.g., Bartels 1988; Sheth, Gardner and Garrett 1988) or service marketing histories (e.g., Fisk, Brown and Bitner 1993). As such, these histories either make no mention of services marketing or, if they do, limit themselves to readily available academic works published from the 1950s onward. In either case, the impression received is that services marketing is somehow new.

Despite our success in illustrating the trend underlying services marketing development, limitations exist. Our focus on a single industry leads to the issue of whether banks were unique among service organizations in their adoption of a service-orientation. No comprehensive services marketing history across service industries exists, and we are thus unable to offer a firm response to the issue. But on face value, it is unlikely that banks were unique. Trade press articles reveal that bankers were highly cognizant of what was occurring in the marketing and advertising industry in general. Likewise, managers in insurance, transportation and hospitality industries had easy access to the wealth of printed material available on marketing and advertising. For example, in life insurance, the adoption of agency methods, corporate branding (e.g., Prudential's use of the Rock), segmentation efforts to reach specific nationality groups (e.g., Germans by Metropolitan) and specific income groups (low income groups by Prudential), all complete by 1900, suggest cross-fertilization of ideas and awareness of general marketing techniques (Carr 1975; James 1947). Further research into service industries other than banking, however, is required before a definitive answer on whether the banking industry was unique can be offered.

REFERENCES

American Bankers Association (1935), *School Savings Banks*. New York: American Bankers Association.
A.W. Shaw Company (1918), *Advertising and Service*. Chicago, IL: A.W. Shaw Company.
Baley, O. (1922), "What Chicago Banks are Doing for Women Depositors," *The Bankers' Monthly*, 36 (July), 18-19+.
The Bankers' Magazine (1899a), "The Duties of Bank Employees," 59 (July), 73-75.
_____ (1899b), "The Value of Advertising," 58 (February), 183-184.
_____ (1908a), "How Banks are Advertising," 77 (August), 258.
_____ (1908b), "A New Emblem," 77 (July), 90.
_____ (1908c), "Backing up Advertising," 77 (April), 594.
_____ (1908d), "Banking Publicity," 76 (February), 238.
_____ (1909), "How Banks are Advertising," 78 (July), 1006.
_____ (1911), "The Bank's Appeal to Women," 82 (March), 389.
_____ (1915), "Banking Publicity," 91 (December), 821-822.
_____ (1917), "Experience with the Women's Department," 95 (August), 187-191.
_____ (1920), "The New Business Department," 104 (April), 394-395.
_____ (1922), "Cultivate Old as Well as New Customers," 100 (March), 707+.
_____ (1930), "Five Cents Savings Bank Takes Nickels," 121 (July), 140.
The Bankers' Monthly (1928), "Chicago History Dramatized," 45 (May), 27.
Bartels, R. (1988), *The History of Marketing Thought*. Columbus, OH: Publishing Horizons.
Berry, L.L. and A. Parasuraman (1993), "Building a New Academic Field—The Case of Services Marketing," *Journal of Retailing*, 69 (Spring), 13-60.
Bourne, C.E. (1928), "Advertising a Bank with 900 Branches," *The Bankers' Magazine*, 117 (December), 1031-1036.
Carr, W. (1975), *From Three Cents A Week ... The Story of the Prudential Insurance Company of America*. Englewood Cliffs, NJ: Prentice-Hall.
Clarke, J.I. (1922), "The Spirit of Service," *Journal of the American Banking Association*, 13 (September), 136-137.
Cleland, R.G. and F.B. Putnam (1965), *Isaiis W. Hellman and the Farmers and Merchants Bank*. San Marino, CA: Huntington Library.
Cross, I.B. (1927), *Financing an Empire: History of Banking in California*. Chicago, IL: S.J. Clarke.
Currier, E. (1920), "Selecting the Dress for Your Printed Message," *The Bankers Monthly*, 37 (July), 25-26+.
Davis, L.J. (1919), "Telling the Story of Your Mechanical Aids," *The Bankers' Monthly*, 36 (November), 28.
Dean, L.R. (1914), "Selling Bank Service," *The Bankers' Magazine*, 89 (November), 513-516.
De Bebian, A. (1921), "Advertising Within the Bank," *The Bankers' Magazine*, 102 (February), 244+.
Densch, E.C. (1920), "Every Bank Needs a Slogan," *The Bankers' Monthly*, 37 (April), 30-31.
Douglas, W.W. (1922), "Does Your Bank Force Read Your Copy?" *The Bankers' Monthly*, 39 (July), 23.
Downs, L.A. (1929), "Service is Perishable," *The Bankers' Monthly*, 46 (January), 15-16+.

Du Four, C.J. (1921), "How Alameda Has Educated Children," *The Bankers' Monthly*, 38 (November), 25.

Ecklund, O.F. (1925), "The Personal Touch in Your Letters to Newcomers," *The Bankers' Monthly*, 42 (May), 30-31.

Ekrich, A.A. (1910), "Modern Used by Our Progressive Banks," *The Bankers' Magazine*, 80 (March), 417-419.

Ellsworth, F.W. (1920), "Merchandising Ideas of 'Department Store of Finance'," *Printers' Ink*, 113 (December 23), 77-78+.

The EquitableEnvoy (1929), "New Type of Central Information File Adopted by New Business: Findex in Operation," 9 (August), 11.

Fisk, R.P., S.W. Brown and M.J. Bitner (1993), "Tracking the Evolution of Services Marketing Literature," *Journal of Retailing*, 69 (Spring), 61-103.

Flint, M.H. (1927), "Solicitation Management," *The Bankers' Monthly*, 48 (August), 25-26.

Gail, H.E. (1919), "Safe Keeping of Bonds as Business Getter," *The Bankers' Monthly*, 36 (February), 8-9.

Griffith, J.H. (1907), "Ought Bank Clerks to Be Good-Natured," *The Bankers' Magazine*, 74 (January), 87-88.

Guaranty Trust Company of New York (1916), *The Argentine Republic*. New York: Guaranty Trust Company of New York.

————— (1917), *The War Tax Law*. New York: Guaranty Trust Company of New York.

Handerson, C.H. (1923a), "Merchandising 'Save-at-Shop' Banking to Employers and Employees," *Printers' Ink*, 125 (October 25), 97-98+.

————— (1923b), "Why Not Advertise Banks Like Soaps and Soup," *Printers' Ink*, 123 (June 7), 97-98+.

Harlow, A.F. (1916), "How the Banks Taught a City to Save," *The Bankers' Monthly*, 30 (July), 28-33.

Harrington, R.E. (1926), "How Louisville Bankers are Winning School Savers," *The Bankers' Monthly*, 34 (January), 18+.

Heitzman, B.E. (1926) "Keeping in Contact With Customers Through the Central File," *The Bankers' Monthly*, 43 (March), 17-18.

Hill, O.W. (1907), "The Night and Day Bank of New York City," *The Business World*, 8 (September), 827-835.

Holdsworth, J.T. (1928), *Financing an Empire: History of Banking in Pennsylvania*. Chicago, IL: S.J. Clarke.

Hollander, S.C. (1984), "Herbert Hoover, Professor Leavitt, Simplification and the 'Marketing Concept'," in *1984 Winter Educators Conference Proceedings*, P. Anderson and M. Ryans, eds. Chicago: American Marketing Association, 260-263.

Husband, J. (1933), *One Hundred Years of Greenwich Savings Bank*. New York: Greenwich Saving Bank.

Ingraham, A.M. (1912), "Advertising to Present Depositors," *The Bankers' Magazine*, 84 (February), 227-228.

James, C.F. (1938), *The Growth of Chicago Banks*. New York: Harper & Brothers.

James, M. (1947), *The Metropolitan Life: A Study in Business Growth*. New York: Viking Press.

————— and B.R. James (1954), *Biography of a Bank: The Story of the Bank of America N.T. & S.A.* New York: Harper & Brothers.

Jess, S. (1907), "Uniting the Work of the Receiving and Paying Tellers," *The Bankers' Magazine*, 75 (July), 117-118.

Kerman, F. and B.W. Griffin (1926), *New Business for Banks*. New York: Prentice-Hall.

Kittredge, E.H. (1923), "House Organs For Banks," *The Printing Art*, 41 (July), 453-457.

Knapp, G.P. (1925), "Controlling the Bank's New Business Department," *The Bankers' Monthly*, 42 (April), 12-13+.

The Kodak Magazine (1929), "The Recordak Corporation," 9 (January), 3-4.

Lovelock, C. (1984), *Services Marketing*. Englewood Cliffs, NJ: Prentice-Hall.

MacGregor, T.D. (1913), *Bank Advertising Plans*. New York: Bankers Publishing Company.

———— (1914), "Pertinent Points," *The Bankers' Magazine*, 88 (May), 496.

———— (1917), *The New Business Department*. New York: Bankers Publishing Company.

———— (1918), "How Banks Get 'New Business'," *Printer's Ink*, 102 (March 14), 106+.

Mann, H. (1908), "Home Banks Increase Deposits," *The Bankers' Magazine*, 77 (September), 405-408.

McGraw-Hill (1990), *Money Matters: A Critical Look at Bank Architecture*. New York: McGraw-Hill Publishing Company.

Mills, G.E. and D.W. Holdsworth (1975), "The B.C. Mills Prefabricated System: The Emergence of Ready-Made Building in Western Canada," in *Occasional Papers in Archeology and History*, No. 14: *Canadian Historic Sites*. Ottawa, Canada: Indian and Northern Affairs.

Moorehouse, H.E., correspondence with E.B.B. Reesor (1909), "Women as Bankers," *The Bankers' Magazine*, 79 (October), 511-514.

Morehouse, W.R. (1913a), "A Method for Stopping Unnecessary Withdrawals," *The Bankers' Magazine*, 87 (December), 633-35.

———— (1913b), "Employees' Contest for Securing New Deposits," *The Bankers' Magazine*, 87 (July), 17-21.

———— (1914), "Letters that Pull and Hold Business," *The Bankers' Magazine*, 88 (February), 157-63.

———— (1918), *Bank Deposit Building*. New York: Bankers Publishing Co.

———— (1919), *Bank Window Advertising*. New York: Bankers Publishing Co.

Mottram, R.H. (1930), *Miniature Banking Histories*. London: Chatto and Windus.

Neibel, O.J. (1930), "Five Basic Sales Policies and Their Application to Banking," *The Bankers' Monthly*, 47 (April), 9-10+.

New York Times (1910), "Night Bank Opens in Times Square," (September 5).

An Old Cashier (1885), "Advice to Bank Clerks," *The Bankers' Magazine*, 39 (April), 736-37.

Ollerenshaw, P. (1987), *Banking in Nineteenth Century Ireland: The Belfast Banks, 1825-1914*. Manchester, UK: Manchester University Press.

O'Reilly, G.A. (1924), "Taking a Novel Slant on Bank Merchandising," *The Bankers' Monthly*, 41 (July), 40-43.

Payne, W. (1905), "The Workings of a Model Bank," *The World's Work*, 9 (February), 5872-5875.

Reihl, C.W. (1906), "Practical Banking: Analysis of Accounts," *The Bankers' Magazine*, 73 (August), 280-287.

Report of the Commissioner of Education (1898), "School Savings Banks," 1 (no. 5, part 1), Washington, DC: U.S. Government Printing Office, 160-164.

The Review (1909), "Banking by Machinery," 6 (May), 4-5.

———— (1914), "A Currency Washing Machine," 11 (July), 42-43.

Robinson, C.E. (1924), "Handle Dormant Accounts with Care," *The Bankers' Monthly*, 40 (September), 27+.

Rose, W.G. (1922), "Why the Teller is Able to Make or Break Friendships," *The Bankers' Monthly*, 39 (March), 22.

Rule, W.G. (1947), *The Story of the Oldest Bank West of the Mississippi*. St. Louis, MO: Boatmen's National Bank of St. Louis.

Say, J.B. (1821), *A Treatise on Political Economy*. New York: A.M. Kelly (reprinted 1964).

Sheth, J.N., D.M. Gardner and D.E. Garrett (1988), *Marketing Theory: Evolution and Evaluation*. New York: John Wiley & Sons.

Shostack, L. (1977), "Breaking Free from Product Marketing," *Journal of Marketing*, 41 (April), 73-80.

Shoyer, W.T. (1955), *A Century of Saving Dollars: 1855-1955*. Pittsburgh, PA: Dollar Savings Bank.

Tinsley, J.F. (1921), "The Operation of an Industrial Savings Plan During Commercial Depression," *The Bankers' Magazine*, 102 (April), 565-567.

Tymeson, M.M. (1955), *Worcester Bankbook*. Worcester, MA: Worcester County Trust Company.

Vincent, W.D. (1913), "Service as an Advertisement," *The Bankers' Magazine*, 87 (June), 49.

Welton, A.D. (1923), *The Making of a Modern Bank*. Chicago, IL: Continental and Commercial Banks of Chicago.

Wilson, J.F. (1906), "Cost of Handling Checking Accounts," *The Bankers' Magazine*, 73 (September), 412-417.

Woodworth, L.D. (1921), "Christmas Savings Clubs, 1920," *Journal of the American Bankers Association*, 14 (July), 17-20.

"MANAGEMENT SERVICE QUALITY" IN A SERVICES MARKETING SETTING

Deborah L. Cowles and Tracy L. Tuten

ABSTRACT

This study examines whether customer perceptions of the quality of a firm's management play a direct role in creating satisfied customers. Findings suggest that customers use tangible cues (e.g., an unresponsive manager, employee negative word-of-mouth) as well as inferential cues to assess the quality of management. Moreover, customer perceptions of management service quality (MSQ) directly influence customer satisfaction and perceptions of service quality.

INTRODUCTION

The nexus between management and marketing is perhaps no more apparent—and important—than in a services marketing setting. Indeed, from the beginning of the services marketing literature to today's increasingly sophisticated inquiries into the complexities of the service economy, the simultaneous production and consumption of most services continues to be recognized as a critical difference between goods and services (Bateson 1992).

Advances in Services Marketing and Management, Volume 6, pages 125-146.
Copyright © 1997 by JAI Press Inc.
All rights of reproduction in any form reserved.
ISBN: 0-7623-0176-7

In the case of goods, producers and consumers rarely come together. In the case of services, the customer:

> actively inputs into the design of the tactics, participates in the joint producing/consuming act, provides feedback during the consumption process (not just afterwards as is the case for goods) and experiences ... the effects of whatever mix modification takes place during the service delivery process (Bell 1981, p. 163).

The *service encounter* is at the heart of the goods/services distinction. Some researchers have described the service encounter—when the service employee comes in contact with the service customer—as "interactive marketing," while others have labeled the encounter as the "moment of truth" in services marketing (e.g., Carlzon 1987; Grönroos 1990a). Regardless of the terminology, service customers' satisfaction and impressions of quality are shaped by not only the outcome of the service production process but also the service encounter experience, including contact with the service employee (Bitner 1992, 1990; Bitner, Booms and Mohr 1994; Bitner, Booms and Tetreault 1990; Crosby, Evans and Cowles 1990; Crosby and Stephens 1987; Holbrook 1994). As a result, management issues are at times difficult to distinguish from marketing concerns.

The services marketing literature has been expanded to include human resource and management issues as they relate to service employees. For example, Berry (1995) asserts that top-performing service firms implement their service strategies "through people" by (1) competing for talent (hiring), (2) developing skills and knowledge (training), (3) empowering servers to serve, (4) developing a work environment in which teamwork thrives and (5) both measuring and rewarding service excellence. While the impact of such factors most certainly influences customer satisfaction and perceptions of quality achieved "through" the service employee, the perspective of this study is that management's impact on the service employee also affects service customers *directly*. This assertion is consistent with criticism of the management literature which suggests that researchers often view "organizations from the top down (management's perspective) or the inside out (employee's perspective) but rarely from the outside in (customer's perspective)" (Dean and Bowen 1994, pp. 408-409). The purpose of this study is to examine empirically whether customer perceptions of a service firm's management of customer contact personnel may play a direct role in the development of strong customer relationships.

MANAGEMENT'S ROLE IN CUSTOMER SATISFACTION

A number of different perspectives can be taken when considering management's role in shaping customer satisfaction and perceptions of service quality. Typically, in a services marketing setting, management is thought to influence customers indirectly—*through* the service provider—as well as through its impact on other service variables (e.g., service systems, corporate image). For example, the "gap analysis" approach to assessing customer perceptions of service quality includes many management-related variables (e.g., teamwork, supervisory control systems, role conflict, role ambiguity, employee-job fit, technology-job fit, upward communication, levels of management, management commitment to service quality) in at least three of the five "gap" categories (Brown and Swartz 1989; Parasuraman, Zeithaml and Berry 1985; Zeithaml, Berry and Parasuraman 1988). Also, Grönroos (1990a) has focused on organizational variables such as structure, cross-functional cooperation and internal marketing as critical to managing "moments of truth," or service encounters. However, the "gap" model depicts explicitly and Grönroos implies that such factors play an *indirect* role in shaping customer perceptions of service quality. Indeed, most published research in this area suggests that organizational variables (e.g., management policies, procedures, actions) impact service customers via the contact employee (Bitner 1992, 1990; Parasuraman, Zeithaml and Berry 1985).

Similarly, Bateson (1992) conceptualized the relationships among the service firm, the service employee and the service customer as a "three-cornered fight" (Figure 1A). Focusing on the broad concept of relationship control, Bateson characterized (1) the relationship between service firm and contact employee as a tradeoff between autonomy/control and efficiency; (2) the relationship between firm and customer as a tradeoff between satisfaction/control and efficiency; and (3) the relationship between the contact employee and the service customer, a matter of perceived control. In Figure 1A, the *indirect* influence of management on customers would follow "path" $A <> B <> C$, such that management policies, procedures and actions, as well as the relationship between management and contact employees, would affect customers *through* the service provider.

Much research in the services marketing literature has focused on relationship $B <> C$ (contact employee-service customer)—that is, the "moment of truth." Additionally, some studies have considered the firm's influence on customer satisfaction and perceptions of service quality from the perspective of relationship $A <> C$ (service firm-service customer). For example, Crosby and Stephens (1987) found that in addition to satisfaction with the service outcome and the contact person, a customer's overall satisfaction is based on satisfaction with the service company. To some extent, studies incorporating the concept of company image into models explaining customer satisfaction and perceptions of service quality address relationship $A <> C$ (e.g., Clow 1993). Finally, the services marketing literature has called for a balance among the relationships depicted in Figure 1A (Bateson 1992; Parasuraman, Zeithaml and Berry 1988).

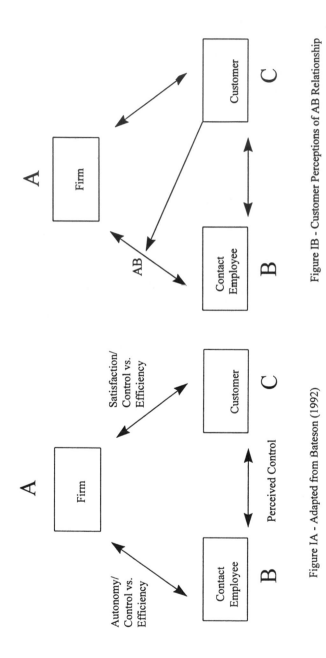

Figure IA - Adapted from Bateson (1992)

Figure IB - Customer Perceptions of AB Relationship

Figure 1. Three-Cornered Fight Between Firm, Employees and Customers

128

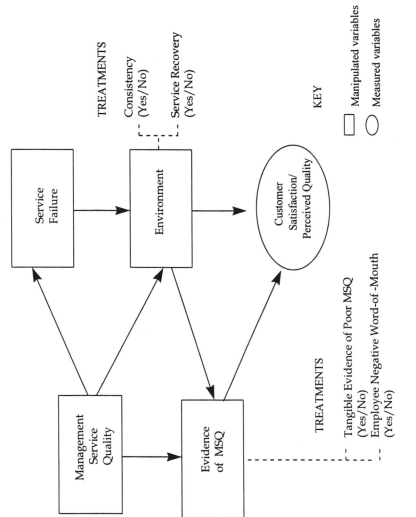

TREATMENTS

Consistency
(Yes/No)

Service Recovery
(Yes/No)

TREATMENTS

Tangible Evidence of Poor MSQ
(Yes/No)

Employee Negative Word-of -Mouth
(Yes/No)

KEY

☐ Manipulated variables

○ Measured variables

Figure 2. Conceptual Model

The relationship of particular interest for this discussion is shown in Figure 1B as $C > (A <> B)$. It represents the customer's view of the relationship between a firm and its service employees. Also, Figure 1B suggests that customer satisfaction and perceptions of service quality may be influenced not only *indirectly* by service firm-service employee interactions ($A <> B$) and *directly* by service employee-service customer interactions ($B <> C$) and the service firm-service customer relationship ($A <> C$), but also by customer perceptions of management's relationship and interactions with its employees ($C > [A <> B]$). In terms used by Bateson (1992), because customers are often inside the "service factory," they are privy to information about relationships between a firm and its employees, including struggles between autonomy/control and efficiency. Schneider (1980) has observed that organizational climate (e.g., "enthusiast," "bureaucratic") affects both the customer and the employee.

The conceptual model guiding this study (Figure 2) was developed to explore whether customer perceptions of management's relationship with service employees *directly* impact customer satisfaction and perceived service quality. The model relies on a concept labeled "management service quality" which assumes that customers make judgments about the quality of management just as they assess the quality of services provided to them.

MANAGEMENT AS A SERVICE TO EMPLOYEES

The extant services marketing literature supports the general concept of management as a service, albeit mainly from the employee's perspective. For example, Berry (1981) has long commented on the need for service firms to view employees as "internal customers" of management. In a public sector service setting, C. Cowles (1994) found that some of the services provided by immediate supervisors (e.g., consultation, providing needed information in a timely manner) can be evaluated in the same way that customers evaluate service quality. Specifically, the characteristics of tangibility, reliability, responsiveness, assurance, empathy and equity, as they manifested themselves in a supervisory situation, were shown to have a direct bearing on an employee's job satisfaction and desire to remain in his or her current employment position. For the past two decades, the business literature increasingly has recognized that meeting the needs of an organization's employees is tantamount to creating satisfied customers (e.g., Berry 1995).

From a somewhat different perspective, a primary tenet of the quality literature (e.g., Deming 1986; Juran 1989) is a focus on management's role in developing processes and providing resources that both inspire and enable employees to meet customer expectations. Moreover, top-performing companies have long held that providing competent management is an ethical obligation (Smith and Quelch 1993). Thus, management services consist of those which enable employees to perform their job functions to the satisfaction—even to the "delight" (Deming 1986)—of service customers. Ostensibly, the higher the quality of services provided by management to the contact employee (the internal customer), the better the service provided by the contact employee to the external customer. As such, the quality of aggregate services provided by management to contact employees is referred to in this discussion as management service quality (MSQ).

The marketing literature also provides support for both the potential role and the potential importance of the MSQ construct. From both the firm's and the customer's perspectives, contact employees represent a corporate resource integral to the creation of customer satisfaction and the delivery of quality. In the same way that customers are impacted by management's care for physical property (i.e., tangibles [Shostack 1977]), customers may also be influenced by management's care for human resources, particularly contact employees.

Bitner (1990) found that service customers are influenced by environmental factors such as tidiness, or the lack of tidiness, of a service facility. Customers link such environmental cues to form customer satisfaction and quality evaluations (Folkes 1988). These cues may also shape customer assessments of MSQ. For example, in Bitner's study (1990) of the role of physical surroundings in service encounter outcomes, study participants could have attributed an untidy customer service area either to the individual service employee or to the quality of the service firm's management function. Similarly, D. Cowles (1995) found that a service firm's reputation for consistency and reliability of quality service had a bearing on the attributions service customers' made concerning service failures. In situations where retail service firms had a reputation for *inconsistent* service quality, customers were more likely to attribute a *favorable* response to a service failure *to the service employee*. On the other hand, in situations where customers perceived the firm to provide *consistent* and *reliable* service, an employee's *favorable* response to a service failure was attributed *to management policies and procedures*, including hiring, training, compensation, and so forth. These findings suggest that customers can and do evaluate MSQ. Thus, the questions arise: (1) Do customers regularly evaluate MSQ and, if so, how do they make their MSQ assessments? (2) Do customers' MSQ evaluations influence satisfaction and perceptions of overall service quality? The first question is addressed in the services marketing literature, while the second is the focal point of this study.

HOW CUSTOMERS DEVELOP AND USE PERCEPTIONS OF MSQ

According to Shostack (1977), points of contact in the service system serve as cues that help customers shape their performance expectations, evaluations of service experiences and, ultimately, satisfaction. These tangible cues are especially important in service settings because of the intangible nature of services. In the case of high-contact services, customers are inside the "factory" when services are produced. This contact makes a wide variety of cues available during the service encounter, and these cues may be used to develop perceptions of MSQ. The "line of visibility" refers to a demarcation in the production process, behind which service systems and performances are not visible to the customer. This line presumes that while much of the organization and many of its systems cannot be observed by service customers, part of the service production process is visible to the customers (Bateson 1992). As depicted in Figure 2, this study considers two of the many ways in which customers use directly observable evidence available during a service encounter to make MSQ evaluations (supervisory control systems and communication with customer contact personnel), as well as two aspects of the retail environment which customers use to draw inferences about the quality of management (response to service failure and consistency of service quality).

Direct Observations of MSQ Evidence

Although Zeithaml, Berry and Parasuraman (1988) place three of their five potential service quality "gaps" behind the customer's line of visibility, customers can observe and evaluate many of the elements thought to comprise these gaps. For example, in many situations, customers can either interpret or make inferences from cues in the environment, or they can observe directly whether (1) employees are working as a team (teamwork), (2) management has selected the right kind of employee for a particular position (employee-job fit), (3) management provides adequate and competent supervisors (supervisory control systems), (4) the firm has numerous layers of bureaucracy (levels of management) and (5) management provides an adequate number of properly trained employees with adequate resources available to them (management commitment to service quality). Even when a customer's information concerning such factors is limited or incomplete—even inaccurate—perceptions and attitudes can be influenced nonetheless.

In addition to using direct observations of management policies and procedures to evaluate MSQ, service customers also can acquire information about MSQ from customer contact personnel. Although the services marketing literature has acknowledged word-of-mouth communication (WOM) among customers as an important component of the promotional mix for intangible products (e.g., Brown and Reingen 1987; Davis, Guiltinan and Jones 1979; George and Berry 1981), this study recognizes that customers also can communicate directly with customer contact personnel. Word-of-mouth communication pertaining to MSQ between an employee and a customer can be attributed to a number of factors, including conflict between the service provider's role and the constraints imposed by the organization (Rogers, Clow and Kash 1994; Schneider 1980) and the desire to maintain social relationships (Folkes 1994).

Conflict and resultant stress on the part of customer contact personnel are important aspects of Bateson's "three-cornered fight" (1992). Schneider (1980) found that service providers experience stress when company policies and procedures prevent them from providing a level of quality they perceive they are capable of providing. He also found that a conflict resolution strategy used frequently by service providers during situations of service failure or other forms of stress is to explain the problems with management of the organization to the customer in an attempt to reduce stress and seek sympathy from the customer. Similarly, Rogers, Clow and Kash (1994) found that empathy and clear lines of communication—including WOM—between service employees and service customers, as well as between service employees and their employers, serve to minimize employee stress in frontline retail service settings. Thus, the customer can develop perceptions of MSQ using this communication as a primary source of information.

Folkes (1994) asserts that WOM between a service provider and a customer can also occur as a means of repairing a disrupted social relationship. In a service failure situation, a contact employee may communicate reasons for the firm's poor performance hoping to cause the customer to attribute blame away from the service provider in order to secure social aspects of the service relationship (Hill, Baer and Kostenko 1992; Weiner 1992). Bitner (1990) also described communications in which service providers offered explanations for service failures. Employee WOM that comments specifically on the quality of management or the nature of the employee's relationship with management could be used by customers to develop perceptions of MSQ. Like other forms of WOM, employee communications used to shape customer MSQ evaluations could be positive or negative and would be largely out of the control of management. The increasing use of service recovery in service settings (Berry and Parasuraman 1991; S. Brown 1994; Johnston 1996) provides ample opportunity for employee-customer WOM to occur.

Customers Make Inferences about MSQ

In addition to directly observing evidence concerning MSQ, customers also are capable of drawing inferences about the quality of management from a variety of cues present in the retail environment. This study considers two of these environmental cues: employee response to a service failure and consistency of service quality. Empowering employees to provide service recovery has been referred to as "enlightened management" (Aspery 1993). Customers who observe contact employees afraid to make service recovery decisions might infer that the cause of the fear was management policies and procedures (e.g., Deming 1986).

Service reliability has been recognized as being central to services marketing excellence (Berry and Parasuraman 1991). Over the past decade, studies considering how customers make evaluations of service quality have concluded that reliability—consistency of quality service, performing the service dependably—is the most critical dimension (Berry and Parasuraman 1991; Parasuraman, Zeithaml and Berry 1988; Zeithaml and Bitner 1996). D. Cowles (1994, p. 4) observed that when "a customer receives good service consistently when frequenting a specific retail store (as opposed to receiving good service from a specific contact person), the customer attributes the cause of the good service to be internal to the retail store." As such, consistency in high quality service delivery should reflect favorably on MSQ.

Research Hypotheses

Figure 2 depicts the conceptual model underlying the study which tests empirically whether and how customers develop perceptions of MSQ and, if so, whether those perceptions influence satisfaction and evaluations of service quality. Two hypotheses were tested:

Hypothesis 1.   Customers use direct and indirect evidence available to them to assess MSQ.

   A.   Tangible evidence (direct customer observation of a manager's inattention to a service failure) and negative information about management communicated to a customer by a contact person will have a negative impact on customer perceptions of MSQ.

   B.   Consistency of service and a contact employee's willingness to engage in service recovery in the face of service failure will have a positive influence on customer perceptions of MSQ.

Where the first hypothesis focuses on factors which shape customer perceptions of MSQ, the second hypothesis considers the influence those perceptions have on customer satisfaction and evaluations of service quality, as depicted in Figure 2.

Hypothesis 2.   Customer perceptions of MSQ will exhibit a positive relationship with satisfaction and perceptions of service quality, such that as customer perceptions of MSQ become more favorable, satisfaction and service quality evaluations will be more favorable.

METHODOLOGY

A $2 \times 2 \times 2 \times 2$ between groups experiment was conducted to test the two hypotheses. The experiment used scenario vignettes and a projective technique which permitted subjects to focus on and respond to the same stimulus. Such vignettes have been shown to be helpful in measuring complex variables and can provide "good approximations to realistic psychological and social situations" (Kerlinger 1986, p. 476).

Treatments and Measures

Each scenario contained one of two conditions for the four treatments: (1) *consistency* of good service during previous store visits (versus *inconsistency*); (2) *tangible [i.e., observable] evidence* of management's lack of adequate supervisory control (versus *no such evidence*); (3) *employee negative WOM* regarding management (versus the *absence of such communication*) and (4) the presence of *service recovery* following poor service (versus *no service recovery*). Two of the treatments (tangible evidence and employee negative WOM) were intended to manipulate cues used directly by subjects to shape perceptions of MSQ, while the other two treatments (consistency and service recovery) manipulated cues that permit subjects to draw inferences about MSQ. Sixteen scenarios resulted from the conditions and treatments (see Figure 3). Appendix A shows one of the 16 scenarios used in the study.

A situation of service failure was used as the premise for treatments since (1) employees are more likely to engage in the kind of "blaming" depicted in the scenario, which would provide evidence of the quality of management for the customer (Bitner 1990; Hill, Baer and Kostenko 1992) and (2) customers are more likely to make attributions about service quality in a service failure setting (Folkes 1994). The scenarios were developed through a three-step procedure. Students of an undergraduate marketing class turned in written descriptions of both positive and negative service encounters. The two researchers analyzed these descriptions looking for the presence of the independent variables. Scenarios that depicted the independent variables and resembled many of the student descriptions were developed for the experiment.

Undergraduate business students ($n = 424$) of a major university in the southeastern United States took part in the study. Following random assignment to a treatment cell and exposure to one scenario, each subject responded to items contained in a questionnaire. A majority of the participants (60.5%) was 25 years of age or younger, 26.9 percent was ages 26-35, with the remaining participants over 36 years of age. Nearly one-half of the participants (48.1%) worked part-time while pursuing their education; 32.7 percent were employed on a full-time basis. More than half of the subjects (50.2%) was male and 46 percent was female, with the remaining 3.8 percent not reporting this

Service Failure															
Consistency								No Consistency							
ENWOM				No ENWOM				ENWOM				No ENWOM			
Tangible		No Tangible		Tangible		No Tangible		Tangible		No Tangible		Tangible		No Tangible	
R	NR	R	NR	R	NR	R	NR	R	NR	R	NR	R	NR	R	NR

Key: ENWOM = Employee negative word-of-mouth communication.
Tangible = Tangible evidence.
R = Service recovery, NR = No service recovery.

Figure 3.   The Block Design

information. Finally, the following student classifications were represented: sophomore standing, 7.7 percent; junior, 22.7 percent; senior, 41.4 percent; and graduate level, 17.8 percent.

Subjects evaluated the scenarios as "believable" and "realistic" (overall mean scores of 1.59 and 1.44, respectively, 1 = very believable/realistic and 5 = not very believable/realistic), with no significant differences in these scores between treatment groups or experimental cells. A check of the manipulations indicated that all four treatments had the desired effect. Based on a five-point scale of agreement (1 = strongly agree, 5 = strongly disagree) and using an independent samples t-test to examine group mean score differences, subjects in the recovery treatment group agreed that the contact person attempted to make things right following service failure (2.38), in contrast to subjects who were exposed to the scenario in which no recovery attempt was made (3.78), $p = .000$. Study participants in the employee negative WOM treatment group agreed that such communication occurred (1.96), compared to those whose vignette did not involve employee NWOM (3.48), $p = .000$. Subjects exposed to the scenario depicting tangible evidence of a lack of supervisory control agreed that such a situation existed in the scenario (2.84), versus 3.29 in the group not exposed

Table 1.   Measures and Reliabilities

Item(s) Used to Measure Construct	Cronbach's Alpha
Management Service Quality (MSQ)	0.72
Managers of this department provide prompt supervision of employees. (1 = strongly agree, 5 = strongly disagree)	
Management of this firm provides employees with the support to do their jobs better. (1 = strongly agree, 5 = strongly disagree)	
Encounter Satisfaction (ENSAT)	0.80
How did you feel about your service experience on this particular occasion? (1 = delighted, 5 = terrible)	
I was satisfied with this specific service experience. (1 = strongly agree, 5 = strongly disagree)	
My decision to shop at this store on this occasion was a wise one. (1 = strongly agree, 5 = strongly disagree)	
Overall Satisfaction (OVSAT)	0.84
Based on your experience, how satisfied overall are you with this store's service? (1 = very satisfied, 5 = very dissatisfied)	
In general, I am satisfied with this retail store. (1 = strongly agree, 5 = strongly disagree)	
Compared to other, similar stores that you have done business with, how would you rate your satisfaction with this store? (1 = very satisfied, 5 = very dissatisfied)	
Overall Quality (OQUAL)	0.80
Based on everything you know about the store described in the scenario, rate the overall quality of this store. (1 = excellent, 5 = poor)	
When compared to other stores that provide the same type of service, the store described in the scenario is: (1 = superior, 5 = inferior)	
If asked, I would definitely recommend this store as a place to shop for gifts. (1 = strongly agree, 5 = strongly disagree)	
The quality of service provided by this store is outstanding. (1 = strongly agree, 5 = strongly disagree)	

to such direct evidence ($p = .001$). Finally, participants responding to scenarios in which the service firm had provided consistently good service during previous visits agreed that such consistency existed (1.90), compared to 4.31 for subjects responding to the scenario in which a lack of consistency in service quality was described ($p = .000$).

Management service quality (MSQ) was measured by subjects' agreement or disagreement with items contained in Table 1, that is, "Managers of this department provide prompt supervision of employees," and "Management of this firm provides employees with the support to do their jobs better." Together, the two MSQ items were acceptably reliable (Cronbach's coefficient alpha = .72); however, the need to develop a better measure of this construct is discussed later.

The key dependent variables (*encounter satisfaction, overall satisfaction* and *perceived overall quality*) were based on research by Bitner and Hubbert (1994), who reported that the constructs represent three distinct customer assessments. Bitner and Hubbert define encounter satisfaction as the perceived service level compared to the expected service level, concluding that it reflects the customer's feelings about a discrete interaction with a firm. In contrast, overall satisfaction occurs at multiple levels of the organization. In addition to multiple service encounter experiences with a firm, it includes a satisfaction evaluation of the contact person, the core service and the institution as a whole. Finally, perceived overall quality is a consumer's overall impression of the relative superiority/inferiority of the organization and its services. As shown in Table 1, the three measures adapted from Bitner and Hubbert (1994) were highly reliable, with coefficients alpha ranging from .80 to .84.

ANALYSIS AND RESULTS

Table 2 contains the results of an analysis of variance which shows that all four treatments had a significant influence on customer perceptions of MSQ, findings which support both Hypotheses 1A and 1B. Moreover, within each treatment group, mean MSQ scores for "YES" and "NO" conditions were significantly different (based on independent samples t-tests which examined differences between group mean scores, $p < .001$). Results were in the hypothesized directions, suggesting that customers are aware of MSQ. The results indicate further that customers use direct/observable evidence in the retail service environment, as well as other cues from which they can draw inferences, as means of assessing MSQ.

Table 3 shows the results of three analyses of variance conducted to examine the impact of MSQ on the dependent variables. In the analyses, the variable measuring customer perceptions of MSQ (a manipulated condition derived from the four treatments) is used as a covariate. Tangible evidence and employee negative WOM were designed to influence perceptions of MSQ *directly*, and thought to relate exclusively to the MSQ construct. The other two treatments, consistency and recovery, were thought to influence not only customer evaluations of encounter satisfaction, overall satisfaction and perceived overall quality but also customer perceptions of MSQ (indirectly via

Table 2. Effects of Treatment Variables on Perceptions
of Management Service Quality (MSQ)

Dependent Variable: MSQ (Customer Perceptions of Management Service Quality)

Source of Variation	F	Sig. of F
Main Effects	15.209	0.000
TANGIBLE	8.703	0.003
EMPNWOM	6.632	0.010
CONSISTENCY	30.040	0.000
RECOVERY	12.724	0.000
2-way interactions (none significant)		0.419
3-way interactions (none significant)		0.786
4-way interactions (none significant)		0.323
Explained	4.640	0.000

Cell Means: Overall Mean = 4.00

	Mean Scores of Treatment Variables			
Condition	TANGIBLE	EMPNWOM	CONSISTENCY	RECOVERY
YES	4.12	4.11	3.80	3.87
NO	3.89	3.90	4.22	4.13

inference). Therefore, it was necessary to control for MSQ differences created by the two "indirect" treatments, while testing for differences between groups based on the influence of the MSQ construct.

Table 3 shows that MSQ accounts for a significant amount of the variation among groups in all three analyses. While consistency and service recovery

Table 3. Impact of Management Service Quality (MSQ), Service Recovery
and Service Consistency on Customer Satisfaction
and Perceptions of Service Quality

	Encounter Satisfaction (Sig.)	Overall Satisfaction (Sig.)	Perceived Quality (Sig.)
Covariate	0.000	0.000	0.000
MSQ	0.000	0.000	0.000
Main effects	0.000	0.000	0.000
Recovery	0.000	0.004	0.142
Consistency	0.114	0.000	0.000
2-way interactions	0.090	0.034	0.871
Explained	0.000	0.000	0.000

Table 4. Impact of MSQ on Dependent Variables by Treatment Group

	Treatments		Dependent Variables		
Treatment Group	Consistency	Recovery	Encounter Satisfaction	Overall Satisfaction	Perceived Quality
Overall mean			3.97	3.40	3.55
Group 1—mean	YES	NO	4.17	3.22	3.41
MSQ beta			0.29^b	0.27^b	0.26^b
Treatment beta			3.01^a	2.11^a	2.34^a
Group 2—mean	NO	NO	4.28	3.88	3.90
MSQ beta			0.42^a	0.46^a	0.51^a
Treatment beta			2.49^a	1.90^a	1.71^a
Group 3—mean	YES	YES	3.71	2.99	3.17
MSQ beta			0.54^a	0.51^a	0.48^a
Treatment beta			2.14^a	1.15^a	1.44^a
Group 4—mean	NO	YES	3.72	3.53	3.76
MSQ beta			0.38^a	0.49^a	0.43^a
Treatment beta			1.78^a	1.50^a	1.93^a
Adjusted R^2			0.97	0.97	0.97
F			1691.17	1627.10	1990.40
Sig. of F			0.000	0.000	0.000

Notes: [a] $p < 0.001$ (sig. of treatment).
[b] $p < 0.01$ (sig. of treatment).
* Lower score indicates more favorable evaluation.

140

have varying levels of impact on encounter satisfaction, overall satisfaction and perceived overall quality, customer perceptions of MSQ are instrumental in shaping customer satisfaction and perceptions of service quality. Results depicted in Table 3 are consistent with those reported by Brown, Cowles and Tuten (1996): (1) service recovery appears to have a more significant, positive impact on encounter satisfaction, and (2) service consistency exerts a greater influence on more enduring customer outcome measures (i.e., overall satisfaction, perceived quality).

Although both interesting and predictable, the results in Table 3 do not directly support the second hypothesis. As anticipated, the treatment, recovery and consistency have a significant impact on satisfaction and perceived quality; moreover, cell means depicted in Table 4 show that the impact is in the anticipated direction. For example, subjects exposed to the "no prior consistency" and "no offer of service recovery" scenario were least satisfied and perceived the lowest level of quality (i.e., highest mean scores), and subjects exposed to the "consistency" and "service recovery" scenario had the lowest average scores, meaning that overall they were most satisfied and perceived the highest level of service quality.

However, a separate analysis, also contained in Table 4, was needed to explore further both the direction and the degree of influence exerted by MSQ on the dependent variables. In regression analyses, dummy variables captured the influence of the covariate (MSQ) in each cell and the influence of the treatments themselves, shown as MSQ Beta and Treatment Beta, respectively. Due to the experimental design, it was necessary to "force" the regression through the origin so as not to fall into the "dummy variable trap." Results show that in the case of all four cells, MSQ relates positively and significantly with each of the dependent variables. As perceptions of MSQ increase, customer satisfaction and perceptions of service quality increase.

DISCUSSION

The research presented here suggests that MSQ is a valid and measurable construct and that it may be important in a number of ways. First, a customer's assessment of MSQ appears to relate directly to customer satisfaction and perceptions of service quality. That is, customers evaluate cues, both direct (e.g., tangible evidence of supervisory control, employee WOM) and indirect (e.g., consistency of prior service quality, service recovery actions), as they determine their satisfaction and assess the quality of service. Whether MSQ evaluations influence how customers make attributions about service experiences and service outcomes is an area requiring further inquiry.

Also, MSQ addresses the issue of motivating employees through classic reward structures. Reward structures are typically thought of as intrinsic or extrinsic, and tangible or intangible, with the primary focus of management on tangible, extrinsic rewards. The construct of MSQ provides a sense of how employees evaluate the reward structures as internal customers. Moreover, it provides managers with a better sense of the long-term consequences of poor MSQ.

Finally, the empirical evidence presented here suggests that MSQ is a direct influence on customer perceptions of encounter satisfaction, overall satisfaction and service quality. These findings indicate a need for service firms to focus on *all* relationships depicted in Figure 1B, including the customer's view of the relationship between the firm and the service provider. Focusing on MSQ provides two benefits. When a customer views a positive level of MSQ, satisfaction (and, ultimately, patronage) is promoted. Second, when management increases the level of service quality provided to employees, the service provider's ability to serve the customer is improved. In other words, the customer is pleased with the service quality provided by management to the service providers, and this service quality enables the service providers to better serve the customer. The result is increased customer satisfaction and overall perceptions of service quality. Clearly, as the service industry becomes increasingly competitive, the role of management will become more visible and more critical to the customer.

LIMITATIONS

Despite its strong and consistent results, this study has a number of limitations. A common issue in empirical research is the limited generalizability of results when using a student sample. However, in this study, the population of interest is a population of customers. Each student in the sample has acted in the role of customer, a factor that should enhance generalizability. At the same time, two-thirds of the participants (66.8%) had worked in a retail setting at some time, a factor that could influence attitudes concerning contact personnel and/ or management. Because subjects were assigned randomly to treatment groups, this characteristic of the sample did not appear to influence the experiment's internal consistency.

Several authors have questioned the validity of role-playing research methods. Typically, they argue that role-playing behavior does not represent participants' true reactions to experimental situations. They suggest that the reactions result from participants' guesses as to how they would react in a given setting, participants' beliefs concerning certain courses of action and behavior demanded by the role-playing situation (Shamdasani and Sheth 1995). However, a primary advantage of scenarios as they were used in this study is that a set of highly controlled experimental manipulations enable inferences concerning causal relationships among a set of observed variables (K. Brown 1994).

It is also important to point out that this research was conducted in the context of service failure. While it seems reasonable that poor quality service may heighten customers' attention to cues used to evaluate MSQ, it is plausible that outstanding service quality may also have the same effect. Is it possible for a service firm to distinguish itself from its competitors on the basis of excellent MSQ? According to Berry, most service firms suffer from mediocrity in this area (1993). Firms with reputations for providing excellent MSQ may be able to attract the best service employees.

DIRECTIONS FOR FUTURE RESEARCH

Future research should include a comparison of various influences on encounter satisfaction, overall satisfaction and perceived quality, including MSQ and related constructs. Such a comparison would help determine the relative level of influence which MSQ and the other determinants have on these variables. In other words, if MSQ is only mildly influential given the effects of service provider behavior, then the retail strategy should focus on the service provider. However, if MSQ makes a significant contribution given other factors at work, then it should be included as a viable strategy.

Future research also may shed light on whether customers' propensity to assess MSQ may be increasing. As companies continue to "downsize" and grow "flatter," customers—who are also employees in other settings—should have more knowledge about how firms function and what management's role should be in the delivery of customer service. Indeed, such an awareness is a goal of managing for quality training programs, and an outgrowth of empowering employees.

If MSQ is an important determinant of customer satisfaction and perceptions of service in a wide variety of service settings, then a better measure of the construct is needed. Is MSQ, from the perspective of the customer, unidimensional? Or, it is possible that customers might distinguish among various aspects of MSQ (e.g., immediate supervision of contact employees, service recovery policies, layers of management), each of which could exert a somewhat different influence on customers?

The business literature suggests that MSQ is capable of influencing the consistency of customer service as well as the ability—and the willingness—of the service providers to recover in cases of service failure. So, in this regard, MSQ would have a direct effect on consistency and recovery and an indirect effect on customer satisfaction. Because consistency and recovery are demonstrated determinants of customer satisfaction, the link between MSQ and consistency/recovery is a valuable area of future research for marketers.

From one perspective, the relationship between MSQ and operational outcomes (e.g., zero defects, empowerment) has been a territory of the quality literature (e.g., Deming 1986). Recognition of MSQ's role in customer perceptions contributes to the blurring of traditional boundaries between functional areas of business (e.g., Grönroos 1990b). Customers' perceptions should become the direct concern of previously behind-the-scenes management and production specialists.

APPENDIX

Sample of Scenario Vignette

Imagine that you are the customer in the following service encounter:

You have gone to a large department store to purchase a gift for a friend. You are in a bit of a hurry, because you told your friend that you would be stopping by her house shortly with a gift. The department store is one that you have shopped in several times before. The service you have received in past visits has typically been good and you like the selection the store offers. This time, as you are browsing through the items, you notice three salespersons talking nearby. Although you have been looking for some time now, none of the salespeople has approached you to offer assistance.

A manager walks over to the group of salespeople. However, the manager does not seem to notice that, despite the presence of customers, the salespeople continue to chat with each other.

Having found a suitable gift, you are ready to be checked out. As you approach the sales counter, you notice that the group of employees has walked away. Spying another salesperson nearby, you ask if she can ring up your merchandise. She says that will be fine, but could you please bring the merchandise to her counter. As the salesperson is bagging the gift, she says, "I am sorry that you had to wait for assistance; management hasn't done a good job of training new staff lately. Could I gift wrap your gift at no charge to thank you for your patience?"

Your present problem can be summarized in the following manner.

You have gone to a store for a gift. You have been to the store before and have been consistently pleased. You receive no assistance from the salespeople and have to wait despite the fact that a manager was aware of your presence. The sales associate who does help you tells you that management has been doing a poor job of training new staff. The sales associate also tries to make your experience better by offering to gift wrap your item at no charge to you.

REFERENCES

Aspery, J. (1993), "Planning for the Inevitable," *Management Services*, 37 (2), 16-17.
Bateson, J. (1992), "Perceived Control and the Service Encounter," in *Managing Services Marketing*, J. Bateson, ed. Fort Worth, TX: Dryden Press, 123-132.

Bell, M.L. (1981), "Tactical Service Marketing and the Process of Remixing," in *Marketing of Services*, J.H. Donnelly and W.R. George, eds. Chicago, IL: American Marketing Association, 163-167.

Berry, L. (1981), "The Employee as Customer," *Journal of Retail Banking*, III (1), 33-40.

_____ (1993), "Improving America's Service," *Marketing Management*, 1 (3), 28-38.

_____ (1995), *On Great Service: A Framework for Action*. New York: The Free Press.

_____ and A. Parasuraman (1991), *Marketing Services: Competing Through Quality*. New York: The Free Press.

Bitner, M.J. (1990), "Evaluating Service Encounters: The Effects of Physical Surroundings and Employee Responses," *Journal of Marketing*, 54, 69-82.

_____ (1992), "Servicescapes," *Journal of Marketing*, 56, 57-71.

_____, B. Booms and L. Mohr (1994), "Critical Service Encounters: The Employee's Viewpoint," *Journal of Marketing*, 58, 95-106.

_____, _____ and M.S. Tetreault (1990), "The Service Encounter: Diagnosing Favorable and Unfavorable Incidents," *Journal of Marketing*, 54, 71-84.

_____ and A.R. Hubbert (1994), "Encounter Satisfaction Versus Overall Satisfaction Versus Quality: The Customer's Voice," in *Service Quality: New Directions in Theory and Practice*, R. Rust and R. Oliver, eds. Thousand Oaks, CA: Sage, 72-94.

Brown, J.J. and P. Reingen (1987), "Social Ties and Word-of-Mouth Referral Behavior," *Journal of Consumer Research*, 14 (December), 350-362.

Brown, K. (1994), "Using Role Play to Integrate Ethics into the Business Curriculum: A Financial Management Example," *Journal of Business Ethics*, 13 (2), 105-110.

Brown, S.W. (1994), "Service Recovery: New Strategies For What To Do When Things Go Wrong," paper presented at the *Frontiers in Services Marketing Conference*, Nashville, TN: Vanderbilt University (October).

_____, D. Cowles and T. Tuten (1996), "Service Recovery in Retail Settings: Its Value and Limitations," *International Journal of Service Industry Management*, 7 (5), 32-46.

_____ and T. Swartz (1989), "A Gap Analysis of Professional Service Quality," *Journal of Marketing*, 53, 92-98.

Carlzon, J. (1987), *Moments of Truth*. New York: Harper & Row.

Clow, K. (1993), "Antecedents of Consumer Expectations of Service," in *Southern Marketing Association Proceedings*, T.K. Massey, Jr., ed. Atlanta, GA: Southern Marketing Association, 205-209.

Cowles, C.W. (1994), "A Conceptual Model of Management Service Quality as a Determinant of Customer Perceptions of Service Quality," Ph.D. dissertation, Richmond, VA: Virginia Commonwealth University.

Cowles, D.L. (1994), "Prostitution as a Metaphor for Customer Service," paper presented at the *Frontiers in Services Marketing Conference*, Nashville, TN: Vanderbilt University (October).

_____ (1995), "Parasocial Relationship Theory in Transaction Marketing Settings: Exploratory Research Findings," *Proceedings of the Seventh Bi-Annual World Marketing Congress*. Melbourne, Australia: Academy of Science/Monash University, Vol. VII-I (July), 1-23.

Crosby, L., K.R. Evans and D. Cowles (1990), "Relationship Quality in Service Selling: An Interpersonal Influence Perspective," *Journal of Marketing*, 54, 68-81.

_____ and N. Stephens (1987), "Effects of Relationship Marketing on Satisfaction, Retention, and Prices in the Life Insurance Industry," *Journal of Marketing Research*, 24 (November), 404-411.

Davis, D.L., J.G. Guiltinan and W.H. Jones (1979), "Service Characteristics, Consumer Research and the Classification of Retail Services," *Journal of Retailing*, 55 (Fall), 3-21.

Dean, J.W. and D. Bowen (1994), "Management Theory and Total Quality: Improving Research and Practice Through Theory Development," *Academy of Management Review*, 19 (3), 392-413.

Deming, W.E. (1986), *Out of the Crisis*. Cambridge, MA: Massachusetts Institute of Technology, Center for Advanced Engineering Study.

Folkes, V. (1988),"Recent Attribution Research in Consumer Behavior: A Review and New Directions," *Journal of Consumer Research*, 14 (March), 548-565.

_____ (1994), "How Consumers Predict Service Quality: What Do They Expect?" in *Service Quality: New Directions in Theory and Practice*, R. Rust and R. Oliver, eds. Thousand Oaks, CA: Sage, 108-122.

George, W.R. and L.L. Berry (1981), "Guidelines for the Advertising of Services," *Business Horizons*, 24 (May-June), 52-56.

Grönroos, C. (1990a), *Services Management and Marketing: Managing the Moments of Truth in Service Competition*. Lexington, MA: Lexington Books.

_____ (1990b), "Relationship Approach to Marketing in Service Contexts: The Marketing and Organizational Behavior Interface," *Journal of Business Research*, 20 (1), 3-11.

Hill, D.J., R. Baer and R. Kostenko (1992), "Organizational Characteristics and Employee Excuse Making: Passing the Buck for Failed Service Encounters," in *Advances in Consumer Research*, Vol. 19, J.F. Sherry and B. Sternthall, eds. Urbana, IL: Association for Consumer Research, 673-678.

Holbrook, M.B. (1994), "The Nature of Customer Value: An Axiology of Services in the Consumption Experience," in *Service Quality: New Directions in Theory and Practice*, R. Rust and R. Oliver, eds. Thousand Oaks, CA: Sage, 21-71.

Johnston, R. (1996), "Achieving Focus in Service Organizations," *The Service Industries Journal*, 6 (5), 53-71.

Juran, J.M. (1989), *Juran on Leadership for Quality*. New York: Free Press.

Kerlinger, F. (1986), *Foundations of Behavioral Research*. Fort Worth, TX: Holt, Rinehart, and Winston.

Parasuraman, A., V. Zeithaml and L. Berry (1985), "A Conceptual Model of Service Quality and its Implications for Further Research," *Journal of Marketing*, 49 (Fall), 41-50.

_____, _____ and _____ (1988), "SERVQUAL: A Multiple Item Scale for Measuring Consumer Perceptions of Service Quality," *Journal of Retailing*, 64 (1), 12-40.

Rogers, J.D., K.E. Clow and T.J. Kash (1994), "Increasing Job Satisfaction of Service Personnel," *Journal of Services Marketing*, 8 (1), 14-26.

Schneider, B. (1980), "The Service Organization: Climate is Crucial," *Organizational Dynamics*, 9 (Autumn), 52-65.

Shamdasani, P. and J. Sheth (1995), "An Experimental Approach to Investigating Satisfaction and Continuity in Marketing Alliances," *European Journal of Marketing*, 29 (4), 6-23.

Shostack, L. (1977), "Breaking Free from Product Marketing," *Journal of Marketing*, 41, 73-80.

Smith, N.C. and J.A. Quelch (1993), *Ethics in Marketing*. Homewood, IL: Irwin.

Weiner, B. (1992), "Excuses in Everyday Interaction," in *Explaining Oneself to Others: Reason-giving in a Social Context*, M. McLaughlin, M.J. Cody and S.J. Read, eds. Hillsdale, NJ: Lawrence-Erlbaum, 131-146.

Zeithaml, V., L. Berry and A. Parasuraman (1988), "Communication and Control Processes in the Delivery of Service Quality," *Journal of Marketing*, 52, 35-48.

_____ and M.J. Bitner (1996), *Services Marketing*. New York: The McGraw-Hill Companies.

OPERATIONALISING THE QUALITY OF INTERNAL SUPPORT OPERATIONS IN SERVICE ORGANISATIONS

Javier Reynoso and Brian Moores

ABSTRACT

In the service sector literature, both marketers and organisational behaviorists emphasise the importance of the internal dynamics of the organisation in terms of a network of customers and suppliers interacting together to satisfy customers. Although the relevance of internal customers within the context of the service delivery process is frequently referred to in that literature, there is in fact a somewhat surprising paucity of published research on the topic. The research project reported here was aimed firstly at identifying and measuring those factors which determine how internal customers perceive the quality of the support they receive from other parts of the organisation. The second objective was to identify the organisational factors which enable support units to deliver the quality of service expected by internal customers. It is felt that this research project has contributed to the existing work on organisational processes related to service quality. It has confirmed that, along with customers, employees are able and prepared to produce scaled assessments of the service they themselves receive

Advances in Services Marketing and Management, Volume 6, pages 147-170.
Copyright © 1997 by JAI Press Inc.
All rights of reproduction in any form reserved.
ISBN: 0-7623-0176-7

from other parts of the organisation. Results indicate that these can be captured as a limited number of perceptual dimensions. The research also contributes to the identification of organisational determinants of internal service quality. The results show sets of variables at different levels of analysis, which were felt to be facilitating or inhibiting factors in the delivery of support services to other units. All in all, this work has contributed to a better understanding of the dynamics involved in the customer service delivery process using an internal service approach.

THE IMPORTANCE OF INTERNAL SUPPORT OPERATIONS

Internal Customers and Internal Dynamics

The concept of the internal customer in services evolved originally through the idea of selling jobs in the service sector with the purpose of making the job more attractive for the employee (Sasser and Arbeit 1976). This idea has been addressed subsequently in wider terms as internal marketing by a number of authors (e.g., Berry 1981; Grönroos 1990; Gummesson 1990). Their belief is that if management wants its employees to deliver an outstanding level of service to customers, then it must be prepared to do a great job with its employees. Of particular relevance in this regard is the contribution to the debate by Stershic, who claims the following:

> As obvious as it may seem to recognise employees as the critical link in delivering service quality and customer satisfaction, rarely are they the focus of such research. Obtaining and understanding the employee perspective is a critical tool in managing customer satisfaction (1990, p. 45).

Researchers in organisational behaviour have confirmed the importance of the internal marketing concept introduced by marketers. In this respect, some scholars have provided data on the ways in which staff and organisational issues are reflected in customer satisfaction and behaviour (Parkington and Schneider 1979; Schneider and Bowen 1985; Schneider, Parkington and Buxton 1980). These various papers have demonstrated that staff and customer perceptions, attitudes and intentions share a common basis and are related to each other.

Service organisations can be described as open systems with highly permeable boundaries in which the perception of organisational practices is visible both to employees and customers. In their definitive contribution to "internal service climate," Schneider and Bowen (1985) found that when employees describe the human resource practices of a company as being service-oriented, customers also hold favorable views of the quality of service they receive. This suggests that a service-oriented organisation should treat frontline employees as "partial customers," that is, as individuals deserving the same treatment that management wants the customers to receive (Bowen and Schneider 1988).

Based on these findings, these same authors suggest that this idea of treating the employee as a customer could also be considered in the internal dynamics of the organisation. In their 1985 paper, Schneider and Bowen argue that it is important to realise that organisational members not only serve external customers but also have internal customers. In other words, in any organisation, staff are both receivers and providers of some services. This particular piece of research, which constituted the first major validation of the relationship between employee attitudes and customer satisfaction, marks the beginning of internal customer research.

Common concerns are emerging from organisational behaviour and marketing researchers regarding the organisational dynamics surrounding the production and consumption of services. Bowen (1990), for example, identifies those issues where the literature of both academic fields converge in their thinking and points to aspects of service operations demanding of interdisciplinary research. One of the issues he addresses is the need for additional research on the aforementioned relationship between employee behaviour and customer satisfaction. He claims that this prospect offers a natural intersection of interests in organisational behaviour and marketing.

In the service sector today, both marketers and organisational behaviourists emphasise the importance of the internal dynamics of the organisation in terms of a network of customers and suppliers interacting together to satisfy customers.

Internal Operations in the Service Delivery Process

In attempting to provide an integrated discussion of the service production and delivery process, Gummesson (1993) presents what he labels a multi-perspective approach. This consists of four service models each associated with four groups of actors—namely, customers, contact staff, support staff and management. He argues that all these perspectives, along with that of the owners, need to be taken into account before one can claim to possess a comprehensive appreciation of the service delivery process. All five groups hold different perspectives, each of which is relevant to the whole service experience. Although the relevance of internal customers within the context of the service delivery process is frequently referred to in the literature by marketers and organisational behaviourists, there is something of a paucity of published research relating to the support staff's perspective. Some service researchers, for instance, have emphasised the complexity of improving the effectiveness and efficiency of internal service delivery (e.g., Davis 1993). Davis (1993) provides an overview of some of the main issues related to internal services including typical dysfunctions, and suggests general guidelines to improve them. Particularly, Davis claims that there is an increasing need among organisations to make internal service departments more accountable and cost-effective. The author argues that research is required to develop measures of internal service effectiveness. The research on bank employees by Lewis and Entwistle (1990) is a valuable contribution, as are those of Gremler, Bitner and Evans (1994) and Vandermerwe and Gilbert (1991, 1989) which are referred to later.

Internal Support Activities and Customer Satisfaction

A number of writers have addressed the importance of the internal support activities and operations as the key link to external customer satisfaction (e.g., Adamson 1988; Davis 1991; Heskett et al. 1994; Jablonski 1992; Milite 1991; Sanfilippo 1990). In this same vein, the quality of internal service operations has been identified as one of the essential elements of an overall service quality strategy (e.g., Feldman 1991; Nagel and Cilliers 1990) yielding to long-term cost savings and increasing financial gains (e.g., Davis 1991; Rowen 1992). It has also been associated with the quality culture of organisations (e.g., Albert 1989; McDermott and Emerson 1991).

In further pursuit of these arguments, some scholars have contributed to the establishment of a theoretical framework within which the internal customer concept could be explored and debated. This concept has been addressed in the light of the internal processes involved throughout the service production system. Shostack (1992, 1987, 1984), for example, considers service as a system formed by interdependent and interactive systems. Similarly, Grönroos (1990) describes the service production process as a network of systems built up by interrelations and interdependence among a number of subprocesses. He argues that every service operation comprises internal service functions which support one another and that if poor internal service exists, the final service to the customer will be damaged. George (1990) also supports this proposition, claiming that a large number of support persons who do not come into contact with customers do themselves nonetheless indirectly influence the service ultimately provided to customers. He argues that these supporting personnel should recognise the contact employees as their internal customers.

Research on service quality has demonstrated the aforementioned importance of the internal customer-supplier relationship in relation to the achievement of customer expectations. The findings from an extensive research project conducted in different service companies by the research team of Parasuraman, Zeithaml and Berry (Parasuraman, Zeithaml and Berry 1985; Zeithaml, Berry and Parasuraman 1988; Zeithaml, Parasuraman and Berry 1990) have revealed that internal customer-supplier relationships play a particularly important role in the discrepancy or gap which can and does exist between service quality specifications and the actual service delivered when employees are unable or unwilling to perform the service at the specified level. The authors found that one of the key factors that contributes to this discrepancy is a lack of teamwork.

Towards an Internal Service Strategy

Another set of writers claim that to be aware of the existence of internal customers is not, of itself, sufficient. They argue that it is necessary to determine internal customers' needs and expectations (e.g., Chung 1993; Koska 1992; Ludeman 1992; Plymire 1990). Other contributors have gone beyond this initial proposition and have focused on planning the implementation process for an internal customer strategy throughout the organisation (e.g., Cirasuolo and Scheuing 1991; Davis 1991; Vandermerwe and Gilbert 1991, 1989). Although the approaches differ slightly, some common sequential steps can be identified. These are the following:

- The creation of internal awareness;
- The identification of internal customers and suppliers;
- The identification of the expectations of internal customers;
- The communication of these expectations to internal suppliers in order to discuss their own capabilities and/or obstacles to meeting these requirements;
- As a result of this previous point, internal suppliers should work to make the necessary changes so as to be able to deliver the level of service required and, finally,
- Obtain a measure for internal customer satisfaction. Feedback should be given to internal suppliers if services are to be improved.

One of the areas that is attracting particular attention within such a framework is that of measuring the quality of the internal service being provided in terms of needs and expectations (e.g., Davis 1992; Garrett and Turman 1992; Thornberry and Hennessey 1992), satisfaction (Gulledge 1991) and internal service performance being measured against service standards documented in internal contracts (Koehler 1992).

Service Quality Dimensions

External Service Dimensions

Various researchers have contributed to the identification of service quality dimensions which could be used to operationalise this concept. What are the criteria used by customers in assessing the quality of the service they receive?

Attempts to answer this question in different settings studied from different perspectives have, perhaps not surprisingly, produced various sets of quality dimensions which are useful in measuring external service quality. Perhaps the most publicised is that proposed by Parasuraman, Zeithaml and Berry, who originally identified 10 criteria from research with customers in different types of services (Parasuraman, Zeithaml and Berry 1985, 1988; Zeithaml, Berry and Parasuraman 1988; Zeithaml, Parasuraman and Berry 1990). They subsequently consolidated seven of the 10 original dimensions into two broader categories resulting in five general criteria. It should be pointed out that a number of writers, including, for example, Vandamme and Leunis (1993) and Babakus and Boller (1992), have criticised the SERVQUAL approach mainly on the grounds of the transferability of these generic criteria across sectors. Other observers have argued, with some justification, that the scores secured from the Expectation element of their twin-scale approach is illusory insofar as "excellent" would appear to be a logical response to a prompt as to what is expected from a service experience (see, e.g., Carman 1990). Other authors have also identified quality dimensions (e.g., Baker 1987; Garvin 1987; Norman 1988). In a first attempt to summarise research contributions on this topic, Gummesson (1992) provides a comparison of general quality dimensions as well as examples of specific criteria for a number of service activities.

Internal Service Dimensions

Just as the quality as perceived by customers can be captured in the form of sets of dimensions or criteria, so too is it felt that the quality of internal services that units receive from those departments which support their activities could be meaningfully categorised. That being the case, then the ensuing groupings could be referred to as internal service quality dimensions, recognising that in some circumstances there might still exist a need to identify and measure the type of harder criteria commonly featured in internal service level agreements.

Unfortunately, in spite of the prevalence of articles which refer to the importance of identifying such internal service dimensions, only the papers by Vandermerwe and Gilbert (1991, 1989) and the more recent one by Gremler, Bitner and Evans (1994) could be considered as being methodologically useful. Some see the measurement of the quality of internal services as being conceptually no more complex than adopting or adapting the existing findings from customer-based research. Zeithaml, Parasuraman and Berry (1990, p. 180), for example, claim that "SERVQUAL, with appropriate adaptation, can be used by departments and divisions within a company to ascertain the quality of service they provide to employees in other departments and divisions." This simplistic proposition has obvious appeal but, in reality, research is called for before such a sweeping generalisation can be justified. If there is a justified concern about the transferability of the SERVQUAL criteria across sectors, then there is every reason to believe that this same reservation would hold when one focuses on internal as distinct from external customers. In this vein, Davis (1993, p. 319) claims that "more research like that of Vandermerwe and Gilbert (1991), which compares internal and external provision of services and investigates ways of closing the gap between user needs and provider delivery, is particularly desirable." The results reported here will be seen to support this proposition.

Organisational Determinants of Internal Service Quality

While a reasonable amount of work has been conducted into the identification and measurement of service quality dimensions, there have been very few contributions related to those organisational factors which actually determine the quality of service delivered to customers. Gummesson claims:

> Quality dimensions are of importance to customers and consequently also to the service provider. In the latter sense they also become internal dimensions. Other quality dimensions are usually not of particular interest to customers; they are part of the internal quality management of the organisation, how quality is achieved (1992, p. 201).

These so-called "internal dimensions" refer to the organisational determinants of service quality. Those are the organisational variables that internally influence the ability of service organisations to satisfy customers' expectations.

In continuing their research project based on the gaps model of service quality, the Parasuraman, Zeithaml and Berry team has presented a collection of organisational variables which constitute its extended model of service quality (Zeithaml, Berry and Parasuraman 1988; Zeithaml, Parasuraman and Berry 1990). The model contains a set of constructs which potentially affect the magnitude and direction of each of the four service quality gaps.

In pursuing this issue further, the team conducted an exercise to empirically test the extent to which those organisational factors influence the quality of service as perceived by customers (Parasuraman, Berry and Zeithaml 1991). The authors tested five propositions, the first four pertaining to antecedents of the service-provider gaps illustrated in the extended model, namely, Marketing Information (Gap 1), Standards (Gap 2), Service Performance (Gap 3) and Communication (Gap 4). They examined the relationship between the size of each of these gaps and the corresponding set of their hypothesised constructs. The fifth proposition examined the positive relationship between the size of these four gaps and the size of the Service Quality gap (Gap 5). The authors found only partial support for the propositions tested in the study.

Being the first attempt of its kind, it seems that the most important contribution of the study is the fact that it raises crucial issues for future research. The team claims that the measurement procedures and sampling methodologies employed were subject to design limitations.

Similar to the issue of service quality perceived by customers, there are a few pieces of research which have attempted to provide initial evidence about those organisational factors which may influence the quality of internal support services.

Mohr-Jackson (1991), for example, attempts to broaden the marketing orientation with an added focus on internal customers. The author presents the results of a phenomenological assessment of the characteristics of the marketing concept and the employee activities that influence its implementation. From an analysis of 54 in-depth interviews conducted in 50 organisations, Mohr-Jackson identifies variables such as education and training, involvement and contribution, and empowerment and reward structures as being associated with the ability to meet internal customers' needs.

Clearly, the variables identified by the author refer only to the organisational level of analysis. As a consequence, they provide only a partial view of those factors involved in the internal service perspective. This is not, perhaps, all that surprising given that the interviews were conducted only with corporate executives.

Pfau, Detzel and Geller (1991) report on a pilot study conducted by The Hay Group aimed at the identification of specific organisational factors that contribute to high internal customer satisfaction. They surveyed the internal customers of 50 corporate and 25 purchasing departments of industrial, financial and service companies. In this way, they were able to identify units rated high and low in internal service. As the survey also included the staff of the supplier departments, the authors present those organisational characteristics that typified both high- and low-rated units on internal service quality. In a discussion of the implications of these results, the writers highlight a number of areas that, in their opinion, seem critical to internal service quality. They go on to suggest a number of steps to shape the process required to successfully drive internal customer satisfaction.

In summary, in order to improve the quality of internal support services, not only do organisations need to know who their internal customers are and to understand their needs, but changes within the organisation also have to be implemented if internal services are to be improved. The development and maintenance of an organisation's service-oriented culture will result from its strategy, structure, processes and employees. Results such as those reported by Pfau and his team are useful in identifying those organisational determinants related to internal service.

OPERATIONALISING INTERNAL SUPPORT OPERATIONS

In relation to the successful delivery of internal services in organisations, researchers have emphasised the value of departmental expectations as part of the process required to successfully drive internal customer satisfaction (Davis 1992, 1991; Mohr-Jackson 1991; Pfau, Detzel and Geller 1991; Vandermerwe and Gilbert 1991, 1989). In this view, it is important to observe that only a few contributions have provided any empirical evidence about such internal customer expectations, and even fewer results exist on the organisational determinants which influence the successful or unsuccessful delivery of those departmental needs.

Furthermore, despite the strong and direct link identified by a number of authors (e.g., Parasuraman, Berry and Zeithaml 1990; Schneider and Bowen 1985), the relationship between the quality of the internal service staff receive and the quality of service they provide to their own customers remains little researched. Therefore, the research project reported here was aimed at the following:

- Identifying and measuring those factors which determine how internal customers perceive the quality of the support they receive from other parts of the organisation; and
- Identifying those organisational factors which enable support units to deliver the quality of service expected by internal customers.

The research described here is based on previous studies reported elsewhere (Moores and Reynoso 1993; Reynoso 1993). The main part of the studies involved British hospitals, including one in the private sector. Exploratory case studies had been conducted to secure a basic knowledge and understanding of interdepartmental relationships from a service perspective. Results indicated that, in the internal dynamics of the organisation, departments do harbor expectations about different units that support their activities. It was possible to identify 10 initial conceptual criteria underlying these departmental expectations, namely, reliability, responsiveness, competence, communication, understanding, courtesy, credibility, access, tangibles and confidentiality. In addition, the analysis of factors that either facilitate and or inhibit the meeting of such departmental expectations revealed a whole range of components involved in the internal network of services. It seemed that a number of factors regarding the individual, the group, the inter-group, the organisation and the environment could be driving or inhibiting the service delivery process.

Design and Development of Questionnaires

Those previous studies, which had been essentially qualitative, provided an initial framework of the internal dynamics involved in the service delivery process in the organisation. In particular, the internal customer-supplier chain seemed to be an appropriate vehicle for connecting both the external and the internal environments of the organisation with customer service. Valuable evidence was obtained about the relation between customer service and the internal network of services required to support it. In this respect, it is also essential to couple qualitative and quantitative service quality research (Parasuraman, Berry and Zeithaml 1990). Empirical studies are also needed for operationalising that relationship. A contribution in these terms demands an interdisciplinary effort which incorporates both the marketing and organisational issues involved. This paper turns next to the quantitative research which was conducted to refine, validate and test the results that had been obtained previously. Results obtained from those exploratory studies shaped the design of two separate instruments: an internal customers' questionnaire and an internal suppliers' questionnaire.

Internal Customers' Questionnaire

This questionnaire refers to the perceptions that units have about the internal services they receive from other units within the hospital. Thus, internal service quality is considered a construct of a perceptual, evaluative nature. One distinctive characteristic is that the performance of the supplier unit is assessed by the staff in other units using an internal service perspective. This construct is conceptualised as a multidimensional notion using the 10 perceived internal service quality dimensions previously obtained. A total of 49 statements representing these 10 dimensions were included in the initial version of the internal customers' questionnaire.

Items were developed in order to measure how organisational units perceive the quality of the support they receive from other units. Statements were included for each of the 10 main themes obtained from exploratory studies. Based on the concerns that researchers have expressed about measuring customers' expectations and perceptions in two separate lists (e.g., Babakus and Boller 1992; Carman 1990; Vandamme and Leunis 1993), the scale was designed incorporating both parts in its wording. In the original version of the questionnaire, each item was measured on a six-point scale ranging from "falls far short of my expectations" to "exceeds my expectations."

Internal Suppliers' Questionnaire

This questionnaire was also designed based upon the results obtained previously. This relates to those organisational factors which are felt to impact upon a support unit's ability to deliver the quality of service expected by internal customer units. The instrument was designed in four sections, bearing in mind that the factors identified before were representing different levels of analysis, namely, the individual, the group, the inter-group, the organisation and the environment. Accordingly, the four sections were designed to obtain data about individual members (member data), supplier units (member and relational data), relationships between customer and supplier units (relational data) and the hospital as a whole and its ambiance (global data).

For each of the constructs included in the questionnaire, items representing operating variables were identified from various sources—first, from existing organisational measures (particular reference should be made to Gladstein 1984; Mowday, Steers and Porter 1979; Price and Mueller 1986; Rizzo, House and Lirtzman 1970; Van de Ven and Ferry 1980), and second, from organisational studies of service quality (Parasuraman, Berry and Zeithaml 1991; Schneider and Bowen 1985). Third, a set of other items were generated to produce an integrated instrument for measuring those factors which influence the ability of departments to support other units to undertake their work. Items from previous instruments were not simply imported into the questionnaire. Each item was given an internal service orientation, but at the same time, care was taken to preserve the core meaning. During this process, several versions were produced and modified in light of feedback provided by a range of colleagues.

Both these questionnaires were tested in two separate pilot studies. First, the internal suppliers' questionnaire was locally administered in one large teaching trust hospital using structured interviews with staff from a variety of support departments. As a result, the instrument underwent modification. Second, both questionnaires were remotely tested in another large district hospital. Each of the two questionnaires was completed by a sample of work units selected as internal customers and suppliers, respectively. A refined version of each of the two instruments was produced prior to their empirical test and important methodological and logistical issues were identified as a result of this second pilot experiment.

Empirical Test of the Questionnaires

The revised versions of both questionnaires were empirically tested in a large National Health Service (NHS) teaching hospital and the original private institution.

The internal customers' questionnaire consisted of 45 items relating to the 10 internal service dimensions which had emerged from the qualitative stage, one item that asked internal customers to provide an overall satisfaction rating of each of the 10 support units involved and other summary items. All the items were worded positively and each of them was to be answered using an integrated six-point scale ranging from "completely fails to meet our expectations" to "exceeds our expectations." The overall satisfaction item was answered on a five-point scale ("very dissatisfied/satisfied"), and for the summary items, a five-point scale ("strongly disagree/agree") was adopted.

Each item was answered in relation to each of the selected support units. The names of the units were listed on top of each of the five pages of the questionnaire indicating, whenever necessary, the specific part of the unit or service involved in the assessment (i.e., catering only for patients, admissions in medical records).

As for the support staff completing the internal suppliers questionnaire, instructions were given in relation to each of the four sections. In part A, the correct identification of the internal supplier unit by all members of different groups was emphasised. As questions in section B concerned the dyad relationship, the frame of reference of respondents had to be a specific department; otherwise, the unit of analysis would have been only the group as in the previous section. Thus, individual customer units were listed at the beginning of this section in each questionnaire. In sections C and D, staff were reminded that the questions were focused on various organisational and personal issues respectively. A shortened version of the questionnaire was used with the senior management team of each hospital.

At the NHS hospital, nine wards were selected as a sample of internal customers. These represented a diversity of clinical areas such as Trauma and Orthopedics, General Surgery, Ear Nose and Throat, Dermatology, General Medicine and Gynecology. Ten support units were identified as the sample of internal suppliers (e.g., x-ray, pathology, porters, catering, pharmacy, medical records, hematology). Interviews with each of the nursing managers responsible for the selected wards confirmed the assumed relationship between each ward and those 10 support units. The correct match between each internal customer-supplier relationship was, of course, essential if appropriate responses from nursing staff were to be obtained. For each ward, all members of staff were scheduled into one of 84 designated one-hour sessions extending over a three-week period. In the same way, for each support unit a heterogeneous minimum sample of half of the staff was selected. Whenever possible, all members of the staff were included in the sample. The objective was to obtain a sample of people representing the different activities involved during the delivery of the service considered for each internal supplier unit. At each session, respondents were provided with an overview of the research and a brief explanation as to what was required of them. Any questions were raised and answered at the beginning of each session, after which the respondents completed the questionnaires. In the case of the wards, a total of 176 persons were scheduled, producing a 94 percent response rate. A total of 296 members of support staff were involved in the survey, resulting in a response rate of 92 percent.

In the case of the private hospital, seven wards were selected for the survey. These represented a variety of clinical areas covering Cardiology, General

Medicine, Ear Nose and Throat, Intensive Care, Gynecology, Urology, Orthopedics, Pediatrics and Ophthalmology. Ten support units were identified and included in the sample of internal suppliers. The selected units were functionally equivalent to those included in the public hospital. Both questionnaires were distributed either to the senior sister in each ward or to the manager in each department. All nursing and clerical staff were included in the sample. They totaled 144 and the response rate was 41 percent. In the same way, all support staff from each department were involved in the survey. The total sample consisted of 255 persons and the overall rate response was 31 percent. Responses were lower than those obtained in the NHS facility, primarily on account of the fact that, in this case, the survey was conducted remotely. Both types of questionnaires were returned directly by respondents using a self-addressed envelope over a period of three weeks.

Perceived Quality of Internal Support Operations

Dimensionality

Responses obtained with the internal customers' questionnaire from both hospitals were analysed using pooled data (i.e., for each item, raw data about all 10 support units were considered together). This procedure was deliberate because the basic objective at this stage was to determine whether or not internal service dimensions which would be meaningful in assessing the quality of a variety of internal services in hospitals could be identified.

From the qualitative studies referred to earlier, it will be recalled that 10 conceptual dimensions had been identified and labeled using content analysis. Thus, the 45-item scale was factor-analysed using principal component analysis constrained to 10 factors. An initial factor pattern emerged using Varimax orthogonal rotation for the 10-factor solution. However, many items exhibited high loadings on more than one factor. This was not completely unexpected due to the dependent nature of the hypothesised dimensions which had become apparent during the qualitative stage. The 10-factor solution was therefore subjected to oblique rotation using the Oblimin procedure in SPSS-Windows 6.0 to facilitate interpretation of the factors. A purification process followed as it was crucial to obtain clear, distinctive factors, both in the statistical and in the intuitive sense. Thus, items were relocated or excluded from the content of the factors initially obtained. They included those items with loading lower than 0.30, those with low face validity and those with loading greater than 0.30 in more than one factor which did not make any sense in the solution. Eventually, it was felt that a nine-factor solution comprising 32 items provided the best interpretation of the data.

Only two of the 10 hypothesised dimensions did not appear in the obtained solution, these being courtesy and access. Items related to these two constructs

Table 1.   Internal Customers' Questionnaire: Summary of Results

Service Dimensions and Items	Cronbach's Alpha Coefficient		
	Public	Private	Total
Helpfulness Helpfulness of unit when we need it Willingness of unit to cooperate with us	0.93	0.88	0.92
Timeliness Ability of unit to deliver service within certain time Ability of unit to deliver service at required frequency Speed of unit in responding to our service requests Ability of unit to deal with patients promptly	0.89	0.88	0.89
Communication Unit consults with us on those decisions which impact our activities The feedback we get from this unit Unit keeps us informed about progress, problems or changes Willingness of unit to ask us for support Unit keeps patients informed Willingness of unit to listen to us	0.94	0.94	0.94
Tangibles Condition and appearance of facilities and equipment of unit Condition and appearance of materials and products provided by unit Condition and appearance of written information provided by unit	0.87	0.83	0.86
Reliability Ability of unit to provide necessary information Ability of unit to provide accurate information Ability of unit to provide actual service required Ability of unit to provide service right the first time Exent to which unit tries to sort problems out	0.91	0.87	0.90
Professionalism Skills unit members appear to possess to perform service Experience unit members appear to possess to perform service Knowledge unit members appear to possess to perform service The advice unit provides us with	0.92	0.92	0.92
Confidentiality Unit's handling of confidential information The discretion unit displays in dealing with delicate situations	0.83	0.83	0.83
Preparedness Suitability of resources in unit to perform the service The way unit is organised so as to be able to perform the service	0.84	0.76	0.82

(continued)

Table 1   (Continued)

Service Dimensions and Items	Cronbach's Alpha Coefficient		
	Public	Private	Total
Consideration	0.90	0.88	0.89
Trust unit appears to have in us			
Extent to which unit appears to value our ward's contribution			
Understanding unit has of our needs, problems and constraints			
Extent to which we can rely on unit's honesty			
Total scale reliability	0.98	0.97	0.98
Percent of variance explained	80.9	79.5	80.4

were confused with other factors. The other eight original criteria were in some way present in the content of nine factors obtained. Communication, Confidentiality and Tangibles remained unaltered in their core structure, resulting in the same three dimensions. The content of the original reliability, responsiveness and competence dimensions was regrouped, resulting in five modified dimensions, namely, Helpfulness, Timeliness, Reliability, Professionalism and Preparedness. Finally, the two criteria hypothesised as understanding and credibility were merged into one modified service dimension labeled as Consideration. A summary of the nine internal service dimensions obtained along with their associated items is presented in Table 1.

Reliability and Validity of the Scale

Content validity.   The reliability for each of the nine dimensions was high. As can be seen from Table 1, Cronbach's Alpha coefficients using the total sample ranged from 0.83 to 0.94, and the total-scale reliability obtained was 0.98. These results indicate good internal consistency among items within each dimension. The percentage of variance extracted by the nine factors was 80.4 percent. Reliabilities were also high for the subsamples of both the NHS and private hospital. Table 1 shows alpha scores, total-scale reliability and percentage of variance explained for the two independent samples. These results provide further evidence about the content validity of the dimensions.

Discriminant validity.   Factor analyses of the data obtained at each of the two hospitals were conducted to ascertain the extent to which the factor structure obtained with pooled data was consistent using data from each of the two independent sub-samples. Consistency of the factor structures secured separately from the two hospitals would provide further evidence about the discriminant validity of the identified dimensions. Thus, the 32 items included in the general solution were factor-analysed using oblique rotation. All in all, the nine-factor solution requested was almost identical in both the two hospitals. Data from the NHS hospital produced exactly the same nine factors originally obtained from the pooled analysis. Very few items exhibited loading above 0.30 in more than one factor.

In the case of the private unit, eight of the nine service dimensions emerged, again with few items loading on more than one factor. The two items referring to confidentiality were confused with those of empathy. A possible explanation for this could be the fact that confidentiality in the private hospital was more likely to be associated with patient matters and not with departmental activities, as the hospital operates an open-door policy.

Convergent validity. The explanatory power of the scale was also assessed. To do so, the association between internal service dimensions scores and responses to the question concerned with overall internal service satisfaction was evaluated. This question contained five ascending categories, ranging from very dissatisfied to very satisfied. The correspondence between the overall satisfaction score and the internal service dimensions measures was analysed using one-way ANOVA. For each of the two hospitals, separate tests were conducted for each of the nine dimensions and for the combined score (average) of them named ISQ to identify significant differences across the five levels of satisfaction. With only two exceptions, values for each service dimension and for the combined ISQ score were significantly different at the 5 percent level across different categories of internal service satisfaction. These results obtained separately from both hospitals indicate a clear relationship between each of the service dimensions values and internal service satisfaction categories. This evidence suggests good validity of the ISQ dimensions in predicting other related measures.

Organisational Determinants of the Quality of Internal Support Operations

A number of organisational constructs had been identified based on those issues considered by interviewees as influential to their department's ability to support other units to undertake their work. These were considered as organisational determinants of the quality of internal support operations.

The internal suppliers' questionnaire was also empirically tested. Data from both hospitals was factor-analysed in order to examine the existence of the constructs identified during the qualitative stage as being influential to their department's ability to support other units to undertake their work. The examination was conducted for each of the four parts of the questionnaire, namely, the work unit, the work unit and its internal customers, the organisation and the individual. Pooled data from both hospitals was factor analysed using Varimax rotation in order to examine the existence of such hypothesised constructs. This procedure was used bearing in mind the fact that, in contrast with the internal customers' questionnaire, many of the items included here had been previously tested in other existing instruments. This had provided evidence of their good content validity. Thus, it was considered that an independent treatment of the variables would be more appropriate in this case. This decision was confirmed later as solutions were obtained containing a high proportion of original variables unaltered in their core.

For each of the four sections, clean and interpretable solutions were obtained. Factor loadings were high in most of the items included in each of the obtained factors. In each of the sections, most of the Cronbach's Alpha scores were high with some moderate values. The careful blend of developed questions with other items from existing measures using the appropriate level of analysis certainly contributed to obtaining clear and distinctive factors. From the 39 original variables included, 26 organisational constructs were obtained: 22 corresponding to original variables unaltered in their core. In addition to those constructs, four structural measures were obtained at the supplier unit level of analysis (size, different job titles, different locations and work-flow interdependence). A summary of the four sets of factors obtained is presented in Table 2.

These results were obtained giving an internal service perspective to items from traditional measures. Thus, it is worth observing that these results not only provide evidence about the validity of the qualitative findings discussed earlier but also are a significant indication that an appropriate operational-isation of the concept of internal customer can be useful in exploring the internal dynamics of the organisation. The set of factors obtained constitutes a representative, coherent and meaningful selection of constructs considered by support staff as being relevant in delivering internal services to other units in the hospital.

Relationship Between Organisational Determinants
and Internal Service Dimensions

The relationship between those organisational determinants involved in providing support to other units and the internal service quality as perceived by internal customer units was also examined. The common unit of analysis to both questionnaires is the internal supplier, and data used represented aggregated scores for each of the 10 supplier units in each hospital. Spearman rank correlations were obtained to measure the relationship between each of the organisational constructs (measured by the internal support unit) and each of the nine internal service dimensions (measured by the internal customer unit). Most of the significant correlations were located at the work unit level of analysis. Few other values related to dyadic and organisational constructs and practically none to variables at the individual supplier unit level. These results seem to suggest that perceived internal service quality is being primarily

Table 2. Internal Service Delivery—Organisational Determinants:
Summary of Results from Factor Analysis

Internal Suppliers' Questionnaire Section	Construct Obtained	Items	Alpha Coefficient	Percent of Variance
The internal supplier unit				64
	Integration	9	0.89	
	Supervision	7	0.90	
	Service control	4	0.84	
	Resources-service fit	4	0.75	
	Standardisation	3	0.67	
	Internal service difficulty	3	0.65	
	Interdependence	3	0.58	
	Internal service variability	3	0.56	
	Internal service pressure	3	0.65	
	Conflict	2	0.72	
	Communication	2	0.51	
The internal customer-supplier interaction				60
	Inter-unit relationships	6	0.79	
	Conflict	6	0.76	
	Awareness	3	0.80	
	Similarity	3	0.68	
	Communication	3	0.68	
	Dependence	2	0.56	
The organisation				73
	Leadership	5	0.81	
	Formalisation	3	0.90	
	Staff's authority	4	0.78	
	Stability	3	0.66	
	Environment	2	0.87	
	Senior management's authority	2	0.67	
	Certainty	2	0.83	
The individual				56
	Commitment	6	0.85	
	Job satisfaction	4	0.70	

driven by characteristics pertaining to the structure and processes within the internal supplier unit (see Table 3). This seems to be an intriguing result as it was expected that more variables at the intergroup level would have appeared significantly associated with internal service dimensions.

The analysis highlights the natural differences in both the internal and external environment of public and private hospitals, resulting in different and meaningful patterns of organisational determinants influencing the same

Table 3. Correlations between Organisational Factors and Internal Service Dimensions

Organisational Construct / Service Dimensions	Helpfulness 1	Helpfulness 2	Timeliness 1	Timeliness 2	Communication 1	Communication 2	Tangibles 1	Tangibles 2	Reliability 1	Reliability 2	Professionalism 1	Professionalism 2	Confidentiality 1	Confidentiality 2	Preparedness 1	Preparedness 2	Consideration 1	Consideration 2	Overall Satisfaction 1	Overall Satisfaction 2
Integration																				
Supervision																				
Service control			67*																	
Resources					67*	64*	68*		66*	75*	78**								66*	
Standardisation																				
Service difficulty																-66*				
Interdependence																				
Service variablity																		-68*		
Service pressure														67*		70*				
Conflict	-85**				-68*				-71*		-65*						-88**		-75*	
Communication	-84**				65*				81**	64*	78**								71*	
Unit size			-64*										72*				-67*			
Job titles																				
Unit locations			79*																	
Individual work flow	-63*	-80*									-68*							-80*		
Sequential work flow		-90**		-90**	-80*												-71*	-90**	-74*	
Reciprocal work flow																				
External work flow																				
Interrelations																				
Conflict																				
Awareness	68*									73*		67*								63*
Similarity																				
Communication		-83**																		
Dependence																				
Leadership																				
Formalisation											-66*									
Staff authority										-66*										
Stability							-71*							-64*						
External environment														71*						
Management authority																				
Certainty																				
Commitment					64*															
Job satisfaction																				

Notes: 1 = Public hospital.   2 = Private hospital.   * Significant at the 1 percent level.   ** Significant at the 5 percent level.

165

internal service dimensions. Also, different variables were significantly correlated with different internal service dimensions, producing interesting and useful associations. Promptness in the NHS hospital, for example, was significantly correlated with two structural variables, standardisation and size of the supplier unit. This suggests that having clear and precise objectives and procedures in a smaller unit contributes to being able to provide a prompt internal service. In the same hospital, reliability was correlated instead to resources-service fit, conflict and communication. Thus, a department having adequate resources, with lower levels of conflict and more frequent communication within the unit, seems to be able to provide a more reliable internal service. These situations seem to indicate the influence different organisational characteristics have on different aspects of the service delivery process.

FUTURE DIRECTIONS FOR RESEARCHERS AND MANAGERS

As this project was exploratory in nature, additional contributions in a number of areas would be expected to follow this project from fellow researchers working in the services management field. Also, the results discussed in this paper will most certainly lead managers to the design and implementation of competitive strategies using the internal service value chain approach developed here.

Additional studies are needed, for instance, to find out the extent to which the internal service dimensions identified could be replicated in other service environments. The dimensionality of SERVQUAL, for example, is one of the common concerns being debated in the service quality literature. It would be sensible to build on that experience with regard to internal service quality. These additional experiments would certainly highlight other interesting directions.

In-depth examination is required to assess the relative importance of the service dimensions. The relevance of these constructs in explaining the perceived quality of the service provided by different functional units is also felt to be an important contribution to this emerging field.

The relative importance of organisational determinants discussed in the previous section, combined with the relative importance of the service dimensions, seems to be an exciting area for both researchers and managers. Internal customers may place different weights on their expectations about different support units. In the case of some support services, to be helpful could be considered by internal customers as relatively more important than, for example, to provide an immediate response. If these two dimensions (helpfulness and timeliness) of the service were indeed facilitated or inhibited by different organisational determinants, managers of different support units would have to set different priorities in the way they would structure, organise and deliver their service to the same internal customer.

Finally, one of the ultimate challenges in this field for both practitioners and academics would be to measure the relationship between the quality of the internal service staff receives and the quality of the service they provide to the external customer.

CONCLUSION

It is felt that this piece of research has contributed to the existing work being made by joint efforts between marketers and organisational behaviorists on organisational and managerial processes related to service quality. It has provided a conceptual framework for a better understanding of the organisational dynamics involved in the customer service delivery process. This framework has resulted from exploring departmental interactions using an innovative perspective: the internal service quality approach.

The work reported here has confirmed that along with customers, employees are able and prepared to produce scaled assessments of the service they themselves receive from other parts of the organisation. Statistical results have indicated that these can be captured as a limited number of perceptual dimensions.

This work has also contributed to the identification of organisational determinants of internal service quality. The results show the different sets of variables which appear to be facilitating or inhibiting factors in the delivery of support services to other units.

It is felt that this approach will add a different orientation to the research literature relating to organisational practices, in particular, group performance. The results have also contributed to the balance between the extensive citations in the literature about the concept of the internal customer and the aforementioned absence of a substantial body of research on this issue.

Finally, it is expected that the conceptual model of internal service quality suggested here will spawn both academic and practitioner interest in both the internal and external environments of service quality. This model, in turn, should serve as a framework for both further empirical research and improvement and the innovation of managerial practices in this fascinating area, with a wide range of practicability and applicability in other industries.

REFERENCES

Adamson, J.D. (1988), "Becoming 'Bilingual' Can Help Solve Those Internal Clashes," *Bank Marketing,* 20 (10), 4, 104.
Albert, M. (1989), "Developing a Service-Oriented Health Care Culture," *Hospital & Health Services Administration,* 34 (2), 167-183.

Babakus, E. and G.W. Boller (1992), "An Empirical Assessment of the SERVQUAL Scale," *Journal of Business Research,* 24, 253-268.

Baker, J. (1987), "The Role of the Environment in Marketing Services," in *The Service Challenge: Integrating for Competitive Advantage,* J. Czepiel, C. Congram and J. Shananhan, eds. Chicago, IL: American Marketing Association.

Berry, L.L. (1981), "The Employee as a Customer," *Journal of Retail Banking,* 3 (1), 33-40.

Bowen, D. (1990), "Interdisciplinary Study of Service: Some Progress, Some Prospects," *Journal of Business Research,* 20, 71-79.

_____ and B. Schneider (1988), "Services Marketing and Management: Implications for Organizational Behaviour," in *Research in Organizational Behaviour,* L.L. Cummings and B. Staw, eds. Greenwich, CT: JAI Press, 43-80.

Carman, J. (1990), "Consumer Perceptions of Service Quality: An Assessment of the SERVQUAL Dimensions," *Journal of Retailing,* 66 (Spring), 33-55.

Chung, R.K. (1993), "TQM: Internal Client Satisfaction," *Business Credit,* 95 (4), 26-39.

Cirasuolo, G. and E. Scheuing (1991), "Using Internal Marketing to Enlighten Co-Workers," *Risk Management,* 38 (7), 42-44.

Davis, T.R.V. (1991), "Internal Service Operations: Strategies for Increasing Their Effectiveness and Controlling Their Cost," *Organisational Dynamics,* 20 (2), 5-22.

_____ (1992), "Satisfying Internal Customers: The Link to External Customer Satisfaction," *Planning Review,* 20 (1), 34-37.

_____ (1993), "Managing Internal Service Delivery in Organizations," in *Advances in Services Marketing and Management,* Vol. 2, T. Swartz, D.E. Bowen and S.W. Brown, eds. Greenwich, CT: JAI Press, 301-321.

Feldman, S. (1991), "Keeping the Customer Satisfied—Inside and Out," *Management Review,* 80 (11), 58-60.

Garrett, M. and K.G. Turman (1992), "TQM in a Health Care Environment," *Internal Auditing,* 8 (2), 78-83.

Garvin, D.A. (1987), "Competing on the Eight Dimensions of Quality," *Harvard Business Review,* 65 (6), 101-109.

George, W. (1990), "Internal Marketing and Organisational Behaviour: A Partnership in Developing Customer-Conscious Employees at Every Level," *Journal of Business Research,* 20 (January), 63-70.

Gladstein, D.L. (1984), "Groups in Context: A Model of Task Group Effectiveness," *Administrative Science Quarterly,* 29, 499-517.

Gremler, D.D., M.J. Bitner and K.R. Evans (1994), "The Internal Service Encounter," *International Journal of Service Industry Management,* 5 (2), 34-56.

Grönroos, C. (1990), *Service Management and Marketing: Managing the Moments of Truth in Service Competition.* Lexington, MA: Lexington.

Gulledge, L.G. (1991), "Satisfying the Internal Customer," *Bank Marketing,* 23 (4), 46-48.

Gummesson, E. (1990), "The Part-Time Marketer," Service Research Center C.T.F. Research Report, Karlstad, Sweden: University of Karlstad.

_____ (1992), "Quality Dimensions: What to Measure in Service Organizations," in *Advances in Services Marketing and Management,* Vol. 1, T. Swartz, D.E. Bowen and S.W. Brown, eds. Greenwich, CT: JAI Press, 177-205.

_____ (1993), *Quality Management in Service Organisations.* New York: International Service Quality Association.

Heskett, J.L., T.O. Jones, G.W. Loveman, W.E. Sasser and L.A. Schlesinger (1994), "Putting the Service-Profit Chain to Work," *Harvard Business Review,* (March-April), 164-174.

Jablonski, R. (1992), "Customer Focus: The Cornerstone of Quality Management," *Healthcare Financial Management,* 46 (11), 17-18.

Koehler, K.G. (1992), "Measuring Service Performance," *CMA Magazine,* 66 (2), 15.

Koska, M.T. (1992), "Surveying Customer Needs, Not Satisfaction, Is Crucial to CQI," *Hospitals*, 66 (21), 50-54.

Lewis, B.R. and T.W. Entwistle (1990), "Managing the Service Encounter: A Focus on the Employee," *International Journal of Service Industry Management*, 1 (3), 41-52.

Ludeman, K. (1992), "Using Employee Surveys to Revitalize TQM," *Training*, 29 (12), 51-57.

McDermott, L.C. and M. Emerson (1991), "Quality and Service for Internal Customers," *Training and Development Journal*, 45 (1), 61-64.

Milite, G. (1991), "Don't Take Internal Customers for Granted," *Supervisory Management*, 36 (7), 9.

Mohr-Jackson, I. (1991), "Broadening The Market Orientation: An Added Focus on Internal Customers," *Human Resource Management*, (Winter), 455-467.

Moores, B. and J.F. Reynoso (1993), "Exploring Interdepartmental Relationships in the Service Delivery Process: A Case Study in the Hospital Industry," in *Proceedings of Workshop on Quality Management in Services III*, Helsinki, Finland: Helsinki School of Economics, 375-395.

Mowday, R.T., R.M. Steers and L.W. Porter (1979), "The Measurement of Organisational Commitment," *Journal of Vocational Behaviour*, 14, 224-247.

Nagel, P. and W. Cilliers (1990), "Customer Satisfaction: A Comprehensive Approach," *International Journal of Physical Distribution and Logistics Management*, 20 (6), 2-46.

Norman, D.A. (1988), *The Psychology of Everyday Things*. New York: Basic Books.

Parasuraman, A., L. Berry and V. Zeithaml (1990), "Guidelines for Conducting Service Quality Research," *Marketing Research*, (December), 34-44.

————, ———— and ———— (1991), "Refinement and Reassessment of the SERVQUAL Scale," *Journal of Retailing*, 67 (Winter), 420-450.

————, V. Zeithaml and L. Berry (1985), "A Conceptual Model of Service Quality and Its Implications for Future Research," *Journal of Marketing*, 49 (Fall), 41-50.

————. ———— and ———— (1988), "SERVQUAL: A Multiple-Item Scale for Measuring Consumer Perceptions of Service Quality," *Journal of Retailing*, 64 (Spring), 12-40.

Parkington, J. and B. Schneider (1979), "Some Correlates of Experienced Job Stress: A Boundary Role Study," *Academy of Management Journal*, 22, 270-281.

Pfau, B., D. Detzel and A. Geller (1991), "Satisfy Your Internal Customers," *Journal of Business Strategy*, 12 (November/December), 9-13.

Plymire, J. (1990), "Internal Service: Solving Problems," *Supervisory Management*, 35 (5), 5.

Price, J.L. and C.W. Mueller (1986), *Handbook of Organisational Measurement*. United Kingdom: Pitman.

Reynoso, J.F. (1993), "Internal Organisational Dynamics in the Service Delivery Process," in *Proceedings of the British Academy of Management Annual Conference*. Milton Keynes, England, 447-448.

Rizzo, J.R., R.J. House and S.I. Lirtzman (1970), "Role Conflict and Ambiguity in Complex Organisations," *Administrative Science Quarterly*, 15, 150-163.

Rowen, R. (1992), "Financial Implications of TQM," *Health Systems Review*, 25 (2), 44-48.

Sanfilippo, B. (1990), "Eight Ideas to Stimulate Internal Service," *Bank Marketing*, 22 (12), 26-29.

Sasser, W. and S. Arbeit (1976), "Selling Jobs in the Service Sector," *Business Horizons*, (June), 61-65.

Schneider, B. and D. Bowen (1985), "Employee and Customer Perceptions of Service in Banks: Replication and Extension," *Journal of Applied Psychology*, 70 (3), 423-433.

————, J.J. Parkington and V.M. Buxton (1980), "Employee and Customer Perceptions of Service in Banks," *Administrative Science Quarterly*, 25 (June), 252-267.

Shostack, G.L. (1984), "Designing Services that Deliver," *Harvard Business Review*, (January-February), 133-139.

_____ (1987), "Service Positioning Through Structural Change," *Journal of Marketing*, 51 (January), 34-43.

_____ (1992), "Understanding Services Through Blueprinting," in *Advances in Services Marketing and Management: Research and Practice*, Vol. 1, T.A. Swartz, D.E. Bowen and S.W. Brown, eds. Greenwich, CT: JAI Press, 75-90.

Stershic, S.F. (1990), "The Flip Side of Customer Satisfaction Research," *Marketing Research,* (December), 45-50.

Thornberry, N. and H. Hennessey (1992), "Customer Care, Much More Than a Smile: Developing a Customer Service Infrastructure," *European Management Journal,* 10 (4), 460-464.

Vandamme, R. and J. Leunis (1993), "Development of a Multiple-Item Scale for Measuring Hospital Service Quality," *International Journal of Service Industry Management,* 4 (3), 30-49.

Vandermerwe, S. and D. Gilbert (1989), "Making Internal Services Market Driven," *Business Horizons,* 32 (6), 83-89.

_____ and _____ (1991), "Internal Services: Gaps in Needs/Performance and Prescriptions for Effectiveness," *International Journal of Service Industry Management,* 2 (1), 50-60.

Van de Ven, A.H. and D.L. Ferry (1980), *Measuring and Assessing Organisations.* New York: Wiley.

Zeithaml, V., L. Berry and A. Parasuraman (1988), "Communication and Control Processes in the Delivery of Service Quality," *Journal of Marketing*, 52, 35-48.

_____, A. Parasuraman and L. Berry (1990), *Delivering Quality Service: Balancing Customer Perceptions and Expectations.* New York: Macmillan.

THE APPLICATION OF GROUP
TECHNOLOGY PRINCIPLES
TO SERVICE OPERATIONS:

A CASE STUDY

Samia M. Siha and Barbara Lutz

ABSTRACT

This paper examines the implementation of group technology principles to an insurance company. Both the traditional layout process and a new layout are discussed. Improvements in various areas of the operation are reported. Decreases in turnaround time, more consistency in underwriting decisions, better service to the agents and reductions in bottlenecks and idle time are some of the reported benefits. The employees, who are an important part of the company, also benefit from the change. They are empowered to make their own decisions and challenged to higher levels of responsibility and accountability. Finally, additional suggestions for improvement are presented.

Advances in Services Marketing and Management, Volume 6, pages 171-187.
ISBN: 0-7623-0176-7

INTRODUCTION

In the life insurance industry today, increasing efficiency and thereby achieving significant improvements in operating costs is viewed as one key to success in the 1990s and beyond.

One major concept in accomplishing this goal is the creation of groups. This is very similar to group technology in the manufacturing arena. The idea of group technology is based on utilizing the advantage of the assembly line in a job shop setting. Employing group technology requires: (1) the identification of the families (groups) of products, and (2) the formation of the cells. Each cell contains the various pieces of machinery necessary to process a family of products. This type of arrangement is called cellular layout.

The cellular layout in an organization facilitates the implementation of Just-In-Time (JIT). Reducing product flow, minimizing work-in-process and improving customer service and quality are some of the JIT objectives that can be accomplished through the use of the cellular layout.

These manufacturing concepts of group technology and cellular layout can be transferred to the services arena. By grouping processes and employees around the natural flows of information, a work cell may be created. For example, rather than separating groups of personnel performing coding, underwriting, or policy issue and auditing from each other, efficiency and productivity will be improved if they are grouped together. So, a group of employees, three data entry staff, one underwriter, two policy issue staff and one auditor can work together to turn in the completed job. When such interrelated processes are grouped together, productivity increases, communication is enhanced and throughput time decreases (Billesbach and Schneiderjans 1989; Feather and Cross 1988).

LITERATURE REVIEW

The concepts of JIT and cellular layout have been widely applied to manufacturing. Many authors have reported the benefits and shortcomings of the cellular layout (i.e., Flynn and Jacobs 1987; Morris and Tersine 1994). The impact of the cellular layout on workers' attitudes was investigated by Fazakerley (1974) and Dale (1979). They identified the following benefits: (1) increased job flexibility and variety, (2) improved worker satisfaction, and (3) increased worker involvement in decision making. Shafer and colleagues (1995) found that the cellular layout has both negative and positive effects on workers' attitudes. The results of these authors' surveys showed signs of weaker organizational commitment, greater role conflict and greater role ambiguity. However, their studies also showed that job characteristics positively mediate the effect of cellular layout on employees' attitudes.

Nonetheless, the application of the group technology concepts is less established for service operations. Feather and Cross (1988) were the first to use the term "work cell" in services. They described how the JIT, OPT and cellular organization concepts could be utilized in administration to simplify the administrative paperwork process. They recommended the establishment of production modules or work cells. Each work cell would be responsible for the whole job as well as the production quality and quantity. Billesbach and Schneiderjans (1989) also explained the application of JIT techniques and group technology in administration. According to them, the application of the cellular organization in administration enhances communication, improves problem-solving, reduces paper flow and improves efficiency and effectiveness. However, the details of the implementation of these techniques to a Fortune 500 company were not reported. The application of group technology in health care was suggested by Gambling (1987) and Harvey (1989). Gambling (1987) suggested that group technology could be applied to the operation of the U.K. National Health Service to help in controlling costs and improving efficiency. He suggested various methods of applying group technology in hospitals and presented a detailed discussion and analysis of these methods. Harvey (1989) explained how the techniques of group technology could be implemented in health and human services. She suggested the creation of small groups (or cells) of practitioners who would treat a homogenous mix of clients. This would reduce waiting time and improve the quality of the service.

The implementation of group technology principles to improve supply chain management was suggested by Shafer and Ernst (1993) and Min and Shin (1994). Shafer and Ernst (1993) introduced a number of ways that group technology principles could be applied in warehousing operations. A case study was presented to illustrate these applications within a distribution warehousing operation. However, the authors did not provide any data or analysis to support their claim. Min and Shin (1994) proposed a group technology classification and coding system for purchasing. The benefits that could be gained from applying the proposed system were presented. Again, no examples of code testing were presented.

In this paper, we study the implementation of group technology principles within an insurance company. First, the traditional (original) process, with its pitfalls, is presented. The implementation steps and a new layout are then discussed. The improvements in the areas of quality, productivity, labor utilization and resource utilization are reported. Finally, some suggestions for improvement are presented.

THE COMPANY

This paper presents a real-life application of the cellular organization (hereafter, we will use cellular organization and group arrangement alternatively) to a medium-sized life insurance company, Century Life of America (CLA). At the time of this study, the company's assets were approximately $1 billion, its life insurance in force was $7 billion and its surplus was $72 million. Total premiums were $93 million.

At the time of this study, CLA served a 40-state region, primarily in the Midwest. Most of its new business and insurance in-force was in the states of Iowa, Minnesota, Wisconsin, Ohio, Pennsylvania, Nebraska and Texas. The life insurance was sold through a captive agency system (i.e., the agent sells primarily through one life insurance company) of about 300 agents.

An analysis of the current cellular organization reveals the extent of operational improvements of this insurance company. At one time, CLA used the "process-oriented" layout. This pre- and post-change examination provides a basis for comparison in the same company.

The Original Arrangement (Process Orientation Layout)

Figure 1 diagrams the original structure of the new business department. The new business area consisted of four underwriters, 18 data entry and file clerks, four underwriting support staff, a part-time medical director, a manager of underwriting, a manager of new business, 12 issue staff, three-and-a-half audit staff members and two supervisors.

The applications were processed in a traditional job shop "process-oriented" fashion. First, an application was "prepped" at a set of workstations, then it moved to "coding" to create a record of the application in the mainframe computer. The file was then sent to the underwriter and on to an underwriting secretary if any correspondence or requests for additional information were needed. The file was then sent back to the coding clerks to manage the file while waiting for requirements. (Requirements are work orders for items needed to make a decision, such as a medical exam, blood chemistry tests, missing information or forms from the agent.) When all items needed were received, the file was released to the underwriter for the final decision, and then the application went to the issue workstation. An auditing unit then prepared the policy, did quality checks and mailed the policy to the agent to deliver to the policyholder.

While the same group of coders managed the underwriter's requirement orders and the pending file, the file was not assigned to any particular person. Everyone worked from central work bins and took files as they had available time. Every time a piece of mail was received, the file was pulled and reviewed by an underwriter. Many times, the file would go back into pending since not all requirements were received.

In this processing arrangement, a file could be in one of over 35 locations. Further, based on the nature of the process-oriented layout, there were many bottlenecks at the different stations: coding, issuing, underwriting, auditing,

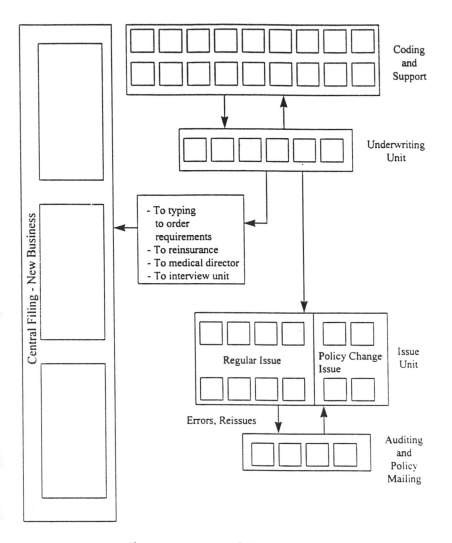

Figure 1. Process Orientation Layout

filing, requirements ordering and mail-matching. Significant delays in the issue "turnaround time" (an insurance term for throughput) were resulting in unacceptable levels of complaints from agents. Furthermore, when agents called in to find out the status of their cases, it took the staff more than a few minutes to respond. It would often be hours (or days) before someone could get back to the agent. As mentioned earlier, there were over 35 possible locations for the file and no good way of tracking the file at any given point in time. These requests were contributing to further delays in processing files since the coding and issue staff were used to find files.

Moreover, it was nearly impossible to track errors since so many people were involved with the same file. As a result, accountability and responsibility were minimal.

Based on complaints from agents and the persistent backlog in coding and issuing, the managers and supervisors of the new business and underwriting area convened to make a major change. The first step was to collect data and analyze it, then decide on corrective direction. The co-authors suggested the organization use the following model common in the literature (e.g., Billesbach and Schneiderjans 1989; Brooks 1994; Savage-Moore 1988) to guide any change:

I.   Assessment
   • Analyze the process and define the causes of the problems;
   • Identify the strengths and the capabilities of the workforce;
   • Identify the problems and what needs to be changed;
   • Choose the appropriate new environment.

II.   Analysis and Goals Setting
   • Identify the work activities needed;
   • Redefine job responsibilities;
   • Install cross-training;
   • Recommend an appropriate layout.

III.   Implementation
   • Recommend how the job is done;
   • Define the tools to get the job done;
   • Institute new performance measurement tools to evaluate the new environment;
   • Get upper management support;
   • Explain the new process to the rest of the staff;
   • Establish an ongoing training program.

IV.   Evaluation and Improvement
   • Measure, evaluate and improve.

Assessment of Process Orientation Layout

As stated earlier, the system did not track each step in the process nor which associates were involved in the handling of the files. This information had to be manually tracked and was only done for specific purposes such as analyzing workflow for this study. The date the application was received was not captured in the system either. The first date of record was the date a computer record of the application was established, that is, at the time of the "coding" of the application information into the system. To determine the length of time from physical receipt of the application to creation of the computer record, a manual tracking process needed to be established. Therefore, these methods were used to collect the data for evaluation:

1. *Manual collection:* In analyzing the workflow to determine the number of hand-offs, the files were physically walked through the process and the number of hand-offs manually tallied. When determining the delay at each hand-off, the time the file was received at that station and the time the file was passed on to the next station was recorded on a paper form designed specifically for this study.

2. *Routine management reports:* Certain management reports were generated monthly which track the progress of files based on calendar days. Reasons for processing delays were also tracked by the system. The management reports tracked the date the application was written, the date the application was entered into the computer, the type of application (whole life, term, annuity), requirements needed (such as a form, a medical, a doctor report), the date the requirement was received and what the final decision was (such as approved, declined, rated extra premium, closed as incomplete). The management reports generated by the system were analyzed on a monthly basis. Total application count (by week, month and year to date), number and percentage of cases approved, declined, rated with extra premium, percentage needing each requirement and number of cases for which each employee was credited with completing the final processing, were tracked.

3. *Ad-Hoc System Report:* Periodically, the number of errors was randomly checked; in addition, the length of time at any one workstation, response time to agent telephone calls and length of time from issue date to policy mail date were tallied.

From the above listed reports and data, it was found that:

- On the average, about 425 life and annuity applications were received per week;
- A file was passed on average to nine different associates in the department and handled 22.5 times before it was mailed to the agent; and
- On average, 45 calendar days elapsed from data coding to the issue date. Another seven calendar days typically passed before the policy was ready to mail.

The success of other life insurance companies with the cellular organization concept spurred CLA management to benchmark these companies. The benchmarking process followed theses steps (Schonberger and Knod 1994):

1. *Selecting the process to be benchmarked.*   The process selected was the new business and underwriting areas. The management team members, who were to oversee the process, were also selected. The team consisted of the vice president of new business and underwriting, the manager of new business and underwriting and the two supervisors of the new business and underwriting areas.
2. *Benchmarking the company's own process.*   The team reviewed both the metrics and the practice of the new business and underwriting areas. The turnaround time was chosen as the metrics. The team documented every step in the process, noting delay, source of error and employees involved.
3. *Choosing the companies to be benchmarked.*   It was decided to perform informal and formal benchmarking. The team members attended workshops and discussion sessions put together by life insurance companies during professional meetings. During these sessions, the concept of cellular organization, its formation, benefits and implementation were explained and discussed. The companies that were informally benchmarked through attending these events were SAFECO, Lutheran Brotherhood and Northwestern National Life. The three companies chosen for visits were Interstate Insurance and American Mutual, both from Des Moines, Iowa, and Security Benefit Life from Topeka, Kansas.
4. *Visiting the site.*   Only the two supervisors visited the above-mentioned companies. They noted the positives and the negatives of these operations from the perspective of implementation at CLA. The entire team analyzed the collected data and developed plans for change and follow through.

Using Assessment Data to Guide Implementation

The following highlights management endeavors to affect change:

- The supervisors shared their findings and the cellular organization concept with all the staff in the new business and underwriting areas. Everyone was allowed to ask questions and the advantages of the new cellular layout were explained (see Table 1). Next, it was time to determine the overall structure of the cell. This includes determining the skills of the existing staff and the requirements of the new cells. The position of the underwriter assistant was suggested and approved. It was determined also to combine the jobs of coding, issuing and auditing to minimize hand-offs. The caseworker concept was created and his or her job responsibility was specified. It was determined also that each team within a cell would serve a specific group of agencies from a certain geographical area.

Table 1. Comparison Between the Process Layout and the Cellular Layout

Attribute	Process Layout	Cellular Layout
Arrangement	By function.	By group; each group serves a certain group of agents.
Focus	On process.	On customer.
Tracking	Very difficult; everyone works from central work bins. File could be in one of 35 locations.	Easy; each file is assigned to a specific case worker with a three-digit ID code assigned to him or her.
Responsiveness	Very long; hours or days.	Very short; a few minutes.
Problem solving	Difficult and takes a considerable amount of time.	Faster and better solutions can be implemented.
Underwriting decision	Non-consistent; any underwriter can make the decision.	Consistent; one underwriter handles a group of agents.
Turnaround time	52 days.	31 days.
Workforce	Narrowly specialized.	Flexible; individuals perform many elements of the job.
Ownership and accountability	Employees do their "part" of the job, but there is no accountability.	Employees serve their "clients" and are accountable to the group.

- Groups of support staff and underwriters were formed to work on specific aspects of the cellular organization concept. The details of the workflow were finalized. This included every aspect of the work process from where to put the mail bins and what to put in the underwriter's in-basket to the new physical layout. Also, the groups defined the tools needed to get the job done.
- The supervisors coached and guided these groups and gave basic structural guidelines. The groups recommended how the various jobs could be done. The supervisors checked to see if these recommendations were consistent with the overall plan and the vision of the company.

After the management approved the implementation groups' suggestions, the groups presented the implementation plans to the rest of the department.

The New Arrangement (Cellular Organization Layout)

Under the cellular organization approach, an administrative services unit was created. In this unit, three support staff prepare the files for the new business/underwriting groups. Prepping the file involves assigning a policy number, verifying payment sent in with the application, putting the file in colored files to correspond with an underwriting group and other

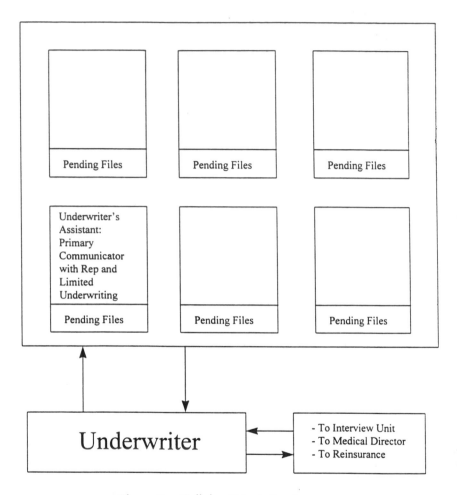

Figure 2. Cellular Orientation Layout

administrative support. These tasks, needed by every group, are more appropriately centrally located rather than dispersed into the groups. Figure 2 shows the work flow within one of the groups. Figure 3 summarizes the tasks of administrative services, the underwriter's assistant and the underwriter under the new organization.

The files are then distributed by the administrative services team to the new business groups. The file is assigned to a support clerk called a caseworker, who is given responsibility for the file from coding to issue, including self-auditing. A desk code field is carried in the computer to assist in tracking the file. Several caseworkers work with one underwriter to serve the agency regions.

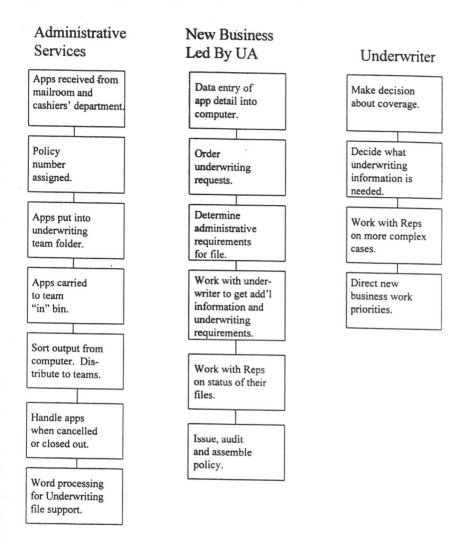

Figure 3.   Task Summary—Cellular Organization Layout

Instead of the file being in dozens of possible locations, there are now less than six. Further, instead of 18 people trying to keep track collectively of thousands of pending files, each caseworker has the responsibility for 50-75 files at any one time. Each caseworker has a three-digit identification code assigned to him or her. A field is carried in the computer with this code to assist in tracking.

Not only were jobs combined and responsibilities expanded, but a few new positions were also created. More specifically, caseworkers now do both coding and issue functions instead of just one or the other. There are four new business groups. These groups consist of one underwriter and six caseworkers. When the groups were formed, each was able to include at least two staff trained in both coding and issue. This was possible because most issue staff under the process-oriented approach had at one time been data entry coders, the entry level position in the department. Cross-training became less time-consuming and the groups became more functional.

One new job created was the underwriter's assistant (UA). Since the company did not have the resources to install jet issue or expert systems, this job was created to off-load the simple cases to support staff, who also could code and issue. Conceivably this person could code, underwrite and issue simultaneously. The UA became the primary communicator with the agent. Routine and status questions previously handled by the underwriter were now handled by the UA. Further, the bimonthly routine of reviewing all pending files, to determine if action could or should be taken despite the file not yet being complete, was transferred from the underwriter to the UA.

In sum, the major differences from the previous process orientation layout were the following:

- The arrangement of personnel;
- The expansion of employees' responsibilities;
- The creation of the underwriter's assistant job;
- The new system of file tracking; and
- The enhancement of the workflow and the elimination of bottlenecks.

RESULTS AND IMPROVEMENTS

Quality and Productivity

A primary reason for moving to a cellular organization approach was to improve service to the field agents. Significant delays in issue "turnaround time" resulted in unacceptable complaint levels from agents. Based on the nature of the process layout, there were many bottlenecks at coding, issuing, underwriting and auditing workstations. This significantly impaired the turnaround time.

When groups were established, the following was accomplished:

- Issue turnaround time went from an average of 52 days to 31. This included all cases, from the most complicated underwriting, requiring many extra requirements, to "clean," no-extra-information-needed cases;
- Turnaround time on "clean cases" went from an average of eight days to five; and

- A total of 95 percent of telephone calls from agents could be answered in the initial call; a delay and call-back were not required. No figures are available on the amount of time that was saved looking for files, but the number of call-backs was virtually cut in half.

From a service standpoint, the change with the largest impact came from the territorial division of applications. Each field agent had one underwriter to deal with and just a few new business associates. This resulted in more consistency in underwriting decisions and a better understanding of expectations in the home office. The group was now linked with the field, expanding the definition of a group. From the home office associates' perspective, a specific set of agents were now their "clients."

Utilization of Labor and Resources

Another objective of the new configuration was cost reduction. Bottlenecks not only lengthened the turnaround process, they created periods of idle time, so associate time was not being used efficiently. The group arrangement provided the following solutions:

- The auditing department was eliminated. New business staff audited their own work. Initially, they worked in pairs to check each other's work, as a transition to self-audits. This saved up to three days of processing and three out of four staffing positions; and
- Reductions in staff in the coding, pending and issue functions. Initially, eight out of 39 positions were eliminated.

No analysis of the savings resulting from the reduced number of telephone calls, shortened cycle time or improved relations with the agents was done. By far the biggest visible savings came from staffing. Fortunately, employee attrition absorbed the reductions.

Impact on Employees

The primary advantage of a "process layout" set-up in processing new business lies in training. Only a small part of the total new business-to-issue process needs to be known by an associate. If business flow is steady, bottlenecks are minimal. However, as controlling costs become more critical and quality becomes much more visible and important, group set-ups better fit these new demands.

A major factor in meeting these demands is job design. Enriching and enlarging the job contributes not only to reaching cost and quality goals but to improving employees' working relationships. These goals were served by

combining the new business, issue and underwriting groups together in the
following ways:

- Working relationships were created between the units in-house and the
  agents. Everyone was working together with the same goal: to get cases
  issued as quickly as possible. Tension between departments was lessened
  because people were doing the whole job; they had much more control
  over a particular case. (Underwriting is still a separate function, but the
  underwriter is in the group and has much more control over work flow
  on particular files.)
- The span of files was reduced, making them more manageable. The
  number of cases an associate had to work with was reduced from 300-
  400 to 50-75. These cases were from a tighter geographic distribution
  which meant associates had four to five sets of state regulations to be
  concerned with versus 40. (The life insurance industry is not nationally
  regulated, so every state has its own regulations. This company was
  licensed to sell in 40 states.)
- Since associates had more control over what they did, more challenging
  jobs, more meaningful work and higher salary levels, this increased job
  satisfaction. They were empowered to make decisions that affected the
  handling of "their" files. Associates were allowed to negotiate the
  requirements with the agents, deviate from the typical procedures
  without supervisor approval, make exceptions and close cases that have
  been opened for a long time. Although job satisfaction was not formally
  measured, it was the subject of staff meetings and it was reported
  favorably.

There are, however, a few negative factors in the cellular organization
approach:

1. *Training.*   It takes much longer for an employee to learn a job. Full
   training went from about six months to two years. This is the most
   significant management challenge in an environment of changing and
   increasing staff levels as well as one that demands immediate results.
2. *Cooperation between the groups.*   The associates in a group tend to
   get territorial; in other words, they do not like to ask for help if they
   are behind and are not always quick to help other groups. This is because
   of group pride, lack of an incentive system to help other groups (there
   is no system to automatically track work that others initiate) and the
   small differences in processing business in different groups based on state
   requirements, underwriter's direction, unfamiliar agents and group
   members.

Determinants of Cellular Organization's Success

Underlying the success of the group technology implementation at CLA were the following key elements:

1. *Using more generalists than specialists.* This is an important element of JIT and group technology implementation. It assures the workforce flexibility that is required in this environment. In the CLA case, it had caseworkers do both coding and issue functions.
2. *Utilizing effective performance measures.* Measuring customer satisfaction, turnaround time, consistency in underwriting decisions, employee satisfaction and providing on-time feedback were very critical to the success of the new process.
3. *Listening to the customers.* That was the driving force for CLA; listen and do whatever it takes to "delight" one's customer. However, CLA had to define its customer. Is it the agent or the policyholder? It was determined (at the time of writing this paper) that the agent was the customer since she or he represented the policyholder. So any delay or lack of prompt responsiveness would make the "customer" unsatisfied.
4. *Benchmarking.* Contacting and visiting companies in the same industry or other industries that applied the technology successfully.
5. *Explaining the benefits to everyone.* The success of any new process depends on people, and an informed, convinced and enthusiastic group can achieve this success.

Future Improvements

The following are suggestions for improving the cellular organization approach at CLA:

- Create levels of expertise, such as entry-level new business, senior new business and underwriter's assistants. This eases the burden of having everyone fully trained in every function. Multiple expertise level in each group allows for flexibility and self-sufficiency of each group. Furthermore, it offers a career development path;
- Improve communication to the field through technology such as electronic mail, computerized file status reports and field access to the mainframe data.
- Use expert systems to underwrite clean cases and prescreen cases for the requirements needed to underwrite; and
- Install an Electronic Data Interchange (EDI) system to facilitate field entry and electronic transfer of applications. This offers further speed in total turnaround time.

CONCLUSION

There is unprecedented demand to process business faster and more cost effectively. This paper has presented the implementation of group technology (arrangement) to a life-insurance company. An implementation process model has been shown and the key elements behind the success of the group technology presented. This analysis of a group arrangement has revealed the potential extent of operational improvements in an insurance company. Decreases in turnaround time, consistency in underwriting decisions, better service to agents and reductions in bottlenecks and idle time are some reported benefits. The employees, who are an important part of the company, have also benefited from the change also. They are empowered to make their own decisions and challenged to higher levels of responsibility and accountability. These benefits concur with the social benefits reported earlier by Fazakerley (1974) and Dale (1979).

However, there are a few negative factors in the cellular organization approach. These include the need for extra training time and lack of cooperation between groups.

For future research, the authors propose an empirical study to survey a number of service organizations to determine the usefulness of group technology implementation. We suggest that the survey address the following issues:

- The type of companies that are most likely to implement group technology. It would seem that service organizations that perform their process in a multi-stage fashion will benefit the most from the cellular organization;
- The impact of group technology implementation on existing systems;
- The benefits gained from implementing group technology. Would it be possible to measure financial and other intangible gain?
- The implementation strategies of group technology used in service organizations. It would be interesting to investigate the correlation between the implementation strategy and the corporate culture;
- The methods of organizing the process to apply group technology; and
- The employee training programs required to implement group technology. Do such programs depend on the classification of the service process? (see Schmenner 1986).

The results of this study could provide a framework for successful implementation of group technology in service. In addition, a model to measure the actual cost savings from applying the cellular organization after all factors (positive and negative) are considered could prove to be very helpful.

REFERENCES

Billesbach, T.J. and M.J. Schneiderjans (1989), "Applicability of Just-In-Time Techniques in Administration," *Production and Inventory Management Journal*, 30 (3), 40-44.

Brooks, D.G. (1994), "The Competitive Edge in Developing a Traditional Manufacturing Business," *Technovation*, 14 (6), 357-362.

Dale, B.G. (1979), "Some Social Aspects of Group Technology," *Work Study*, 10, 19-24.

Fazakerley, G.M. (1974), "The Human Problems of Group Technology," *European Business*, (Summer), 50-56.

Feather, J.J. and K.F. Cross (1988), "Workflow Analysis: Just-In-Time Techniques Simplify Administrative Process in Paperwork Operation," *Industrial Engineering*, 20 (1), 32-40.

Flynn, B.B. and F.R. Jacobs (1987), "An Experimental Comparison of Cellular (Group Technology) Layout with Process Layout," *Decision Sciences*, 18 (4), 561-582.

Gambling, T. (1987) "Baumol's Disease, Group Technology and the National Health Service," *Financial Accountability & Management*, 3 (1), 47-58.

Harvey, J. (1989), "Just-In-Time Health and Human Services: A Client Approach," *Public Productivity & Management Review*, 13 (1), 77-88.

Min, H. and D. Shin (1994), "A Group Technology Classification and Coding System for Value-Added Purchasing," *Production and Inventory Management*, 35 (1), 39-42.

Morris, J.S. and R.J. Tersine (1994), "A Simulation Comparison of Process and Cellular Layouts in a Dual Resource Constrained Environment," *Computers and Industrial Engineering*, 26 (4), 733-741.

Savage-Moore, W. (1988), "The Evolution of a Just-In-Time Environment at Northern Telecom Inc.'s Customer Service Center," *Industrial Engineering Journal*, 20 (8), 60-63.

Schmenner, R.W. (1986), "How Can Business Survive and Prosper," *Sloan Management Review*, 27 (3), 21-32.

Schonberger, R.J. and E.M. Knod, Jr. (1994), *Synchroservice! The Innovative Way To Build A Dynasty of Customers*. New York: Irwin.

Shafer, S.M. and R. Ernst (1993), "Applying Group Technology Principles to Warehousing Operations," *International Journal of Purchasing & Materials Management*, 29 (2), 38-42.

_____, B.J. Tepper, J.R. Meredith and R. Marsh (1995), "Comparing the Effects of Cellular and Functional Manufacturing on Employees' Perception and Attitudes," *Journal Of Operations Management*, 12 (2), 63-74.

A CUSTOMER-BASED TAXONOMY OF SERVICES:
IMPLICATIONS FOR SERVICE MARKETERS

Lawrence F. Cunningham, Clifford E. Young
and Moonkyu Lee

ABSTRACT

Respondent perceptions of how a set of 11 services relate to a classification of service categories were modeled using multidimensional scaling. Two analyses were performed: in the first, the service classifications were used to develop a perceptual space onto which the services were mapped, and in the second, the services were used to develop the perceptual space onto which the classifications were mapped. Results of the analyses provide information on how respondents view the classifications and the services. Managerial and research implications are presented.

INTRODUCTION

The growth of service industries is playing a significant role in the U.S. economy. By 1992, the service sector accounted for 72 percent of its gross

Advances in Services Marketing and Management, Volume 6, pages 189-202.

domestic product and 76 percent of the domestic labor force employment (*The Economist* 1993). It has accounted for most of the recent growth in non-farm employment; 85 percent of all new jobs created in the last decade have been in service industries (Koepp 1987). Such rapid growth in the service economy has inspired a great deal of research in the area of services marketing over the past two decades.

This stream of research, which began with the controversy over the differences between goods and services, is now making remarkable progress, moving its focus toward such issues as the measurement and management of service quality (e.g., Fisk, Brown and Bitner 1993). However, the proliferation of services marketing research would benefit from what seems to be lacking— the development of a sound classification scheme of services. As Hunt (1983) has suggested, classification schemata play significant roles in the development of a research area because they are used for organizing phenomena and theories.

The research in the goods marketing area, for example, has flourished based on such useful classification systems as those developed by Copeland (1924, 1923) and Aspinwall (1958). On the other hand, many empirical studies accumulated in the services area have typically focused on a single or a few industries. The lack of a reliable service taxonomy contributes to researchers being uncertain as to the generalizability of their studies in other service industries. Service marketers also find it extremely difficult to gain managerial insights from the experience in other industries without a proper understanding of the similarities and differences among services (Bowen 1990; Lovelock 1983).

Certainly, several service typologies have been proposed in the past (e.g., Bell 1981; Chase 1978; Hill 1977; Lovelock 1983, 1980; Thomas 1978). However, none of these frameworks was empirically based or customer-driven. Moreover, these typologies typically used only a few classification dimensions, which may not cover the range of qualities that differentiate one service from another.

The purpose of this paper is to develop a service classification scheme from a customer perspective and provide managerial insights for service marketers. To some extent, this research is similar to that of Bowen (1990), who developed an empirically based service classification scheme. Bowen used a cluster analysis to categorize services and described the characteristics of each cluster based on the average ratings on the classifying dimensions. His resulting clusters were thus based on customers' perceptions of the services using the classification descriptions provided. The clusters (i.e., service categories) could then be described based on how they were similar or different on the classifying dimensions.

In contrast, in the current research, customers were asked in a survey about their feelings and perceptions regarding services in terms of seven key dimensions. These perceptions of services were used as a basis for the development of a taxonomy. Multidimensional scaling (MDS) was used in the study to show how classifying dimensions are related to each other, how services are related to each other and how different services are located in the multidimensional classification space. (Also see Iacobucci and Ostrom [1996] for an MDS of services.)

LITERATURE REVIEW

Many authors have suggested that the classification of goods is among the oldest of the commonly accepted theoretical concepts in marketing. They suggest that such distinctions date back to very early in the discipline (e.g., Bell 1986, 1981). While some have suggested that a classification scheme for goods can encompass both goods and services merely by broadening the scope, researchers have examined the issue of service classification for at least the last 25 years. For example, one of the earliest classification attempts examines the issue of ownership versus rental (Judd 1964). Subsequent research efforts considered the type of seller, type of buyer, buyer motives, buyer practice and the degree of industry regulation (Rathmall 1974). Others have attempted to classify goods and services on the basis of the proportion of physical goods and intangible services contained within each product package (Sasser and Arbeit 1978; Shostack 1977).

Some work has chosen to emphasize the nature of service benefits by examining services that affect people versus those affecting goods, permanent versus temporary effects of the service, reversibility versus nonreversability of outcomes, physical versus mental effects and individual versus collective services (Hill 1977). Other efforts have viewed the issue as equipment-based versus people-based services (Thomas 1978).

New and different approaches to service classifications continued into and past the late 1970s. One approach sought to emphasize the extent of customer contact required in the service delivery (Chase 1978), recognizing that product variability is difficult to control in high-contact services because customers exert great influence. Hybrid approaches to service classifications also started to evolve during this period. For example, Kotler (1980) synthesized previous work by considering people-based versus equipment-based services, the extent to which a client's presence was necessary, whether the service met personal needs or business needs, and the orientation of the firm (e.g., public versus private and for-profit versus nonprofit). Other work in the same period emphasized basic demand characteristics, service content and benefits, and service delivery procedures (Lovelock 1980).

Classification work continued in the services area throughout the 1960s, 1970s and 1980s, because individuals interested in services continued to suggest that services have characteristics different from goods (Bateson 1979; Shostack

1977; Zeithaml 1981). Studies in the 1980s emphasized employee/customer interaction as well as the issue of intangibility (Bell 1986). They looked at the service delivery system (Daniel 1982), audience size, customer participation and employee/customer contact (Grove and Fisk 1983; Silpakit and Fisk 1985), as well as multiple versus single-site and the level of customization of the service (Langeard and Eiglier 1983).

Lovelock (1983) suggested that it was possible to derive strategic insights from the classification of services, in that factors had been identified that shape marketing problems and opportunities. Further, the classification of services facilitates the examination of strategies outside the industry because it highlights similarities to otherwise apparently different service industries. Lovelock concentrated on the nature of service delivery, the relationships between the service provider and its customers, the customization of services, the degree of judgment exercised by customer contact personnel, the nature of the demand for the service and the method of service delivery.

Other researchers took different approaches in examining how consumers classify services. For example, Goodwin (1986) looked at the issue of role relationship in service encounters: that is, customer power over the service provider, customer commitment to the service relationship and the strategic implications for each combination.

Bowen (1990) pointed out that none of the classification schemes developed thus far had been empirically based. He classified 10 services (e.g., hospitals, movie theaters, photographic services, restaurants, hotels, and so forth) on the basis of nine criteria (e.g., intangible/tangible, level of customization, employee/customer contact, importance of people, and so forth). As mentioned earlier, the current study also makes an empirical effort in developing a service taxonomy but with an approach different from that used by Bowen.

METHODOLOGY

Service Dimensions

The existing literature has identified several key dimensions which would give rise to significant differences among services (Bell 1981; Bowen 1990; Lovelock 1983, 1980). Seven of the dimensions were selected and used as classification bases in this study. They were selected based on their representing the essential conceptual framework of services and also the ability of the dimensions to be operationalized in the proposed questionnaire. The dimensions were the extent to which (1) a service is performed on a person or a tangible object; (2) a service exhibits a formal relationship between the service provider and the customer or not; (3) the delivery of a service is continuous or involves discrete transactions; (4) service characteristics are customized or standardized; (5) customer contact personnel exercise judgment in meeting individual customer need or not; (6) customers need to go to the service provider versus the service provider comes to customers and (7) a service is provided in association with physical components or not.

Selection of Services

Two criteria were considered in selecting the services: first, the total set of services had to represent a wide range of variations on the classifying dimensions, and second, they had to be well-known to the respondent population. A total of 11 services were chosen based on these criteria: commercial airline service, hospital service (inpatient), physician or clinic health care service (outpatient), university education, commercial dry cleaning service, banking service, radio station broadcasting, fine restaurant, fast food restaurant, movie theater and plumbing service.

Measures

Respondents were asked to rate each of the 11 services on the seven classification dimensions. They were provided with an explanation and several examples for each of the dimensions, which were developed based on the literature.

The Sample

Data was collected through a survey with students in an evening M.B.A. program at a major metropolitan university. These students were selected because most of them were white-collar workers; as such, they were actual customers of the services selected in the study. A total of 65 surveys were completed. Table 1 presents a summary of the demographic statistics of the sample. Note that the students tend to be older and more affluent, with a significant portion being married. This sample appears to be more representative of the populations likely to use these services than the traditional college student.

Analytical Technique

Means aggregating over respondents were calculated for each service on each rating scale. This matrix of means was then used as input to PREFMAP, a variant of MDS (Carroll 1972), to pictorially represent the services and classification properties. PREFMAP constructs a representation of either set of inputs and then relates the second set of inputs on the first representation.

Table 1. Sample Characteristics

Sex	Male	38.5%
	Female	61.5%
Age	20-29	29.2%
	30-39	56.9%
	40 and over	13.9%
Marital status	Married	66.2%
	Single	30.8%
	Other	3.0%
Profession	Professional	32.3%
	Business manager	21.5%
	Administrator	10.8%
	Student	10.8%
	Other	24.9%
Ethnic background	Caucasian	85.9%
	Asian descent	12.5%
	Hispanic	1.5%
Household income	Under 30K	16.1%
	30K to <50K	35.5%
	50K to <80K	35.5%
	80K and over	12.9%

For the current research, either the service classifications or the set of services themselves could logically be used as the basis for the initial representation onto which the other would be mapped. Given that this study was exploratory in nature, with no a priori basis for testing a given set of classifications or services, the data was analyzed both ways, first by representing the classifications and mapping the services, then by representing the services and mapping the classifications.

RESULTS AND DISCUSSION

In the first analysis, two dimensions based on the seven classifications described above accounted for 79 percent of the total variance of the means. A pictorial representation is presented in Figure 1. Figure 2 overlays the 11 services on the classifications in two-dimensional space.

In the second analysis, the individual services were used to derive the initial map. Two dimensions accounted for 76 percent of the total variance. Figure 3 presents the pictorial representation of the 11 services in two dimensions. Figure 4 presents the combined overlay of the 11 services and seven classifications in the two-dimensional space (defined by the services).

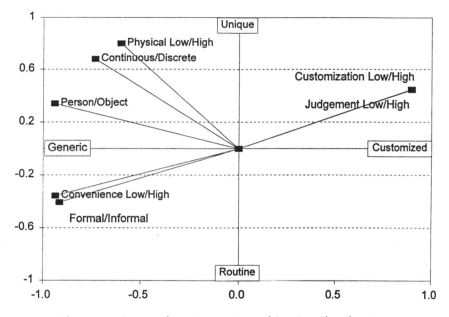

Figure 1.   Respondent Perceptions of Service Classifications

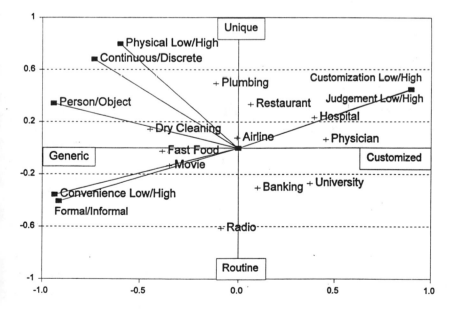

Figure 2.   Combined Service Classifications and Services
in Service Classifications Dimensions

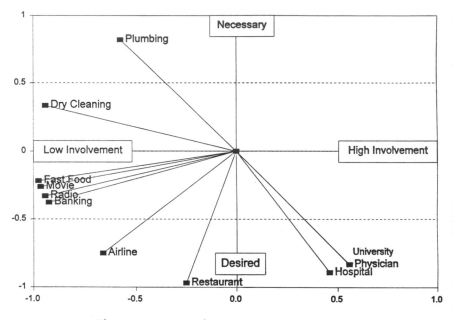

Figure 3.   Respondent Perceptions of Services

The results of the MDS analysis indicate that respondents view the a priori classification of services in a number of different ways. As shown in Figure 1, there were three distinct quadrants of consumers' perceptions of classifications. The upper-left quadrant contains classifications such as a physical component, continuous/discrete transactions and services done to a person/object. The lower-left quadrant contains perceptions for convenience and the formalization of the relationship. The upper-right quadrant suggests respondents perceive judgments involved in the providing of the service and the degree of customization in the service very similarly.

After examining the various quadrants, the researchers assigned descriptions to the various axes. As can be seen in Figure 1, we described the horizontal axis as a continuum between generic and customized services. We described the vertical axis as one that distinguishes unique versus routine service. These descriptions were used as a basis for describing consumer perceptions of services in Figure 2. These descriptions seem to work fairly well; for example, respondents seem to perceive plumbing as a uniquely occurring service which is slightly more generic than customized in nature. They perceived a fine restaurant as somewhat unique and slightly customized.

This map succinctly summarized perceptions of attributes of many services. For example, dry cleaning, fast food and movies are perceived as more generic

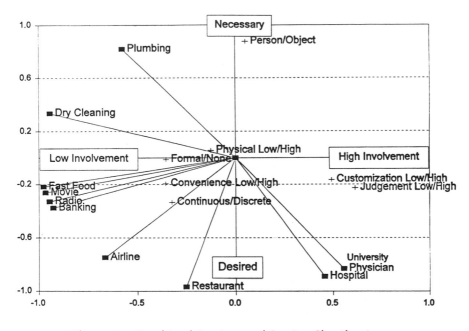

Figure 4. Combined Services and Service Classifications
in Service Dimensions

in nature. Dry cleaning is thought to be slightly unique while movies are slightly more routine. Banking and radio are routine although banking is thought of as somewhat more customized. An interesting service is the university, which is thought to be somewhat routine and customized. Health care services (physician and hospital) are considered customized in nature, with a somewhat greater uniqueness for hospital services.

Looking at Figure 3, services are viewed from a somewhat different perspective. We have described the horizontal axis to be a continuum of low to high involvement on the part of the service recipient. The vertical axis is tentatively described as a continuum from necessary services to desired services. Hospital and physician services are displayed in the lower-right quadrant, reflecting desired services and relatively high involvement on the part of the customers. Airline services and fine restaurant services are desired but relatively low involvement services. Fast food, the movies, radio and banking are predominantly low involvement. Lastly, plumbing is viewed as somewhat more necessary and entailing slightly higher involvement than dry cleaning, although both are low involvement services.

Note that respondents perceive service classifications defined by the high physical component of the product, no relationships, high convenience and discrete transactions as being on the low side of involvement. It is also important that high convenience and discrete service transactions are on the desired side of the perceptual map. High customization and high judgment are somewhat desired and reflect high involvement. The object side person/object classification is basically viewed as necessary and neutral involvement. Finally, as with Figure 2, Figure 4 presents the combination of service and classifications but mapped in the service perception space instead of the classification space.

CONCLUSIONS

The service classification schemes developed in this study provide important insights for services marketing academicians and practitioners alike. These taxonomies have advantages over those proposed previously in that: (a) they have been empirically generated on the basis of service customer perceptions and (b) they have illustrated not only how service characteristics are correlated but also how similar services are perceived compared to each other in terms of these characteristics (cf. Bowen 1990; Lovelock 1983). This information should help service marketing researchers in defining the range of the applicability of their study results.

The taxonomies also serve as a basis for the contingency approach to formulating business or marketing strategies (Ginsberg and Venkatraman 1985; Hambrick and Lei 1985). The contingency approach has been built upon the assumption that there is no universal set of strategies that is optimal for all businesses or companies. Instead, it suggests that there are groups of strategies that are effective within a particular context or for a class of settings. Therefore, the contingency approach lies somewhat between two extreme viewpoints, that is, "broad-brush" research and industry-by-industry approach (Lovelock 1983). The service dimensions developed in this study can be used as contingency variables in building up mid-range theories.

One of the assumptions underlying the classification schemes is that consumers understand and categorize services in terms of the dimensions identified in the schemes. This implies that consumers also use these dimensions in determining similarities and differences among services. Thus, the taxonomies will assist service marketers in finding out the bases for their positioning and differentiation strategies.

The service taxonomies will also facilitate cross-fertilization of ideas among service firms. Companies can learn not only from their industry peers, but also from success or failure cases outside the industry. In fact, they can generate many innovative ideas by benchmarking a successful firm within their taxonomical group. However, without such taxonomies, they would have great difficulty in determining whether a certain case would be applicable to their business. The classification schemes show the service firms (a) how they are perceived by consumers and (b) to what types of service businesses or industries they are perceived to be similar or dissimilar and on what bases they are perceived to be similar or dissimilar to such businesses.

Managerial Implications

The service taxonomy shown in Figure 2 has implications for targeting and positioning strategies. The generic-customized dimension is concerned with the characteristics of services per se, whereas the unique routine dimension is related to service usage situations (or market segments). Firms can use different strategies depending on the service/market conditions under which they are operating. Customization versus standardization has long been a strategic choice in services marketing. The classification system indicates one situation where services need to be customized, that is, the customized-unique condition (e.g., hospitals, physicians and restaurants). Firms or service providers that belong to the generic-unique group (e.g., airlines, plumbers and dry cleaners) can benefit from offering similar services across several market segments (i.e., combined target market approach). With services that are generic in nature or standardized to a great extent, firms should have as their strategic focus the development of new markets. Under the generic-routine condition, service companies (e.g., fast food restaurants, movie theaters and radio stations) should expand the current market by offering new menu items, movies or programs (i.e., single target market approach). Since the market size is limited in this case, advertising and sales promotion may have only short-term effects on sales. Finally, service providers in the customized-routine situation (e.g., universities and banks) should offer several different programs for different segments (i.e., multiple target market approach). In this case, the market usually consists of some distinct segments. Firms can prosper by capturing most of those segments by providing several variants of their services. The strategic implications of the taxonomy are summarized in Table 2.

The service classification in Figure 4 offers some insights into service consumer behavior as well as advertising/promotional strategies. The shopping behavior of the customers of high involvement-necessary services (e.g., auto

Table 2.   Implications of the Results of Figure 2 for Services Marketing Strategies

	Generic	versus	Customized Services
Unique	Combined Target Market Approach:		Customization:
	"Catch two birds with one stone"		"Everybody is different"
versus	Single Target Market Approach:		Multiple Target Market Approach:
Routine services	"Stick to your knitting"		"Different strokes for different folks"

Table 3. Implications of the Results for Service Consumer Behavior
and Promotion Strategies

	Low Involvement versus	High Involvement of Customers
Necessary	Habitual buying:	Complex buying:
versus	Value appeal, price incentives	Informative advertisements
	Variety seeking:	Cognitive dissonance:
Desired services	Emotional appeal	Rational appeal, confirmative advertisements

insurance and long-distance telephone companies) can be characterized as complex buying. Service companies should use informative ads because customers need factual information about the service. Consumers of low involvement-necessary services (e.g., plumbers and dry cleaners) make habitual decisions. Sales promotion, price incentives and the emphasis on service value can be used effectively in such situations. Customers of low involvement-desired services (restaurants, movie theaters, radio stations, banks and airlines) need some "eye-openers" because they tend to be variety-seekers. Emotional appeal or feeling ads can stimulate the demand in this case. Lastly, buyers of high-involvement and desired services (e.g., professional services such as universities, physicians and hospitals) can be convinced by rational appeal or thinking ads. However, since professional services are highly intangible, and thus perceived to be similar among alternatives, customers tend to feel discomfort (or so-called cognitive dissonance) even after the purchase. In this situation, service providers should occasionally use ads that confirm their customers' choice to reduce the dissonance and build customer loyalty. The advertising and promotional implications of the taxonomy are outlined in Table 3. In creating promotional or advertising themes for services, intangible concepts need to be conveyed by simple, tangible cues, for example, symbols, signs, metaphors or artifacts that effectively deliver the message (George and Berry 1981; Hill and Gandhi 1992; Shostack 1977).

The results of this research suggest certain similarities to the a priori classifications and taxonomies of services that have been offered in the literature and discussed previously in this paper. Such linkages seem to suggest that the service strategies for these industries may be viewed with some of the same criteria from the consumer's perspective. Given that all services are not the same, these taxonomies clearly suggest that service strategies pursued by firms in these various industries should be different, exploiting the now empirically demonstrated knowledge of how services industries are similar and different. These results imply the opportunity for cross-fertilization of managerial concepts in and between these industries in terms of service strategy, and also in terms of other strategies that constitute the marketing mix, for example, pricing behavior and distribution strategies (see Table 2). The most important area for cross-fertilization may be in the area of promotional strategy (see Table 3). Further, researchers can now see what service industries logically group together when analyzing services. For example, a researcher seeking to understand service loyalty might analyze industries from similar classifications or companies from a number of different but related industries, resulting in a true cross-sector of service classification and industries.

REFERENCES

Aspinwall, L.V. (1958), "The Characteristics of Goods and Parallel Systems Theories," in *Managerial Marketing,* E.J. Kelly and W. Lazer, eds. Homewood, IL: Richard D. Irwin, 434-450.

Bateson, J.E. (1979), "Why We Need Service Marketing," in *Conceptual and Theoretical Developments in Marketing,* O.C. Ferrell, S.W. Brown and C.W. Lamb, Jr., eds. Chicago, IL: American Marketing Association, 131-146.

Bell, M.L. (1986), "Some Strategy Implications of a Matrix Approach to the Classification of Marketing Goods and Services," *Journal of the Academy of Marketing Science,* 14 (1), 13-20.

_____ (1981), "A Matrix Approach to the Classification of Marketing Goods and Services," in *Marketing of Services,* J.H. Donnelly and W.R. George, eds. Chicago, IL: American Marketing Association, 208-212.

Bowen, J. (1990), "Development of a Taxonomy of Services to Gain Strategic Marketing Insights," *Journal of the Academy of Marketing Science,* 18 (1), 43-49.

Carroll, J.D. (1972), "Individual Differences and Multidimensional Scaling," in *Multidimensional Scaling: Theory and Applications in the Behavioral Sciences,* Vol. 1, R.N. Shepard, A.K. Romney and S.B. Nerlove, eds. New York: Seminar Press, 105-153.

Chase, R.B. (1978), "Where Does the Consumer Fit in a Service Operation," *Harvard Business Review,* 56 (November-December), 41-52.

Copeland, M.T. (1923), "The Relation of Consumers' Buying Habits to Marketing Methods," *Harvard Business Review,* 1 (April), 282-289.

_____ (1924), *Principles of Merchandizing.* Chicago, IL: A.W. Shaw Co.

Daniel, P. (1982), *Service Industries: Growth and Location.* Cambridge, UK: Cambridge University Press.

The Economist (1993), "The Final Frontier," (February 20), 63.

Fisk, R.P., S.W. Brown and M.J. Bitner (1993), "Tracking the Evolution of the Services Marketing Literature," *Journal of Retailing,* 69 (1), 61-103.

George, W.R. and L.L. Berry (1981), "Guidelines for the Advertising of Services," *Business Horizons,* 24 (4), 52-56.

Ginsberg, A. and N. Venkatraman (1985), "Contingency Perspectives of Organizational Strategy: A Critical Review of Empirical Research," *Academy of Management Review,* 10 (3), 421-434.

Goodwin, K. (1986), "Using Consumers' Roles to Classify Services," in *Creativity in Services Marketing: What's New, What Works, What's Developing,* M. Venkatesan, D.M. Schmalensee and C. Marshall, eds. Chicago, IL: American Marketing Association, 159-163.

Grove, S. and R.P. Fisk (1983), "The Dramaturgy of Service Exchange: An Analytical Framework For Service Markets," in *Emerging Perspectives in Service Markets,* L.L. Berry, G.L. Shostack and G.D. Upah, eds. Chicago, IL: American Marketing Association, 45-49.

Hambrick, D.C. and D. Lei (1985), "Toward an Empirical Prioritization of Contingency Variables for Business Strategy," *Academy of Management Journal*, 28 (December), 763-788.

Hill, D.J. and N. Gandhi (1992), "Services Advertising: A Framework to its Effectiveness," *Journal of Services Marketing*, 6 (4), 63-76.

Hill, T.P. (1977), "On Goods and Services," *Review of Income and Wealth*, 23 (December), 315-338.

Hunt, S.D. (1983), *Marketing Theory: The Philosophy of Marketing Science*. Homewood, IL: Richard D. Irwin.

Iacobucci, D. and A. Ostrom (1996), "Perceptions of Service," *Journal of Retailing and Consumer Services*, 3 (4), 195-212.

Judd, R.C. (1964), "The Case for Re-Defining Services," *Journal of Marketing*, 28 (January), 58-59.

Koepp, S. (1987), "Pul-eeze! Will Somebody Help Me?" *Time Magazine*, (February 2), 28-34.

Kotler, P. (1980), *Principles of Marketing*. Englewood Cliffs, NJ: Prentice-Hall.

Langeard, E. and P. Eiglier (1983), "Strategic Management of Service Development," in *Emerging Perspectives on Services Marketing*, L.L. Berry, G.L. Shostack and G.D. Upah, eds. Chicago, IL: American Marketing Association, 68-72.

Lovelock, C.H. (1980), "Toward a Classification of Services," in *Theoretical Developments in Marketing*, C.W. Lamb and P.M. Dunne, eds. Chicago, IL: American Marketing Association, 72-76.

———— (1983), "Classifying Services to Gain Strategic Marketing Insights," *Journal of Marketing*, 47 (Summer), 9-20.

Rathmall, J.M. (1974), *Marketing in the Services Sector*. Cambridge, MA: Winthop Publishers.

Sasser, W.E. and S. Arbeit (1978), "Selling Jobs in the Service Sector," *Business Horizons*, 19 (June), 61-65.

Shostack, G.L. (1977), "Breaking Free from Product Marketing," *Journal of Marketing*, 41 (April), 73-81.

Silpakit, P. and R.P. Fisk (1985), "Participatizing the Service Encounter: A Theoretical Framework," in *Service Marketing in a Changing Environment*, T.M. Bloch, G.D. Upah and V.A. Zeithaml, eds. Chicago, IL: American Marketing Association, 117-121.

Thomas, D.R.E. (1978), "Strategy is Different in Service Business," *Harvard Business Review*, 56 (July-August), 158-165.

Zeithaml, V.A. (1981), "Home Consumer Evaluation Processes Differ Between Goods and Services," in *Marketing of Services*, J.H. Donnelly and W.R. George, eds. Chicago, IL: American Marketing Association, 186-190.

THE ROLE OF MOOD AND HEDONIC ORIENTATION ON THE PERCEPTION OF WAITING

Gian Luca Marzocchi

ABSTRACT

Perception management has gained widespread acknowledgment as an effective approach to managing waits in the service delivery process. In this perspective, the comprehension of psychological states intervening as mediating variables between the objective attributes of the wait (length, fairness, etc.) and the overall evaluation of the service become extremely important. The purpose of this study, conducted in the retailing sector, is to shed additional light on the queuing experience per se and on some of its antecedent states. Specifically, three major areas are investigated: the psychological dimensions underlying the queuing experience evaluation; the role played by the hedonic/utilitarian value of the buying behavior itself on the perception of waiting; and the impact of mood on the queuing evaluation process. The empirical factor structure obtained through the scale development procedure consists of two correlated but distinct dimensions, suggesting a portrayal of queuing in both intellectual and emotional terms. The results also display a significantly higher tolerance to wait for those customer showing a strong hedonic orientation and a positive mood. Discussion explores implications of the findings for service-industry managers and researchers.

Advances in Services Marketing and Management, Volume 6, pages 203-223.
Copyright © 1997 by JAI Press Inc.
All rights of reproduction in any form reserved.
ISBN: 0-7623-0176-7

INTRODUCTION

Time is an important concept in the marketing literature, one that can be seen either as a consequence (dependent variable) or as an antecedent (independent variable) of consumer behavior (Jacoby, Szybillo and Berning 1976). For example, in the literature on "time budgets" and allocation of time (Feldman and Hornik 1981; Hendrix, Kinnear and Taylor 1978; Hornik 1982; Venkatesan and Anderson 1985), researchers seek to use demographic variables to explain how people differ in the times they allocate across activities, that is, their lifestyles.

In this paper, time—specifically *waiting time*—is regarded as an independent variable that might be used to help explain satisfaction with a service encounter. Little research has been conducted on the impact of waiting duration on satisfaction, despite the widespread acknowledgment of waiting as a likely key dimension customers evaluate when they engage in the process of judging a company's service. Only recently has an emerging stream of research begun to emphasize the negative relationship linking overall service evaluations and waits occurring during the service delivery process (Dube-Rioux, Schmitt and Leclerc 1988; Katz, Larson and Larson 1991; Larson 1987; Maister 1985; Taylor 1994). The dichotomy pointed out in these contributions is that between *operations management* and *perceptions management* as separate (but not necessarily conflicting) approaches to the waiting experience (Fitzsimmons and Sullivan 1982; Lovelock 1992; Sasser 1976). The difference between the two techniques is straightforward: while operations management tries to reduce the *actual* waiting time, perceptions management attempts to minimize the *perceived* waiting time as subjectively experienced and reported by any single customer. In this latter perspective, the comprehension of psychological states and emotions intervening as mediating variables between the "objective" attributes of the wait (length, fairness, etc.) and the overall evaluation of the service becomes extremely important (Taylor 1994).

This paper deals with one of the most problematic and managerially provoking kinds of wait: the end-of-process wait (queue) in a grocery store (the expression *end-of-process* is used here, instead of the more common *post-process*, to explicitly distinguish from those situations in which the wait is experienced when the customer is technically and psychologically out of the service delivery system—that is, the usual traffic jam following a major sporting event in a large city). End-of-process waits are usually perceived as most distressing because the service is over, no more value can be received by the service provider and nevertheless the customer is forced to stay idle, virtually captive of the service company. The grocery setting provides an additional problem: the business-specific end-of-process wait is totally unbeneficial for the customer, who is now confronted with the most painful transaction of the overall shopping expedition, the act of paying, by definition putting value in the pockets of the service provider. The purpose of this paper is to shed additional light on the queuing experience and on some of its antecedent states. More specifically, it aims to answer three broad research questions: (1) What are the psychological dimensions underlying the queuing experience perception and evaluation? (2) Is there any impact of the customer's *hedonic-utilitarian* shopping value on the queuing experience perception and evaluation? (3) Is there any impact of customer's *mood* on the queuing experience perception and evaluation?

It can be noted that this research does not specifically address the relationship between waiting and overall service evaluations. This relationship has been taken as an a priori assumption not to be tested further; rather, the focus of this paper is on the antecedents of the queue, which, in turn, are expected to affect satisfaction.

OPERATIONS MANAGEMENT VERSUS PERCEPTIONS MANAGEMENT

Operations management represents the most popular approach to the task of balancing demand against capacity, a physical problem in capacity-constrained service organizations (Fitzsimmons and Sullivan 1982; Lovelock 1992; Sasser 1976). The approach focuses on accurate blueprinting and reengineering of the service delivery system in order to achieve a process as quick and smooth as possible, reducing if not eliminating the insurgence of waits. Two basic solutions are proposed to the problem of fluctuating demand and consequent unplanned waiting lines:

> One is to tailor *capacity* to meet variations in demand. This approach, which falls within the province of operations and human resource management, requires an understanding of what constitutes productive capacity and how it is constrained. The second is to manage the level of *demand*, using marketing strategies to smooth out the peaks and fill in the valleys to generate a more consistent flow of requests for service (Lovelock 1992, p. 156).

Perceptions management, acknowledging that implementation obstacles such as budget constraints could hinder the pursuit of such goals, takes a different path in tackling the waiting issue. In this perspective waiting is regarded as a "necessary evil," somehow inevitable unless one accepts a disproportionate increase in overhead costs due to the oversizing of contact personnel, equipment and service facilities. Accordingly, the focus shifts to a better understanding of the perceptual dimensionality of waiting, trying to pinpoint and modify the most stressful psychological components of the experience.

> The logic behind perceptions management ... is that when it comes to customer satisfaction perception is reality. If customers think that they are satisfied, then they are satisfied.

Similarly, if customers think that their wait was short enough, then it was short enough, regardless of how long it actually was. A major benefit of perceptions management is that it is often very inexpensive to implement (Katz, Larson and Larson 1991, p. 44).

The difference between the two approaches is that while operations management tries to reduce the *actual* waiting time, perceptions management attempts to minimize the *perceived* waiting time as subjectively experienced and reported by any single customer. It is implicitly assumed that the relationship existing between real and perceived measures of time is hardly linear. Thus, the comprehension of psychological states and emotions intervening as mediating variables between the objective attributes of the wait (length, fairness, etc.) and the overall evaluation of the service becomes an extremely relevant research issue (Taylor 1994).

Operations versus Perceptions in Retailing

In the context of the present research, it might be useful to explore how these two different strategies can (or cannot) be applied to retail management, and specifically to the grocery store. Looking at *operations management* first, it is obvious that managing demand is not an easily actionable solution, given the relative insensitivity of customers' shopping time to pricing or communication strategies. It is well-known that the finite nature of time forces individuals to make choices among activities according to their perceived utility (Feldman and Hornik 1981; Hornik 1982). The main divide is the one between work and non-work activities, with the former usually given the highest priority, and the latter further split into three homogeneous categories of activities: necessities, homework and leisure. Shopping is usually included in the necessities category, but this assumption can be regarded as somewhat controversial (for some individuals, shopping is more fun than work, as we shall see later when exploring the hedonic/utilitarian continuum); it is nevertheless undeniable that work dictates the time available residually for shopping, and not the reverse.

Techniques aimed at tailoring capacity to the unavoidable fluctuations of demand appear to be quite feasible in grocery stores. Two popular approaches are the use of part-time clerks (e.g., extra workers are temporarily hired during the Christmas season) and the cross-training of employees (e.g., stockers are shifted to operate cash registers when lines start to be too long). Unfortunately, the picture in contemporary retailing is not always so clear. Typical capacity-tailoring strategies such as the utilization of temporary workers, part-time labor forces and flexible work hours are much less easily implemented in the heavily unionized European countries than they are in the U.S. setting. And while the practice of swapping personnel between check-outs and shelf-stocking is still a solid and viable approach in small independently owned supermarkets (where store dimensions, reduced number of cash registers and low average tickets allow both the cross-training of employees and their impromptu reassignment according to the judgment of the store manager), this is not applicable in modern superstores and hypermarkets: an average hypermarket can easily operate more than 50 or 60 check-outs simultaneously. The high average bill, the connected security problem and the availability of multiple electronic payment systems are all factors that dictate the hiring and training of specialized cashiers; symmetrically, logistics related to the huge dimensions of these stores make stocking a heavily industrialized task, again demanding specifically skilled people.

The result is an increased inflexibility in the management of human resources: check-out shifts have to be planned in advance (usually two weeks), and very little room exists for last minute adjustments. Time series, on monthly and weekly bases, can help tailor capacity (e.g., percentage of check-outs open) to demand (customer flow), but inaccurate forecasts are too common and bring two kinds of costly consequences: if demand exceeds capacity, it immediately translates into unsatisfactorily long queues; if, on the contrary, the number of open check-outs is disproportionately high compared to the customers' inflow, the waste of monetary resources is directly proportional to the level of "overservicing" measured by idle check-out clerks.

This is where *perceptions management* can be quite helpful. On the one hand, comprehension of the behavioral principles governing queuing can drive retailers toward a better understanding of people's expectations and perceptions of waiting, with a view to making it more bearable, perhaps even enjoyable (Mudie and Cottam 1993). The net gain would be an increased satisfaction with the queuing experience and, hence, with the overall shopping expedition. On the other hand, the knowledge of those factors that exert the major influence on the queuing experience evaluation can be exploited in the capacity planning stage, allowing a tailoring of the capacity not to the *actual* demand but instead to a sort of *tolerance-weighted* demand. This new measure can be ideally obtained by weighting the actual demand (customers' outflow) with a *sensitivity* coefficient, measuring and summarizing those factors affecting the tolerance to wait of customers standing in queue.

The basic assumption under which this approach can be managerially exploitable as a productivity tool is obvious: some of the factors affecting sensitivity to queuing must exhibit a relatively stable time pattern, on a daily or weekly basis. If this condition holds, capacity planning (i.e., check-out personnel shifts) can be accommodated to fit the forecast levels of weighted demand, capitalizing on those customers that show a higher tolerance to the waiting time. Later in this paper, some factors hypothesized to affect this sensitivity level will be examined.

The Previous Study

A previous study (Marzocchi 1995) attempted to shed some light on the queuing experience in the retailing (grocery) sector. A two-pronged approach was followed. The research focused on the queuing experience per se, trying to empirically explore some of the propositions assumed by the previous literature as likely to influence customers' satisfaction with waiting times. Some of the relations investigated have been (according to Maister 1985): unoccupied times feel longer than occupied times; unexplained waits are longer than explained waits; unfair waits are longer than equitable waits; the more valuable the service, the less painful the wait; and solo waiting feels longer than group waiting. Surprisingly, results indicated that some of the propositions developed in the service context regarding the psychology of wait did not hold, at least in their original meaning, in the specific setting of grocery stores. Specifically *expenditure, loneliness* and *usage of time* did not influence significantly the overall evaluation of a specific queue (findings consistent with Katz, Larson and Larson [1991]).

The study focused also on factors exogenous to the psychology of customers and related instead to the service delivery system: environmental factors, cashiers' and other customers' behavior and malfunctioning equipment were regarded as having a potential impact on the global waiting satisfaction. It appeared that the *crowding-space* dimension was the most relevant, followed by a *personnel* factor. Finally, it was attempted to sort customers into homogeneous groups according to their queuing behavior, also trying to profile these clusters on the basis of some specific social, demographic or buying behavior traits. This last step produced mixed evidence: demographic variables failed to significantly distinguish among clusters, but a loyalty factor and a sophistication factor (i.e., usage of credit cards, a behavior that in Italy is strongly associated with income and schooling) emerged as explanatory variables of the different levels of satisfaction with waiting.

RESEARCH OBJECTIVES

The present research aims to broaden our understanding of the queuing experience in the retailing sector, deepening and enlarging the scope of the previous study (Marzocchi 1995). Specifically, we focus on the following research objectives.

Dimensions Underlying the Queuing Experience Evaluation

A first investigation of the empirical factor structure underlying the *queuing* construct was performed in our previous study through exploratory factor analysis. In the present study, a more thorough analysis is performed in order to capture the psychological states associated with the waiting process: this research aims to define an extended set of items tapping the different facets of the phenomenon and result in a new questionnaire instrument. An exploratory factor analysis is replicated on the new sample, and the hypothesized structure is tested through confirmatory factor analysis. The relative impact of the different dimensions on the endogenous construct *queuing evaluation* is also tested.

Impact of *Hedonic-Utilitarian* Shopping Value on the Queuing Experience Evaluation

In the time-perception literature, Hornik (1984) first introduced the concept of "enjoyment" as a predictor variable of self-estimated waiting time. Specifically, he postulated that consumers who regard shopping as a relatively enjoyable activity will underestimate the time in line more than individuals who regard the activity as relatively unenjoyable. Consumer researchers have since recognized the substantial duality of the shopping experience: shopping is regarded as a sort of work, whose meaning has to be searched for in the utilitarian value of the goods and services purchased, but shopping can also provide a more intrinsic and emotional reward, connected with the hedonic value (increased arousal, fantasy fulfillment, escapism, etc.) of the buying behavior itself. From a hedonic consumption perspective, products do not represent objective entities but are regarded as subjective symbols, able to cause reactions, judgments and evaluations differentiated from customer to customer. The "entertainment" potential of the shopping expedition prevails, and a less central role is given to the benefits to be gained by the product usage itself. An extensive body of literature witnesses the relevance of the issue (Babin, Darden and Griffin 1994; Hirschman and Holbrook 1982).

The hedonic-utilitarian shopping value is relevant to the present study because a positive relation between the hedonic orientation of a customer and his or her evaluation of waiting can be hypothesized: for people with a high hedonic score, the queuing experience represents, at least to a certain extent, a welcomed extension of a pleasurable experience. This is supposedly not the case with customers with a strong utilitarian orientation: any additional minute spent in the retailing environment due to a check-out queue is perceived as a pure cost, diminishing the net value of the shopping expedition.

The present study focuses on the hedonic dimension, given the specificity of the setting in which the analysis was performed, that is, a grocery store. It is assumed that the accomplishment and task-completion dimensions typical of utilitarian shopping orientation are taken for granted from people shopping at a grocery store. The image of work that can also be fun, commonly applied to shopping in major retail malls (Babin, Darden and Griffin 1994), appears to also apply to grocery shopping, as described by participants of focus groups in the qualitative phase of this study. Consequently, a common core of utilitarian shopping value was assumed for all customers, with hedonic value playing the major role in discriminating among different buying typologies. Two different kinds of effects are hypothesized: a direct effect from hedonic orientation to queuing evaluation, and an indirect effect with mood as an intervening variable between hedonic orientation and queuing evaluation (empirical evidence suggests that shopping can alleviate depression or loneliness [Tauber 1972]).

Hypothesis 1. Hedonic orientation has a positive effect on queuing evaluation; the total effect can be decomposed into a direct one (Hypothesis 1a) and an indirect one, assuming mood as an intervening variable (Hypothesis 1b).

Impact of Mood on the Queuing Experience Evaluation

The expression *antecedent states* encompasses those temporary physiological and psychological states that a consumer brings to a consumption activity (antecedent states are, in turn, just one example of the broader category of the so-called *situational influence factors*, namely, those temporary environmental and personal factors that form the context within which a consumer activity occurs). Mood is a typical antecedent state whose impact on consumer behavior in the retailing setting is receiving increasing attention. Mood is commonly regarded as a type of feeling state, general and pervasive but relatively transitory, with no specific target, not attention-getting and usually not resulting in a sudden change in behavior. It consists of "thinking about positive or negative material and in having easy access to a substantial amount of additional compatible material in memory" (Clark and Isen 1982, p. 77). Moods are distinguished from emotions which are usually more intense, more focused and more attention-getting than the former.

Positive moods appear to enhance the likelihood of performing an extensive set of behaviors (Clark and Isen 1982; Gardner 1985): it appears that a positive mood makes one kinder both to oneself and to others. Moods are also supposed to affect evaluations and information retrieval processes, for example, a positive relation has been shown between positive mood and the amount of money spent and number of items purchased (Gardner 1985; Sherman and Smith 1987). The main objective of this part of the study is to test the impact of mood on the queuing experience perception and evaluation: it can be hypothesized that positive mood affects the evaluation of a queuing experience in a congruent way.

Hypothesis 2. Mood has a positive effect on queuing evaluation.

METHODOLOGY

Operationalization and Measurement

The data collection procedure involved a questionnaire organized on the following themes (operationalization and measurement details can be found in Marzocchi [1995]): (1) actual waiting time (as recorded by the interviewer) versus reported (perceived) waiting time, queue length and reported total shopping time; (2) overall satisfaction with the waiting experience (using a seven-point Likert-type scale); (3) a 10-item scale measuring the different facets (e.g., fairness, boredom, etc.) of the specific waiting experience; the items were presented in a seven-point semantic differential format; (4) a 13-item scale measuring specific satisfaction ratings on exogenous dimensions of waiting based upon customers' repeated shopping experience with the store (this part of the questionnaire will not be analyzed in the present work); (5) a three-item scale measuring the consumer perception of hedonic shopping value (using a seven-point Likert-type scale); (6) a three-item scale measuring the customer's mood (using a seven-point Likert-type scale); and (7) information and socio-demographic data on shopping behaviors. The scales measuring *mood* and *shopping value* were adapted from standard scales (Allen and Janiszewski 1989; Babin, Darden and Griffin 1994; Peterson and Sauber 1983).

The Sample

A survey was conducted among a quota sampling of 208 customers of a single large grocery store location located in a mid-size town in northern Italy. The store is owned and managed by a major Italian retail chain, whose management offered sustained cooperation during the implementation of the research design.

The sampling plan was defined according to the day of the week and the hour of the day, in order to reflect the different conditions of crowding, and therefore queuing, experienced by customers; customers were assigned to cells according to the average number of cash receipts issued per hour (store information system data). Customers were approached by an interviewer according to the sampling plan (Hornik 1984; Sudman 1980) at all times of the day between 9:00 a.m. and 9:00 p.m., from Monday to Saturday, over a two-week period in June, 1995.

Two-hundred-and-eight questionnaires were collected, with a negligible refusal rate; 202 of them were retained for the analysis phase. Of these, 162 customers were confronted with a waiting experience; 40 customers were not (their queuing time was zero), but these customers were nevertheless surveyed in order to get an unbiased picture of the real waiting conditions in the store.

To test the representativeness of the sample compared to the population of the store, a preliminary check was performed along some key dimensions of the sample data and characteristics of the average customer as provided by previous location-specific company surveys. The tests showed that no differences were significant between means of age or sale slips in the two groups; similarly, no differences proved significant between distributions of gender or profession. Overall, the present study sample is comparable to the known store population properties.

One additional caution has been taken with the mood scale. As mentioned above, the interviewee was asked to respond to the group of items about mood *after* the check-out wait was over. Questions explicitly asked for a self-assessment of mood prior to the store visit, and interviewers were instructed to make this point very clear to the interviewee: nevertheless, it could not be excluded on an a priori basis that the measures collected were influenced by the queuing itself, acting as a mood-inducing experience.

The scores of two groups of respondents were compared along the three items composing the mood scale. The first group was composed of the 162 people who experienced an actual wait at the check-out desk; the second group was made up of the remaining 40 customers, who spent no time standing in line. Three *t*-tests were run to assess the differences between means of the three variables in the two samples. No differences proved significant at the 0.05 level. Consequently, we can be more confident that the scores on the mood variables were not influenced by the queuing experience. (Of course, this proves nothing in terms of the overall *validity* of a self-reported scale as an instrument to measure such a subtle and transient phenomenon as mood.)

Data Analysis: Overview

In the first stage of the research, an interpretable empirical factor structure for the queuing evaluation construct is sought. Subsequently, confirmatory factor analysis is used to examine the tenability and robustness of the measurement model.

In the second stage, the basic model is expanded through the insertion of another exogenous construct, the hedonistic-utilitarian perceived value of the shopping expedition; the model is further modified to take into account the role played by the customer's mood on the different dimensions underlying the wait. Eventually, the strength of the relationship linking the different psychological dimensions of waiting to the overall satisfaction with the queuing experience is assessed, and the relative contribution of the dimensions estimated.

RESEARCH RESULTS: MEASUREMENT MODEL

Before testing hypothesized theoretical relations existing among constructs, we sought to understand the reliability and validity properties of our measures (cf. Anderson and Gerbing 1988). We first examine the set of indicators underlying the waiting experience. Then, other measures are briefly examined, and the overall measurement model evaluated.

Queuing Experience: Empirical Factor Structure

In order to capture the different facets of the customers' feelings about queuing, three focus groups and five in-depth personal interviews were performed with a total of 24 customers. The aim of this step was to further refine the range of characteristics commonly used in the literature (Hornik 1984; Katz, Larson and Larson 1991; Maister 1985; Taylor 1994) and tested in a previous study (Marzocchi 1995). A total of 10 distinct items were determined: slow, frustrating, boring, disorderly, irritating, inexplicable, unacceptable, stressing, long and unfair.

The analysis of the 10-item correlation matrix confirmed the hypothesized opportunity to collapse the 10 variables related to psychological perception of queuing into a more useful and empirically derived classification (measure of sampling adequacy $= 0.823$ (Kaiser [1974]). Principal axis factoring was used as a first extraction method to investigate the underlying structure. The analysis led to the extraction of three factors, together explaining 69.1 percent of the variance (ascertained through the use of the eigen-value scree plot criterion).

An oblique rotation was performed because it allows for intercorrelations among factors. Besides being theoretically justified by the research design, aimed at identifying the hypothetical correlated dimensions underlying a construct, an oblique rotation was chosen in order to ensure consistency with the confirmatory analysis; this also allows for some covariation among the latent constructs. Table 1 shows the resultant factor loadings (the average factor intercorrelation is 0.39).

According to well-established procedures (Churchill 1979), the purification of the scale has been carried out through an iterative process: items failing to load uniquely on a factor, or forming a subscale with an unacceptably low reliability coefficient, have been deleted; reliabilities of the reduced item pool have been recomputed and the factor structure thoroughly reexamined. Several iterations of this sequence of analysis generated a final pool of five items representing two dimensions. Looking at the two factors (i.e., variables loading on them) in search of a meaningful interpretation of their substantial meaning, it seems reasonable to label the first factor as an *affective* one (e.g., *stress*), and the second factor as a *cognitive* one (e.g., *idleness*). In this perspective, a queue seems to be perceived not just as a time-draining necessity, as suggested by the *slow-fast* and *long-short* descriptors (a mainly evaluative and thinking-based reflection), but also as an experience heavily loaded with strong emotional contents (i.e., frustration, irritation and stress).

Table 1.   Exploratory Factor Analysis:
Principal Axis Factoring with Oblique Rotation

Variables	FAC 1	FAC 2	FAC 3
Boring	0.85		
Frustrating	0.81		
Irritating	0.80	0.32	
Stressing	0.61		
Unacceptable	0.41	0.39	
Unfair		0.39	
Disorderly		0.38	-0.31
Inexplicable			
Long			-0.70
Slow			-0.64
Cronbach's alpha	0.89	0.33	0.80

Note: Loadings < 0.30 are not shown.

In order to verify the two-factor emergent structure, a confirmatory factor analysis was run (using the LISREL 8 software [Jöreskog and Sörbom 1993]). The analysis produced a chi-square of 4.9 ($df = 4$, $p = 0.294$), a GFI of 0.988 and a NFI of 0.988, thus confirming the hypothesized dimensionality of the phenomenon; construct reliabilities were 0.80 for the cognitive factor and 0.86 for the affective one. To keep at a manageable level the number of observed variables to be analyzed in subsequent stages of model development (and in order to maintain the ratio of sample size to number of parameters to be estimated in the recommended proportion of at least 5:1), an alternative, more parsimonious structure was also tested, with just two indicators measuring the *affect* latent variable (the item *irritating*, showing the lesser SMC with the factor, has been dropped). This new model, showing a chi-square of 0.29 ($df = 1$, $p = 0.586$), a GFI of 0.999 and a NFI of 0.999, with just a marginal loss in the *affect* construct reliability (0.83 versus 0.86), was retained for use in subsequent analyses (see Table 2).

A potentially more serious methodological question is the one regarding the discriminant validity of the two dimensions; this is a nontrivial issue, especially given the high correlation between the two constructs ($\phi = 0.743$). The standard error of ϕ is 0.056, so a 95 percent confidence interval for ϕ is $0.63 < \phi < 0.85$ which, being less than 1.00, shows that the factors are in fact distinct (Anderson and Gerbing 1988; Bagozzi 1994).

A more formal test of discriminant validity can be performed comparing the model under scrutiny with a more restricted model in which the correlation

Table 2.   Final Stage Exploratory Factor
Analysis: Principal Axis Factoring
with Oblique Rotation

Variables	FAC 1 *Affect*	FAC 2 *Cognition*
Frustrating	0.82	
Irritating	0.84	
Long		0.82
Slow		0.81
Cronbach's alpha	0.83	0.80

Note: Loadings < 0.30 are not shown.

between the two latent constructs has been constrained to unity. A chi-square difference test gives statistical evidence of whether the null model (i.e., less restricted) provides a significant improvement in goodness-of-fit over the nested (i.e., more restricted) one. In the queuing case, the null model has a chi-square of 0.29 ($df = 1$); the restricted model with ϕ fixed to unity has a chi-square of 32.98 ($df = 2$); the significant difference in chi-squares between the two models ($\phi^2(1) = 32.69, p < 0.001$) points to a rejection of the hypothesis that the two constructs are not distinct.

Other Measures: Time, Mood and Hedonic Value

Waiting time was operationalized through two indicators: actual waiting time and number of people standing in line. The latter indicator was included because line length is commonly regarded as a spatial proxy for duration of the line itself. *Mood* was measured with three indicators from the Peterson and Sauber mood scale (1983). *Hedonic value* was operationalized with three indicators from the Babin, Darden and Griffin (1994) hedonic subscale. To keep the ratio of sample size to number of parameters above the minimum range of 5:1, the three measures of hedonic orientation were aggregated to form a single composite (Cronbach's alpha = 0.63). Error variance for the construct consequently was fixed at 0.37, and its loading to 0.79.

Table 3 presents the factor loading estimates and construct reliabilities. The chi-square resulting from the model estimation is 29.48 with 26 degrees of freedom ($p = 0.29$), providing an acceptable overall goodness-of-fit diagnostic.

Table 3.   Measurement Parameter Estimates

	Cognition	Affect	Mood	Time	Hedonism
COGNITION1	0.87				
COGNITION2	0.77				
AFFECT1		0.80			
AFFECT2		0.89			
MOOD1			0.84		
MOOD2			0.62		
MOOD3			0.77		
TIME1				0.82	
TIME2				0.88	
HEDONISM					0.79
Construct reliability	0.80	0.83	0.79	0.83	0.63

RESEARCH RESULTS: STRUCTURAL MODEL

The LISREL model representing the hypothesized causal relationship between constructs of interest to the present study is depicted in Figure 1. Cognition (*Cogn*; ν_1), affect (*Aff*; ν_2) and mood (*Mood*; ν_3) are the endogenous latent variables of the model; time (*Time*; ξ_1) and hedonism (*Hedon*; ξ_2) are the exogenous latent variables.

The exogenous latent variables covariance (ϕ) was fixed at zero, because there was no theoretical reason to allow for an intercorrelation between time spent in line (a situation specific measure) and hedonic shopping value (an antecedent, relatively enduring orientation); for similar reasons, ϕ_{21} was left to be freely estimated, due to the high degree of covariance between the two dimensions of waiting.

Overall Model Fit

Absolute measures of goodness-of-fit exhibit satisfactory results. A chi-square of 35.85 with 28 degrees of freedom ($p = 0.15$) underscores a good fit between the model and the sample data. GFI is 0.96 and NFI is 0.95, giving further support to the global coherence of the hypothesized relations. Also, the Q-plot of normalized residuals shows an almost linear patterning, with a near 45° slope, indicating an acceptable fit between model-based (Σ) and sample (*S*) covariance matrix.

Structural Relationships

The standardized path estimates are given in Table 4. As expected, the actual time spent waiting in line has the overall major influence on the perception

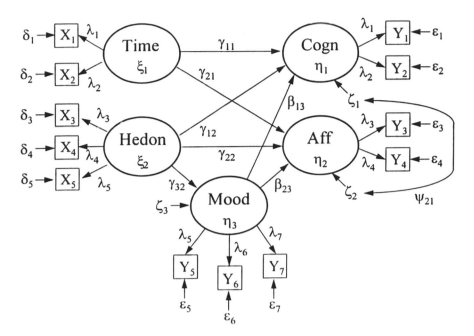

Figure 1. Full Structural Equations Model

of queuing, with a stronger effect on the cognitive idleness factor ($\gamma_{11} = -0.74$) rather than on the affective stress factor ($\gamma_{21} = -0.45$; the minus sign means that the shorter the waits, the more positive the evaluation). The analysis also suggests that hedonic shopping value has a significant effect on both dimensions of waiting, with positive effects on the affective dimension ($\gamma_{22} = 0.41$) and on the cognitive dimension ($\gamma_{12} = 0.35$). Finally, mood seems to have a significant impact on affective reactions to waiting ($\beta_{23} = 0.26$).

Table 4. Structural Parameter Estimates

	Path from:		
	Time	Hedonism	Mood
Path to:			
Cognition	-0.74	0.35	0.05[a]
Affect	-0.45	0.41	0.26
Mood	—	0.17[a]	—

Note: [a] **Not** significant at $p < 0.01$ (all others are significant).

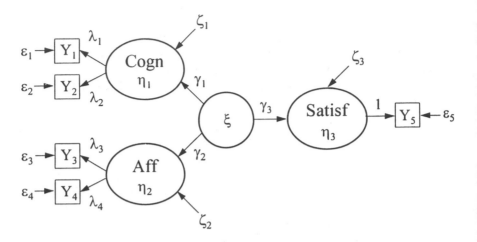

Figure 2.   Second-Order Confirmatory Mode

Second-Order Confirmatory Factor Analysis

As a last step of the analysis, we consider whether the two empirically derived dimensions underlying the waiting experience play a similar or different role in influencing a dependent variable such as satisfaction with waiting lines. This is of theoretical interest; also, previous analyses showed that antecedent variables such as time, hedonic shopping value and mood affect the two dimensions in a very different way; consequently, for a correct estimate of the total (direct and indirect) effect of time, hedonic value and mood on satisfaction, it is necessary to estimate all the complete paths operating through the two intervening variables, cognition and affect. The relative sizes of the paths so calculated can help shed some light on how the causal flows actually work.

One way to represent multidimensional constructs is with a second-order confirmatory factor analysis, which can help reveal the separate effects of the subdimensions of a construct on a dependent variable. This can be accomplished with a model containing a path from the second-order factor to the dependent variable (circumventing multicollinearity problems [Bagozzi 1994]). In the present research, overall evaluation of the waiting experience was regressed on a second-order factor ξ (see Figure 2), with affective and cognitive dimensions loading on this factor. The parameter γ_3 represents the joint effect of the two basic factors on overall satisfaction, and the relative contributions of the cognitive and affective dimensions are roughly proportional to γ_1 and γ_2, respectively.

Overall goodness-of-fit statistics show that the model fits the data well: the chi-square value is 7.52 with 7 degrees of freedom ($p = 0.380$), GFI is 0.98

and NFI is 0.99. While the relatively high level of variance explained for overall satisfaction ($R^2 = 0.71$) supports the hypothesis that the two dimensions jointly play a major role in determining the level of satisfaction with check-out queuing, the relative contributions seem to be significantly different: γ_1 and γ_2 show values of 0.99 and 0.72, respectively, suggesting that cognitive evaluations might contribute more to the prediction of overall satisfaction than affective reactions.

DISCUSSION

The present work addressed three research questions: (1) What are the psychological dimensions underlying the queuing experience perception and evaluation? (2) Is there any impact of the customer's *hedonic-utilitarian* shopping value on the queuing experience perception and evaluation? and (3) Is there any impact of the customer's *mood* on the "queuing experience" perception and evaluation? Results obtained from the analysis phase can be summarized according to this tripartite structure.

The empirical factor structure obtained through the scale development procedure consists of two correlated but distinct dimensions, suggesting a portrayal of queuing in both intellectual and emotional terms. In the cognitive perspective, waiting in line is essentially regarded as a time-wasting experience, evaluated in a way closely (and inversely) proportional to its duration. According to the affective perspective, waiting is a stressful and irritating situation, mainly associated with feelings of captivity and lack of freedom. Customers maintain some degree of rational control over the experience of waiting, because their estimates of perceived queuing times are highly correlated with their actual waiting times ($r = 0.82$).

Structural equations analysis suggests that the hedonic shopping value plays a significant role in influencing both dimensions of waiting. The model supports the hypothesis that perceiving a high hedonic shopping value makes queuing-related negative feelings less likely to occur. The path from hedonic value to cognitive waiting dimension suggests that the decrease in the perceived opportunity cost of queuing time associated with a hedonically valuable shopping experience might make people less conscious of time passing. Additional support for this finding comes from the comparison of average values of "*spread*," computed as perceived waiting time minus actual waiting time and representing the level of "inaccuracy" in the subjective estimation of time spent in line. For the 24 customers exhibiting low hedonic scores, the average value of *spread* was 2.37 minutes; conversely, the 37 customers showing higher hedonic scores overestimated waiting time by only 0.81 minutes (*t*-test for difference between means significant at the 0.01 level). This result seems to support the original hypothesis that high levels of hedonic shopping value, besides positively affecting the emotional side of waiting, make people less aware of the actual passage of time. That is, low levels of hedonic shopping value make people think time is passing more slowly.

Mood displays an impact on the affective dimension of waiting, a finding congruent with the mood literature. Being in a positive feeling state has also been shown to increase one's willingness to strike up a conversation, a finding that our data also confirm: the average mood score for people chatting in line is significantly more positive than for people not engaging in any social interaction ($p < 0.01$).

MANAGERIAL IMPLICATIONS

Undoubtedly, actual waiting time plays the major role in influencing the evaluation retail shoppers make of their queuing experience. Customers are, on average, good judges of the time they spend standing idle in the check-out line. Nevertheless, the results of this study suggest some practical implications for retailers interested in managing perception of waiting times.

Mood, acknowledged as a significant antecedent of an extended set of shopping behaviors, also seems to play a significant role when it comes to queues. While not showing any effect on the *perceived* duration of waits, mood seems effective in moderating undesired emotional outcome of the queuing itself. This means that the usual mood-inducing tactics commonly exploited in retailing to affect buying behavior (lighting, colors, music, etc.) can be usefully applied to waiting management as well.

Perhaps the most promising indications come from the role that hedonic shopping value plays on waiting evaluations. Analyses showed a strong positive effect of hedonic orientation on both dimensions of waiting, suggesting a significantly higher tolerance of waiting for those customers who scored high on the hedonic value. As previously argued, this finding can be used managerially as a productivity instrument under the assumption that the flow of customers who perceive shopping as "fun" exhibits a meaningful and relatively stable time pattern (on a daily or weekly basis).

To explore this opportunity, average hedonic scores were plotted on a hourly basis (see Figure 3). Interestingly, at least for this store, a meaningful pattern seems to emerge, with more positive hedonic levels in early morning and noon customers, and lower levels typical of late afternoon shoppers. Several tentative explanations can be given for this emerging pattern, (e.g., a significant presence of retired customers in the morning opening hours and, on the opposite, the clustering of working people, usually more sensitive to the opportunity cost of their time, in the late afternoon), but this is obviously not the focus of the present study.

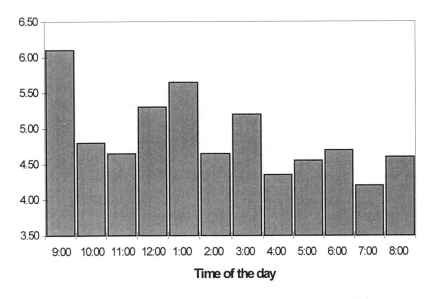

Figure 3. Hedonic Shopping Value Scores (Hourly Breakdown)

What is relevant here is whether this pattern can be found in a consistent way across different locations and different time windows. If this is the case, an interesting opportunity opens up: store managers can reallocate capacity (i.e., redefine check-out personnel shifts) according to the expected hedonic orientation of customers, capitalizing on their higher tolerance to standing in line. In other words, a smaller number of check-outs could be opened, for example, at noon time, which would make *actual* waiting time longer on average, but the overall impact on satisfaction with the queuing experience would be moderated by the high hedonic shopping value of customers, that in turn would make them *perceive* a still acceptably fast, short, fair, unstressing and nonirritating line.

ACKNOWLEDGMENTS

I wish to thank Francesco Cecere and Gian Luca Sacchi for their support in the development and administration of the survey, and the undergraduate interviewers Stefano Dalmonte, Paolo Gatti and Valentino Gaggi for their accurate fieldwork. I would also like to especially acknowledge the helpful comments of Dawn Iacobucci on the manuscript.

REFERENCES

Allen, C.T. and C.A. Janiszewski (1989), "Assessing the Role of Contingency Awareness in Attitudinal Conditioning with Implications for Advertising Research," *Journal of Marketing Research*, 26 (February), 30-43.

Anderson, J.C. and D.W. Gerbing (1988), "Structural Equation Modeling in Practice: A Review and Recommended Two Step Approach," *Psychological Bulletin*, 103 (3), 411-423.

Babin, B.J., W.R. Darden and M.G. Griffin (1994), "Work and/or Fun: Measuring Hedonic and Utilitarian Shopping Value," *Journal of Consumer Research*, 20 (March), 644-656.

Bagozzi, R.P. (1994), "Structural Equation Models in Marketing Research: Basic Principles," in *Principles Of Marketing Research*, R.P. Bagozzi, ed. Oxford, UK: Blackwell, 317-385.

Churchill, G. (1979), "A Paradigm for Developing Better Measures of Marketing Constructs," *Journal of Marketing Research*, 16 (February), 64-73.

Clark, M. and A. Isen (1982), "Towards Understanding the Relationship Between Feeling States and Social Behavior," in *Cognitive Social Psychology*, A. Hastorf and A. Isen, eds. New York: Elsevier/North Holland, 73-108.

Dube-Rioux, L., B.H. Schmitt and F. Leclerc (1988), "Consumer's Reactions to Waiting: When Delays Affect the Perception of Service Quality," in *Advances in Consumer Research*, Vol. 16, T. Srull, ed. Provo, UT: Association for Consumer Research, 59-63.

Feldman, L.P. and J. Hornik (1981), "The Use of Time: An Integrated Conceptual Model," *Journal of Consumer Research*, 7 (March), 407-419.

Fitzsimmons, J.A. and R.S. Sullivan (1982), *Service Operations Management*. New York: McGraw-Hill.

Gardner M. (1985), "Mood States and Consumer Behavior: A Critical Review," *Journal of Consumer Research*, 12 (December), 281-300.

Hendrix, P.E., T.C. Kinnear and J.R. Taylor (1978), "The Allocation of Time by Consumers," in *Advances in Consumer Research*, Vol. 6, W.L. Wilkie, ed. Ann Arbor, MI: Association for Consumer Research, 38-43.

Hirschman, E.C. and M.B. Holbrook (1982), "Hedonic Consumption: Emerging Concepts, Methods and Propositions," *Journal of Marketing*, 46 (Summer), 92-101.

Hornik J. (1982), "Situational Effects on the Consumption of Time," *Journal of Marketing*, 46 (Fall), 44-55.

——— (1984), "Subjective versus Objective Time Measures: A Note on the Perception of Time in Consumer Behavior," *Journal of Consumer Research*, 11 (June), 615-618.

Jacoby, J., G.J. Szybillo and C.K. Berning (1976), "Time and Consumer Behavior: An Interdisciplinary Overview," *Journal of Consumer Research*, 2 (March), 320-339.

Jöreskog, K.G. and D. Sörbom (1993), *New Features in LISREL 8*. Chicago, IL: Scientific Software International.

Kaiser, H.F. (1974), "An Index of Factorial Simplicity," *Psychometrika*, 39, 31-36.

Katz, K., B. Larson and R. Larson (1991), "Prescription for the Waiting in Line Blues: Entertain, Enlighten and Engage," *Sloan Management Review*, 32 (Winter), 44-53.

Larson, R. (1987), "Perspectives on Queues: Social Justice and the Psychology of Queuing," *Operations Research*, 35 (November), 895-905.

Lovelock, C.H. (1992), "Strategies for Managing Capacity-Constrained Services," in *Managing Services*, C.H. Lovelock, ed. Englewood Cliffs, NJ: Prentice-Hall, 154-168.

Maister, D. (1985), "The Psychology of Waiting Lines," in *The Service Encounter*, J. Czepiel, M. Solomon and C. Suprenant, eds. Lexington, MA: Lexington Books, 113-123.

Marzocchi, G.L. (1995), "The Queuing Experience in the Retail Setting," *Proceedings of the 5th EIASM Workshop on Quality Management in Services*, R. Pieters, P.J. Both, A.M. Govaerts, H. Greve, A.Hooijmaijers and M. Van de Ven-Verhulp, eds. Tilburg, The Netherlands: European Institute for Advanced Studies in Management, 335-351.

Mudie, P. and A. Cottam (1993), *The Management and Marketing of Services.* Oxford, UK: Butteworth-Heinemann.

Peterson, R.A. and M. Sauber (1983), "A Mood Scale for Survey Research," in *AMA Educators Proceedings*, P.E. Murphy, O.C. Ferrell, G.R. Laczniak, R.F. Lusch, P.F. Anderson, T.A. Shimp, R.W. Belk and C.B. Weinberg, eds. Chicago: American Marketing Association, 409-414.

Sasser, W.E. (1976), "Match Supply and Demand in Service Industries," *Harvard Business Review*, 54 (November/December), 48-59.

Sherman, E. and R.B. Smith (1987), "Mood States of Shoppers and Store Image: Promising Interactions and Possible Behavioral Effects," in *Advances in Consumer Research*, Vol. 14, M. Wallendorf and P. Anderson, eds. Provo, UT: Association for Consumer Research, 251-254.

Sudman, S. (1980), "Improving the Quality of Shopping Center Sampling," *Journal of Marketing Research*, 17 (November), 423-431.

Tauber, E.M. (1972), "Why Do People Shop?" *Journal of Marketing*, 36 (October), 46-49.

Taylor, S. (1994), "Waiting for Service: The Relationship Between Delays and Evaluation of Service," *Journal of Marketing*, 58 (April), 56-69.

Venkatesan, M. and B.B. Anderson (1985), "Time Budgets and Consumer Services," in *Services Marketing in a Changing Environment*, T.M. Bloch, G.D. Upah and V. Zeithaml, eds. Chicago: American Marketing Association, 52-55.

MANAGING CREATIVITY IN SERVICES

Ravi S. Behara

ABSTRACT

We are now at the threshold of the age of creation—a time when creativity is the key source of value-added and competitive advantage in an ever increasingly global market economy. Creativity is demanded beyond the confines of research and development groups in organizations. Implications for service employees and organizations are discussed in this paper, and a framework for managing creativity in services is proposed. Results of a pilot survey of service firms' practices in this domain are also evaluated. The primary emphasis throughout is that there now exists a *creativity imperative* in services.

INTRODUCTION

Creativity, which is as old as humankind in practice, is not a new concept. Neither is it a new issue in the realms of management theory. Since ideas are the "genetic" building blocks of organizations, creativity is the most important attribute of good management. After recent years of cost-cutting efforts, many companies are looking to enhance creativity in a leaner workplace as a means to spur growth and achieve or retain competitive advantage (Sebastian 1996). So, it appears that we are going back to basics in our attempts to remain competitive.

Advances in Services Marketing and Management, Volume 6, pages 225-250.
ISBN: 0-7623-0176-7

The economies of the United States and other developed countries continue to be dominated by services, which contribute 70 percent of the Gross Domestic Product (GDP) and 70 to 80 percent of the employment in the United States. But the crisis of low productivity that plagues many service operations is the real cause of growth in GDP and employment share (Harker 1995). This issue has been addressed for over a decade through an emphasis on new technologies, quality improvement and, more recently, efforts to reengineer service processes. Such efforts have met with varying degrees of success in implementation. Many service organizations continue their endeavors in these areas, either fine-tuning their successful methods or reattempting to overcome failed efforts. In addition, attempts by organizations to become more creative have only met with sporadic success (Anderson 1992). But the pressures of competition continue unabated.

Successful service organizations continue to maintain an unrelenting pace in their efforts to gain competitive advantage. In addition, such efforts are being played out in an increasingly global marketplace. Both the sources of new challenges and the origins for possible solutions are global in scope. As many countries continue to reduce regulation and open their markets, creative ideas are bound to emerge from many places around the world. Also, greater freedom for the people of the world will result in an increased exchange of knowledge. This will further enhance the possibility that the best ideas could emerge from anywhere in the world. In economies that are becoming more knowledge-based, remaining competitive in this emerging environment is the real challenge of the global economy.

Another key dimension of the current competitive space is the rapid innovation in information and communication technologies. This has contributed significantly to creating an information- and knowledge-intensive environment in which the success of services is dependent more on leveraging intellectual resources than physical assets. The capability to effectively manage intellect is therefore rapidly becoming a crucial executive skill (Quinn, Anderson and Finkelstein 1996).

So, as service organizations head towards the turn of the century, there is an urgent need to look beyond the prerequisites of effectively managing quality and processes. It is essential that the broad-based lead enjoyed by many organizations in services not be allowed to dissipate through complacency. The emergent emphasis on knowledge forces us to look within ourselves for a more comprehensive approach to deal with the reality of ever increasing competitive pressures. In that search for answers, the innate human capabilities of learning and creativity are beginning to take center stage. As a result, there now exists a *creativity imperative* in services.

The discussion in this paper is focused on the management of creativity that is fundamental to the idea generation process. It will elaborate on the various facets of creativity and its management and discuss implications for the management of services. The issues that are addressed help define how individuals and organizations can enhance their creative abilities and bring them to bear on situations that can provide services with competitive advantage. The framework developed in this discussion is designed to aid organizational efforts to develop environments in which human creative potential can be nurtured and tapped for sustained and sustainable growth.

AGE OF CREATION

We are now at the threshold of the age of creation—a time when creativity is the key source of value-added and competitive advantage in an ever increasingly global market economy. The important role of creativity in economic activity is, however, not a new idea. Human creativity has been at the root of all development. But there appears to be an increasing emphasis on the need to be *more* creative. Murakami (1993) refers to this as "creation intensification." In explaining this term, Murakami argues that the agricultural era can be viewed as an externalization of the human pedal function, and the industrial age as the externalization of the human manual functions using machines and energy. The metaphor can be extended to current times. The advent of computers and communication technologies, and their widespread use over the past few decades, can be thought of as the externalization of human sight, hearing, speech, memorization and mental calculations. Hence, the information age is leading to the externalization of the basic human information processing functions.

As we reach the end of the information age, we are heading towards the dawn of the age of creation represented by the term "creation intensification," which:

> refers to the arrival of an age in which society attaches the greatest importance to the creation of new economic values; in which companies attach top priority to the creation of unparalleled technologies, products, systems and businesses; and in which creation plays a more important role than information and ideas play a more important role than data (Murakami 1993, p. 20).

Using the aforementioned metaphor, "humanity is on the verge of externalizing those functions of the brain that are distinctively human—the creative functions" (Murakami 1993, p. 21).

So, it appears that humans are finally beginning to attempt to live up to the name they have given themselves, Homo sapiens—wise being. The demand on human creativity is going to go well beyond merely trying to gain competitive advantage in the marketplace. The key problems of the next century will be how to regulate ourselves in the two critical areas of human proliferation and living in equilibrium with nature (Gaudin 1993). Hence, the technologies and services we create in the future will have to not only be of economic value but also contribute to the long-term quality of life on this planet. Ackoff's (1993) example of the automobile is a case in point. He indicates that while companies around the world are trying to perfect the product and capture new markets, the cities of the world continue to be adversely affected by traffic congestion and pollution. A new approach to transportation services is certainly long overdue. Such larger issues in society, as well as more focused issues within service firms, will need the attention of our creative abilities.

These demands for creativity face demographic challenges in the United States. As we end this century, the number of people in their 20s will drop and the number of people in the labor force aged 40 to 54 will double. This "middle-aging" and "very-olding" of America indicates that we are moving into an uncreative zone or a "creativity bust" (Morrison 1993). Japanese studies at the Nomura Research Institute found that an individual's late 30s were considered to be peak years in creative capabilities, which then appear to deteriorate around age 40 (Murakami 1993). While these views are not universally true, it is a reminder that organizations and individuals need to make efforts to improve and sustain creative abilities in the years ahead.

But the primary challenge that service organizations face in this new age of creativity is how to develop individual creativity and organizations that provide an environment in which individuals and groups can participate in creative work.

CREATIVITY

The fact that change is the only constant in today's environment is clichéd. It is also obvious that the pace of change is accelerating. In addition, many changes are increasingly being made through a disruption of existing processes. But there is one common issue at the basis of change, irrespective of its nature and scope. Change involves either a new product (tangible or intangible), a new process or both. These new products and processes are essentially an implementation of new ideas. So, we find that new ideas are at the core of all the change we are experiencing today. It is also said that necessity is the mother of all invention. The business challenges that we face today provide us with the necessity that seems to inspire the flood of new ideas that drive the unabated pace of change.

The creation of new ideas is the essence of creativity. Creativity has been defined in various ways, some of which are reviewed below. Creativity is seeing and acting on new relationships, thereby bringing them to life (Anderson 1992). Creative behavior is that which results in identifying original and better ways to accomplish some purpose (Shalley 1991; Simon 1985). Simon (1985) states that acts are judged to be creative when they produce something that is novel and that is thought to be interesting or to have social value. More simply, creativity is the act of bringing something into existence that did not exist before (Velthouse 1990). Shalley (1995) defines individual creative behavior in the

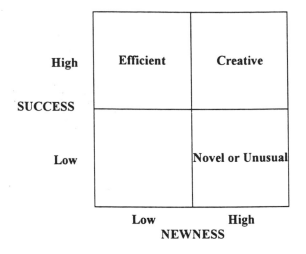

Figure 1. Defining Creative Efforts

context of the work environment as developing novel and appropriate solutions to job-related problems. In management, creativity consists of good problem-solving (Simon 1985). Organizational creativity has been defined as the creation of a valuable, useful new product, service, idea, procedure or process by individuals working together in a complex social system (Woodman, Sawyer and Griffin 1993). Oldham and Cummings (1996) define creative performance as products, ideas or procedures that are novel or original and are potentially relevant and useful to an organization. In an era in which innovation is considered key to competitive advantage, the definition of creativity has evolved beyond being viewed as a human characteristic or a process to a current emphasis on potential or actual outcomes. As Figure 1 indicates, newness and success have become the defining characteristics of creativity.

Hence, creativity at the individual or organizational level essentially involves developing something new that is considered to have value to those affected by it. Creativity is a subset of the wider field of innovation and is confined in this discussion to creative behavior, the creative process and the creation of ideas, goods, services and processes. Innovation, on the other hand, involves successful implementation of the products of creativity. Innovation, in turn, is one of the key drivers of organizational change.

Issues involved in service innovation have only recently begun to receive serious attention by researchers. Quinn and Guile (1988) discuss the management of technology-based innovation in the service industry through case studies that include the typical examples of the FedEx COSMOS IIB package tracking system and Citicorp's development of ATMs. They also address innovations that apply operations research/management science techniques in services. Through these examples, they indicate that many of the essential principles of innovation management in manufacturing environments are equally important in services. More recent studies have taken advantage of the larger knowledge base in manufactured product innovation. For instance, new product development in the financial services sector is investigated by Cooper and de Brentani (1991) and identifies characteristics that distinguish successful service products from failures. Some studies in the development of new services argue for a formally structured approach (Martin and Horne 1993, 1994). On the other hand, Edvardsson, Haglund and Mattsson (1995) find that the service development process consists of four identifiable but overlapping phases: the idea phase, the project formation phase, the design phase and the implementation phase. They state that some improvisation and anarchy are needed, and that creativity and innovation cannot be entirely formally planned. This is not very different from the views commonly held in the area of manufactured product development efforts.

Due to the nature of the discussion, research on service innovation has focused to a large extent on investigating the overall process of new service developed from concept to successful market launches. Lesser emphasis has been placed on the concept creation phase. Iwamura and Jog (1991) investigated innovation in the securities industry to distinguish the innovators from non-innovators, and found that significant differences exist in the management of the idea generation process. This process includes the idea source, the idea generation phase, the internal environment/climate and management's attitude/strategy in supporting the idea-generation process. Such a comprehensive view of new service idea creation is in sharp contrast to earlier studies that indicated new services were a result of intuition, flair, personal fancy or inspiration, or simply luck.

Types of Creativity

Creativity is typically associated with the creation of something new. However, Anderson (1992) clarifies the nature of creativity by describing three broad types of creativity: creation, synthesis and modification. Creation is the making of something new. Synthesis, on the other hand, involves relating two or more existing but previously unrelated events or entities. Modification is the altering of something existing so that it performs a new or improved function. In addition, as a consequence of corporate quality management initiatives, benchmarking has increasingly become an important approach to gaining new ideas. While benchmarked ideas are new to the benchmarking companies, they are established ideas within the benchmarked organizations. Benchmarking within the industry usually results in improvements that help the company catch up with industry leaders through the modification of its

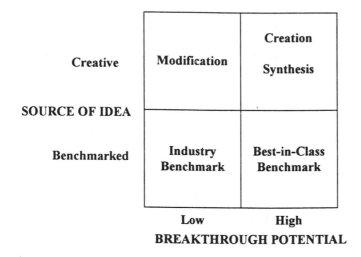

	Modification	**Creation** **Synthesis**
Creative		
SOURCE OF IDEA		
Benchmarked	**Industry Benchmark**	**Best-in-Class Benchmark**

Low	**High**

BREAKTHROUGH POTENTIAL

Figure 2.   Breakthrough Potential of Ideas

current activities. However, benchmarking outside the industry can be viewed as a synthesis of ideas that have been previously unrelated within the industry. The potential for breakthrough solutions is greater in this case. Figure 2 helps classify the different sources of ideas and their potential for resulting in breakthrough and valuable results.

While the three categories of creativity identified above can be defined, they are not easily separated in reality. But Anderson (1992) does highlight an important point that synthesis is the real engine of survival and prosperity and that most of us engage in this type of creative behavior on a consistent basis. All of us already have the seeds of creativity within ourselves, as it is an essentially human trait.

Creative Services

Now, consider some new services that have been introduced. The creative ideas behind the services illustrate the different types of creativity at work. A major issue that is common to most of these services is that they involve "out-of-the-box" thinking. They also demonstrate a strong component of synthesis and the ability of the creators to see connections that others can only discover in hindsight.

Asia represents today's economic growth engine in the global economy. So, it is no surprise that increased business activity makes for a growth market in overnight package delivery services. AsiaOne is FedEx's new network in Asia and the Pacific Rim (FedEx 1996a). It began recently with the opening of a new regional hub at Subic Bay in the Philippines. Subic Bay was a key U.S. military installation in the Asia-Pacific region for a number of years; its location was obviously well-suited for rapid response to areas like Japan, South Korea and Taiwan. In addition, the ultimate pullout of the U.S. military from Subic Bay resulted in well-developed infrastructure being made available for commercial use. A vibrant regional economy, a strategically located base and a well-developed infrastructure combined to form an ideal setting for the hub-and-spoke system of FedEx. Another point to note is that the now famous hub-and-spoke system used by FedEx is conceptually identical to the star configuration that is an established mode of reliable electricity distribution. In addition, the hub-and-spoke structure can now also be seen in airline transportation and computer networks.

FedEx has also begun using the World Wide Web to educate its current and potential customers through the FedEx Learning Lab (FedEx 1996b). In recent years, logistics is receiving greater attention as a source of strategic advantage and as a core competency. A global supplier base, global markets and the success of domestic operations such as Wal-Mart have all contributed to this renewed focus on logistics. Web technology has also seen an unprecedented growth in its use in corporate intranets. There is also an increased focus on learning within firms. FedEx has combined these realities and is marketing its expertise through case studies of how FedEx services add value to an organization and its customers.

While the hype and reality of the World Wide Web (WWW) continues unabated, a small San Francisco company has taken it upon itself to revolutionize the Yellow Pages industry. The BigBook, Inc., is the first value-added Yellow Pages on the WWW (BigBook 1996). The service will provide home-pages for all 11 million U.S. businesses, which will be free to both consumers and listed businesses. In addition to providing details of the goods and services of these businesses, BigBook also provides instant street-level maps for each business and third-party reviews and customer ratings. This service is being provided in an environment in which many start-up businesses are being created on the concept of fee-based home page development. In addition, BigBook expected to include businesses in Canada and Mexico by mid-1996 and planned to expand to Asia, Europe and South America by the latter part of 1996 and 1997. The creation of a free, value-added, global Yellow Pages is an illustration of combining existing technologies and businesses in a unique way.

A combination of existing services to create a consolidated service is a reflection of thinking that goes beyond the bounds of existing convention. The integration of long-distance calling cards and credit cards by AT&T Universal Cards Services is an illustration of this approach. New technology is also a driver in such efforts, as is apparent in the new video-teller machines that some banks are currently testing (Nakashima and Singletary 1996). The major limitation of the typical ATM machine has been the fact that it keeps the customer out of the bank, not receiving the personal service that a face-to-face encounter can provide. This also leads to reduced possibilities of cross-selling services. The combination of ATMs with video-conferencing technologies, both of which are established today, is a way to provide personalized service at remote distances. The use of touch-tone telephones to file tax returns in the United States is another example of the creative use of technology in modifying existing services.

Disney, a name that is synonymous with creativity, has always appealed to the child in all adults. Now, it has developed the Disney Institute, a vacation experience that is aimed at appealing to the adult in adults (Disney Institute 1996). The resort is built around the discovery and exploration of adult interests such as design arts, performing art and films, culinary arts, gardening, outdoor activities and lifestyles. This is a distinctly new concept of an activity holiday for adults, built around everyday activities and not exotic explorations, while maintaining youth and children's activities to facilitate a complete family vacation experience. This different way of thinking, if successful, would represent the creation of a service addressing latent customer needs.

Another illustration of utilizing a new point of view as the basis of creating new services is apparent in the new Integrated Services Digital Network (ISDN) services implemented recently by Bell Atlantic (Bell Atlantic 1996). One of the main problems that poses a hurdle to an even wider use of the WWW is the limit to available channel capacity. This is being experienced by consumers using Internet services via existing telephone services. ISDN technology is capable of providing a transmission capacity that can alleviate many of the delays consumers experience on the WWW. But current ISDN pricing is beyond what most consumers are willing to pay, and telephone companies have not made a significant change to their approach in selling this service—that is, until Bell Atlantic thought of a new pricing approach to ISDN services. Since ISDN services are typically used only for Internet/WWW applications, they would be used by consumers only for a limited time during a week. So customers could be charged a fixed monthly amount for a limited number of hours of usage of ISDN services, very much like many of the Internet services pricing currently in use. By not treating ISDN like other telephone services, Bell Atlantic demonstrated a creative approach to pricing services that was convention-breaking. The validity of this concept has been supported through customer studies that show customer willingness to pay about $40 per month for ISDN services, and reflected in their current pricing structure that is lower than this amount. Such reasoning is also apparent in the development of cable-based modems for Internet services currently being planned. These services are also being planned to be offered at fixed monthly rates, irrespective of the extent of use, like current cable television charges.

The drought of the spring of 1996 inspired the Amarillo National Bank in Texas to offer the "Rainmaker CD" (*Houston Chronicle* 1996). It pays 4.75

percent on any amount from $1,000 to $50,000 over six months. The rate is set to increase by a quarter percentage point for every quarter inch of rainfall, up to two percent for the remainder of the term. Relating rainfall measurements from the National Weather Service to interest rates demonstrates a synthesis that is timely. Even a trace of rainfall ensures a quarter percentage point increase in rates, just to make the offer "user friendly" in a drought situation.

These previous examples are contemporary illustrations of creativity in action in services. They come to the fore and are recognizable because of the associated service products that result. Yet, there are many other important creative ideas that are not in the public eye but are equally important to the effective working of service organizations.

MANAGING CREATIVITY

Creativity is generally considered to be an inherent human trait, although creative ability is often restricted and not allowed to surface. Regardless, individual creativity is the foundation on which an organization's creativity and innovation is developed. Different perspectives have been adopted in studying the creativity of individuals. These include taking a psychological perspective and relating personality characteristics to creativity (Barron and Harrington 1981) and studying the influence of social and contextual conditions on individual creativity (Shalley 1995). Woodman, Sawyer and Griffin (1993) propose a more comprehensive approach in their interactionist model that considers creativity within the context of individual, group and organizational interactions. In considering individual characteristics that affect creativity, they combine other approaches and include cognitive ability and style, personality, intrinsic motivation and knowledge as the key individual characteristics. Of these individual characteristics that affect creativity, limitations to the way we think and intrinsic motivation are discussed further.

One of the individual characteristics that limit creativity is the way we think. This continues to be strongly influenced by the educational system. Ackoff (1993) considers that schools begin the process of killing creativity by influencing children to think in certain predefined ways and through an examination process in which we are continually trying to answer as expected. He also states that this behavior of answering questions by thinking, "What answer do they expect?" continues into the worklife of most adults. This results in thinking for others and not for oneself, thereby inhibiting individual creative thought that requires going beyond mental sets that have been ingrained in our thought processes through a classification-biased educational system.

It is essential to get past mental barriers that come with highly structured education. For example, limitations to different ways of thinking have caused problems for decision makers, and in many cases caused them to become a part of the problem. In response, a Dallas, Texas, consultant brings together senior executives and 10-year-old school children in brainstorming sessions to attack real corporate problems, in which the children make a significant creative contribution that comes from adopting a different perspective (Wise 1991). Many creativity-training techniques are essentially geared towards breaking the limitations in ways of thinking that we impose on ourselves. For instance, in services, we continue to focus to a large extent on either services marketing or services operations as if they are preordained classifications of the reality of managing services. There is little transdisciplinary work in services research. How, then, can we expect to "think out-of-the-box" and develop really creative answers to the situations confronting us?

Motivation is another important barrier to creativity that is internalized and needs to be addressed at an individual level. Motivation theory is too extensive a field of study to address within the context of this discussion. However, we must recognize that intrinsic motivation is considered a key dimension of creativity (Amabile 1990). Further, control of attention or attentional self-regulation is central to motivation (Kanfer 1990). But motivational interventions like evaluations and rewards could adversely affect intrinsic motivation towards a creative task because they are distractive (Woodman, Sawyer and Griffin 1993). Most motivational tools used in services involve rewards and recognition to achieve a set task or predefined behavior that is considered to achieve customer satisfaction. This does not facilitate a creative solution. Consider one typical approach that many services have adopted—to answer customer telephone calls within four rings. This is done even at the expense of a customer who is physically present at the point of service. For instance, think of the number of times the bank teller or a travel agent has interrupted your conversation to answer the telephone inquiry of a customer who has not taken the trouble of coming to the firm in person. The "four rings" criteria has effectively curbed any motivation to provide a creative solution to this situation. An interesting example of tapping into the intrinsic motivation of employees can be seen in Southwest Airlines' recent attempts to thwart United Airlines' no-frills service offerings in California. Southwest Airlines' CEO Herb Kelleher sent out individual videos discussing the situation the company faced to all employees so that they could watch it at home with their families. This approach helped produce a variety of creative responses that included employees from different parts of the country volunteering to go to "the front" in Los Angeles to help the local employees develop new operating methods. Such a response ultimately contributed to Southwest's success in this situation.

Creativity Techniques

While most people still consider creativity training as frivolous or "off-the-wall," it is time to take notice of the fact that many successful businesses organizations are being assisted by leading creativity consulting firms (Wise 1991).

Interest in creativity and related training is on the increase in the United States, Japan and Europe. For example, one-fourth of all U.S. companies with more than 100 employees have some type of creativity training, with at least one-third of the Fortune 500 companies teaching creative thinking in some form (Coates and Jarratt 1994). There has also been a distinct increase in emphasis on creativity by the Japanese in recent years. For instance, Murakami (1993) indicates that many Japanese firms are looking at the creation of entirely new products, systems and businesses as the key focus of corporate strategy, instead of the past focus on share competition based on manufacturing efficiency. This certainly poses a significant competitive threat from an economy that has already demonstrated how it could organize itself around the key concepts of efficiency and quality in the past decades. So, it is time the skeptics paid a little closer attention to this growing interest in creativity. Even some governments are beginning to become attuned to creativity in search of better ways of doing the things they do, as well as in the creation of new government services in a changing world.

Since the fundamental assumption is that creativity can be taught, there are a number of techniques that are adopted in creativity training. These are either individual, group or organizational in context. But most creativity techniques are geared to facilitate "out-of-the-box" thinking. In other words, they are principally targeted at enhancing divergent thinking—something that is considered to be the cognitive key to creativity (Woodman, Sawyer and Griffin 1993). Numerous techniques exist to foster creativity (Van Gundy 1987), including the more popular methods of brainstorming, synectics, thinking through analogies and metaphors, mind-mapping and de Bono's Lateral Thinking. Some of these techniques are briefly discussed below.

Spiral of Knowledge

The creation of knowledge is the essence of successful organizations today. Such creativity is dependent on tapping tacit and subjective insights and intuitions of individual employees, and on testing and disseminating that throughout the organization. This translation of tacit knowledge of an individual to explicit knowledge that can be used by all is achieved through four phases: socialization (learn tacit secrets of the trade), articulation (translate tacit into explicit knowledge), combination (standardize explicit knowledge into products or procedures) and internalization (use explicit knowledge to extend one's own tacit knowledge base). The dynamic interaction of these four stages is referred to as the Spiral of Knowledge (Nonaka 1991). This theory of knowledge-creation requires managers to be comfortable with the concepts of analogies and metaphors in order to articulate their intuitions. Nonaka (1991) describes a three-stage process in converting tacit to explicit knowledge: metaphors are used to link contradictory ideas, the analogies are used to resolve conflicts, and models are used to embody concepts for the rest of the organization to understand. This is illustrated in Matsushita's development of its bread-making machine based on converting the bread-making skills of the expert chef at the Osaka International Hotel into an appropriately designed product. Successful Japanese companies have rallied around metaphors that have been used as "conceptual umbrellas" to guide them. Examples include Sharp's "optoelectronics," Kao's "surface active science," and the "let's gamble" slogan at Honda that led the new-concept car development effort resulting in the "man-maximum, machine-minimum" slogan that translated into "Tall Boy" and ultimately resulted in the "tall and short" Honda-City automobile.

How do these approaches translate into the realm of services? While there is little or no literature that deals with this, the use of metaphors and analogies can be seen when some service company slogans are reviewed. Whether this was the intent of the creators is unsure, but they certainly were developed as an expression of the vision being created for the firm. Nonaka (1991) considers that visions have to be articulated in an open-ended fashion that allows for some variability in interpretation and even allows for some conflicting interpretation. Consider the Ritz-Carlton Hotel slogan "Ladies and Gentlemen serving Ladies and Gentlemen." On the surface, this conflicts with the generally prevalent view of only customer as "king," especially in the people-intensive hotel industry. One of the challenges of this industry is to develop the staff that provide exceptional levels of personal service. The slogan therefore emphasizes the importance and respectability given to all employees, as they are the primary channel of service delivery. It also is a defining concept of how the organization views its employees. The role of a well-articulated metaphor carries additional relevance in services because it helps provide a "tangible" reference to the nature of service. It also provides the impetus to create new or modified services and processes that are aligned with this view of the service. Other examples are Prudential's "Solid as a Rock" to help create products and processes which are financially secure, and Allstate's "You're in Good Hands" slogan that translates into the availability of appropriate insurance products for drivers with less-than-perfect records. Also consider Amsterdam's Schipol Airport's slogan "See. Buy. Fly." This addresses the conflict of viewing an airport as a transit point in one's travels and seeing it as a viable option as a shopping destination. The slogan translates to availability of a variety of products from tulip bulbs to diamonds in well-designed facilities. In addition, typical flight schedules of KLM Airlines also allow just enough time to browse and shop at the airport. It is one of the few airports in the world that has been creatively promoted as an important shopping experience, as articulated by the slogan.

Lateral Thinking

De Bono (1992) coined the term "Lateral Thinking" nearly three decades ago. It is concerned with changing concepts and perceptions. Such thinking leads to creative ideas. The dictionary definition is "seeking to solve problems by unorthodox or apparently illogical methods." The key word is "apparently" since such thinking should be logical in hindsight. Logical explanation of an idea in hindsight is an essential feature of creative ideas and is what distinguishes them from "off-the-wall" ideas. This is why creative ideas appear "obvious" after they have been thought of and implemented by someone else. Specifically, lateral thinking is a set of systematic techniques used for changing concepts and perceptions and generating new ones. It involves explores multiple possibilities and approaches instead of pursuing a single approach. While normal logic is concerned with "what is," lateral thinking is concerned with "what might be" based on changing perceptions. Such thinking is made possible through the use of systematic techniques developed on the basis of the behavior of human perception as a self-organizing information system.

Successful application of lateral thinking in services includes the creation of "living benefits" life insurance by Prudential. These policies allow people to benefit from their life insurance policies while they are alive. Lateral thinking is also credited by Peter Ueberroth for the successful and profitable management of the 1984 Los Angeles Summer Olympics.

De Bono (1992) describes many techniques to facilitate lateral thinking. But the most popular technique appears to be the "six thinking hats" method. The six hats represent six fundamentally different ways of thinking about a given set of issues. Each way of thinking is represented by a different color hat: white hat for information thinking, red hat for intuition and feeling, black hat for caution and logical negative thinking, yellow hat for logical positive thinking, green hat for creative thinking and blue hat for managing the thinking process itself and deciding which hat to "wear" at a given point in time. The six hats method provides a framework for parallel cooperative thinking about the issues at hand instead of the argumentative and adversarial thinking that is dominant in western tradition. Use of this method is established in large corporations such as IBM, DuPont, Prudential and NTT. However, it is just as applicable to help an individual to develop creativity through lateral thinking.

Disruption Thinking

Another approach to "out-of-the-box" thinking is through the disruption of the established patterns of thought. It involves challenging the conventional wisdom. Conventions are current established approaches to the interpretation of issues at hand and represent an unconscious way of thinking and behaving. An example of such disruption can be seen in the point-to-point approach to flying adopted by Southwest Airlines in contradiction to the conventional hub-and-spoke approach of other competitors. Moore and Eastman (1993) of Wells Rich Greene BDDP developed three tools to help disruptive thinking and its application to advertising: the "what if" process, which is a set of proprietary series of questions about the conventions typical in marketing situations; the disruption bank, which consists of marketing and advertising case histories of disruptions that have proven successful in the marketplace; and cross-cultural analysis, which is based on the premise that great ideas transcend physical and cultural borders. The disruptive thinking approach can be seen in hindsight in some breakthrough services such as overnight package-delivery services or no-load mutual funds. The concept is also consistent with strategy gurus Hamel and Prahalad's idea of "stretching the imagination." Furthermore, it is consistent with the current reality of the many disruptive technologies that are constantly changing the nature of services. But it must be noted that while novelty of an idea is sufficient in many advertising situations, novelty alone without inherent value is not sufficient to develop creative service products and processes.

CREATIVITY IN ORGANIZATIONS

A variety of efforts has been made by organizations to enhance creative activity amongst their employees. A summary of key enhancers and inhibitors of creativity as they relate to work context and workplace environment is shown in Table 1. These issues have been identified by a number of practitioners involved in creativity management across a wide spectrum of organizations (Coates and Jarratt 1994; Farnham 1994; LaBarre 1994; Morris 1993; Stevens 1995; Thackray 1995).

Bart (1994) cautions against misinterpretation of the creativity enhancers that have been identified. He provides illustrations of certain forms of bureaucracy in large organizations that are an essential part of fostering creativity and preventing chaos. This is especially pertinent when the innovation phase is also considered. For instance, while "divergent thinking" helps develop new ideas, a complementary "convergent thinking" phase helps achieve closure of the process by selecting the best ideas to implement in a time-constrained business environment. Such a structured process that allows divergent ideas to be expressed is undertaken by Disney to develop feature animations (McGowan 1996). Disney holds three open sessions a year in which line employees are given the opportunity to pitch film ideas to a team of top executives including the CEO. There is also extensive support provided to presenters to enable them to make an effective presentation in an environment that has been created to make them feel safe to express their ideas. Immediate constructive feedback and suitable payment for accepted ideas are an essential part of the process. Disney appears to have created a process that effectively taps into the creativity of all its employees—and keeps ideas and new animation features coming.

Academic investigations into the drivers of organizational creativity continue with a number of hypotheses being proposed in recent literature. The key issue that is addressed is what and how do the different social and contextual

Table 1. Creativity Enhancers and Inhibitors

Enhancers	Inhibitors
Management Attitude	
Commitment to creativity	Emphasis on status quo
Receptiveness to new ideas	Apathy towards innovation
Allow people to take controlled risks	Overly critical personnel evaluations
Limited discouragement in initial stages	Destructive criticism
Promotion of self-empowerment	
Remain flexible as long as possible	
Be creative	
Organizational Culture	
Generally open atmosphere	Resistance to implementation of new ideas
A "safe" climate	Win-lose competitive situations
Encourage intense examination of one's work	Focus on external motivator
Identification and recognition of creativity	Need to look busy at all times
Internal and external encouragement	
Organizational Structure	
Create isolated "creative" units/"skunkworks"	Internal turf and political problems rampant
Allow opportunity for thinkers to connect	
Information Flow	
Diversity in perspectives	Lack of communication and collaboration
Cross-stimulation of ideas	
Exchange of information	
Within-group communication facilitated	
Information transfer within firm	
Information transfer across firm's borders	
Work Process	
New proposals aggressively encouraged	Goal not sufficiently specific
Stimulus provided through development activities	Focus on how work is evaluated
Freedom to pursue ideas	Surveillance/being watched at work
Constructive feedback coupled with rewards	Focus on tangible rewards
Appropriate resources and time	Constrained choice on how work is done
Creativity training	

influences in groups/organizations inhibit or enhance individual creativity. Some of the important hypotheses being investigated by different researchers are now summarized.

Recent Research

An integrated view of creativity in the organization is presented by Woodman, Sawyer and Griffin (1993). They propose a model which interlinks individual, group and organizational characteristics that influence creativity in organizations.

Woodman, Sawyer and Griffin (1993) posit that individual creativity will be increased through open sharing of information, availability of slack resources, cultures that support risk-taking behavior, group diversity, organic organizational designs, and by highly participative cultures and structures. They also consider that creativity is decreased by norms that create high conformity expectations, reward systems that rigorously evaluate and reward creative outcomes, restricted information flow within the system and exchange with the environment, and by autocratic styles of leadership. Creativity is also considered to be impaired when group cohesiveness is very high or very low but to have a positive impact at some intermediate optimal level. The researchers consider an interactionist perspective to be an essential basis for the development of a useful theory of organizational creativity. The creative performance of individuals, groups and organizations is a function of their individual characteristics and contexts. While such a complex model is difficult to study empirically, some efforts have been made to address the interactionist perspective.

Recent research has focused on empirical studies that deal with group and organizational characteristics that influence creativity (Oldham and Cummings 1996; Shalley 1995). Oldham and Cummings (1996) investigated the contributions of personal creativity characteristics and organizational characteristics of job complexity and nature of supervision to the creative performance of employees in a manufacturing environment. They found that the interaction of the personal creativity characteristics measures and the organizational context measures (job complexity, non-controlling and supportive supervision) contributed significantly to the outcome measures of suggestions, patents and rated creativity. The results support the interactionist approach to understanding creativity and suggest that managers should consider personal and contextual factors to increase creativity in organizations. It is suggested that other personal characteristics such as technical skills, cognitive styles, and organizational contexts including goal-setting programs, financial competition and interpersonal competition also be investigated to determine their individual and interactive effects on employee creativity.

Shalley (1995) also investigates the impact of social and contextual factors of coaction, expected evaluation and goal setting on creativity. The subjects of the study were university students. The study indicated that high levels of creativity were achieved when individuals worked alone and when they had a creativity goal. The fact that they worked under expected evaluation had no adverse effect on creativity and was beneficial in certain cases.

The idea of a goal-driven approach to focusing creative effort is also identified by Nonaka (1991) in his discussion on the importance of an effective articulation of corporate vision through analogies and metaphors. He also indicates that the process of creativity is dependent on the personal commitment of the employees and their sense of identity with the enterprise and its mission. Making personal knowledge available to others in the company is also considered important to fostering creativity. He states that Japanese companies implement this through redundancy in organizational design. This is the conscious overlapping of company information systems, business activities and managerial responsibilities. This is done to encourage frequent dialogue and communication that helps create a "common cognitive ground" to facilitate transfer of tacit knowledge between employees. Redundancy is also built in through strategic rotation of employees within the organization. Creativity is also developed by continuously challenging employees to reflect upon and reexamine what they take for granted.

Murakami (1993) indicates that creativity in organizations is enhanced through the development of a target vision that coincides with the aspirations of employees, and when employees are allowed to define their own path to the vision. This is similar to the issues of "shared vision" and "empowerment" that are central to the concept of a learning organization. He also hypothesizes that networked organizations will facilitate creativity through increased exchange of different perspectives among employees. In addition, rewarding creative efforts while they are being carried out is recommended. As indicated by other researchers, an open and free exchange of ideas is also considered to enhance creativity because much of the individual creation in today's complex systems is born out of discussion with other individuals. Finally, he argues that higher corporate earnings rising from implementation of new concepts will help renewed investment in creative efforts.

Murakami (1993) coined the word "creagement," the combination of the words "creation" and "management," and defined it as the management of creation. It requires knowledge of four aspects of corporate activity (strategy implementation, organizational structure, personnel management and information management), at each of the four different stages of the creativity process: hypothesis construction, hypothesis diversification, concept creation and the chain of empathy that links the different parts of the organization together and the organization with the end customer. This matrix of 16 categories provides a comprehensive view of creativity as a value-added activity incorporating a systemic view of the organization.

Another review of Japanese approaches to creativity is provided by Basadur (1992). He discusses the importance attached by Japanese companies to problem-finding. This is because problem-finding is the first stage of creative efforts in organizations and is followed by finding solutions and implementing them in new ways. Organizational emphasis on inducing problem-finding behavior such as anticipating and sensing customer needs is made possible through structural means such as job placement and rotation. Rewards for successful identification, solution and implementation are primarily recognition and job satisfaction, with small monetary rewards. The focus of creativity is both on procedures and products, with importance attached to being involved in the process and not necessarily the quality of any single idea.

The objective is to create "thinking workers" who are "constructively discontent" with their job and the company's products, and are continuously seeking creative ways to improve them. All employees are told that they are expected to create new ideas. This is in direct contradiction of the scientific-management perspective of management as "thinkers." Every employee is considered a "thinker."

Creativity Management Framework

In attempting to study creativity in service organizations, it may be noted that the concepts of creativity and service share a common foundation in knowledge and information. The intangible nature of services is essentially information. That information could be related to an individual or something that is valued. Even the interaction of two humans (customer and service provider) can be interpreted as an exchange of material and psychological information. Hence, services may be considered intangible because of the nature of the underlying information exchange that is involved. Ideas are the product of creativity and are also intangible. The formulation of ideas necessarily involves information that is processed in different ways that are considered creative (see Figure 2: creation, synthesis, modification). So, creative effort is itself a service. It is because of this relationship that an alternative information-centered perspective of organizational creativity may be considered.

Consider the creativity techniques discussed earlier. The Spiral of Knowledge, Lateral Thinking and Disruption Thinking approaches are all involved in managing information and knowledge in ways in which new knowledge can be formed and disseminated in an organization. Yet, all these methods have an unstated requirement—the availability of an information- and knowledge-rich environment in which creative efforts may be attempted. Murakami (1993), Basadur (1992) and Woodman, Sawyer and Griffin (1993) explicitly identify the role of information in creative outcomes in organizations. Yet, the interactionist approach is very appealing from a holistic view of an organization. Therefore, it may be beneficial to evaluate the role of information in organizational creativity utilizing a systemic perspective of the organization.

The Management Systems Model (Cavaleri and Obloj 1993) provides such a systemic approach and is a framework that integrates the five key aspects of an organization: leadership, strategy, structure, process and culture. They represent the social and technical dimensions of an organization. An integration of this model with the informational enhancers of organizational creativity results in the creativity management framework that is shown in Figure 3.

Since the five dimensions of this framework are interrelated, the interactionist perspective of organizational creativity is inherently addressed. Some of the key creativity enhancers under each of the five dimensions are

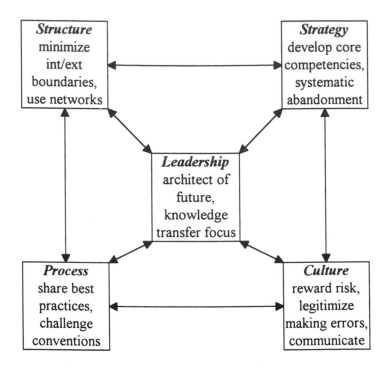

Figure 3.   Creativity Management Framework

also identified. By doing this, the framework provides a bridge from current organizational change efforts (quality, reengineering, organizational learning) in these five areas to new efforts that are required as we enter the age of creativity. It is hypothesized that a concerted and coordinated effort in information management across all dimensions is essential for individual and organizational creativity. But the applicability of the framework to creativity in services needs to be investigated further.

Organizational Creativity Study

A pilot survey study of creativity-related information management practices in service firms was conducted as an initial step in evaluating the appropriateness of the creativity management framework. The companies surveyed included consulting, financial and legal services. These services were selected because they represent knowledge-intensive services and it could be hypothesized they were most likely to be involved in significant information and knowledge-based creative efforts. Senior executives and partners were requested to participate in an anonymous mail survey that examined characteristics influencing organizational creativity and used a 1-5 Likert scale. A summary of results of the 23 respondents is tabulated in Table 2. The low number of responses precludes a more comprehensive statistical analysis ($n = 23$).

Discussion

There appears to be a distinct lack of emphasis on key issues regarded as important to fostering creativity in organizations. For example, a free flow of information is considered a prerequisite for creative efforts. Yet, there appears to be a below-average focus on eliminating internal boundaries and minimizing external boundaries between the organization and its customers, suppliers and partners. Companies are also not adopting a strategy of "systematic abandonment" to a large extent. This approach would involve consistently giving up current products or processes so that new ones may replace them. There is a general tendency in services to reach "steady state" and hope to remain there unless forced to change by external circumstances. This attitude is certainly not conducive to creativity.

Another critical area is that of allowing employees to make mistakes without the fear of penalties. One of Deming's 14 points addresses taking fear out of the workplace. Unless company norms legitimize making errors, there will be fewer people willing to take the risk of coming up with new ideas. Some companies allow their employees to work on original ideas for a portion of the work week. This work is constructively evaluated as it progresses, while no adverse consequences result in the case of failures. It is extremely important to keep coming up with new ideas even if they are not all winners. In fact, not all can be winners, but the success is the process of continuous idea generation. Survey respondents also indicated a low level of internalization of company values by employees. Creative efforts are also suppressed unless company values, like legitimization of making errors, are a part of the tacit knowledge of employees.

Training in services has focused mainly on the teaching of skills to achieve efficiency. Little effort has been taken to teach employees "how to learn." Also, there is a significant emphasis on the external world in Western thought. While this is obviously necessary in services to achieve a customer focus, there should also be an equally important role for introspection. Employees in services place a lower emphasis on reflecting critically on their own behavior. This is reinforced by company norms that penalize any failures. So, instead of learning from mistakes, such opportunities to learn are swept under the proverbial carpet. As a result, companies are not willing to find problems that they may then be able to solve creatively.

Benchmarking from outside the industry is an established technique used to "borrow" ideas and adapt them. While this involves the creative approaches of synthesis and modification, the method is infrequently used in services. Even learning from within the organization appears to be underutilized. There is also

Table 2. Characteristics Influencing Organizational Creativity
(N = 23)

Organizational Characteristics	Mean	SD
Senior Management (1 = very low/5 = very high)		
Spend significant time as an architect designing the future	3.22	0.95
Significantly changed leadership style with lesser controlling	3.31	1.02
Concentrate on internal knowledge transfer and synergy	3.39	0.89
Structure and Strategy (1 = strongly disagree/5 = strongly agree)		
Extensive use of cross-functional teams including customers/suppliers	3.04	1.19
Internal boundaries between functions have been eliminated	2.65	1.23
External boundaries between company and environment minimized	2.96	1.02
Company uses ad hoc management teams or networks	3.35	0.88
Identifying/providing resources for developing core competencies	3.39	1.12
Culture and Values (1 = strongly disagree/5 = strongly agree)		
Company rewards risk-taking in innovation	3.04	1.06
Professed company values internalized by employees	2.83	1.03
Internal communication is frequent and with candor	3.44	0.90
People are heard regardless of position	3.35	1.11
Work environment supports continuous learning	3.48	0.95
Company norms legitimize making errors	2.78	0.80
Training and Learning (1 = very low/5 = very high)		
Employees are trained in "how to learn"	2.66	1.12
Managers have ability to deal with ambiguity	3.36	0.90
Information shared willingly, openly and in a timely manner	3.39	0.94
Employees reflect critically on their own behavior	2.68	0.84
Product and Process Innovation (1 = strongly disagree/5 = strongly agree)		
Company has strategy of "systematic abandonment"	2.52	1.67
Reliance on spontaneous entrepreneurship from within	3.22	1.09
Extensive use of benchmarking from outside the industry	2.26	1.21
Employees encouraged to challenge conventional thinking	3.35	0.83
Effective dissipation of internal best practices/innovations	2.78	0.80
Internal competition between teams used to innovate	2.22	0.80
Company uses anthropologists to study work practices	1.22	0.42
Company uses IT to enhance organizational memory	2.52	1.56
Outcomes (1 = very low/5 = very high)		
More innovative new products	3.05	1.07
Employee adaptability	3.05	0.90
Employee commitment	3.32	1.00

a below-average effort on effective dissipation of internal best practices and innovations. This may be expected since more effort is required to eliminate internal barriers within the organization, despite senior management claims to be making efforts in the areas of internal knowledge transfer and synergy. Internal competition is also not utilized to create new products and processes.

This may also be expected in an environment where failure is not accepted as an integral part of learning.

Information technology is being used in services to improve delivery processes as well as in developing new services. But there is little effort being made to use technology to develop databases of ideas and development histories that employees may use to enhance their creativity. Once again, there is a lack of emphasis on information handling and sharing. It is also interesting to note that while services involve a significant human element, the use of anthropologists to study service activities has been extremely limited.

Services were evaluated along a number of organizational characteristics that have been identified in literature as key to influencing creative behavior in organizations. The results show below average performance along many of these dimensions. Hence, it is no surprise that the number of innovative new products, employee adaptability to a rapidly changing business environment and employee commitment to organizational vision are all at average levels. Service organizations have to look into the future and acknowledge that many of them are not prepared for the inevitable new reality of the age of creation. A *creativity imperative* in services is not a hypothetical scenario but a business reality.

CONCLUSIONS

The primary purpose of this paper is to highlight the *creativity imperative* in services today. Issues related to individual creativity and organizational creativity were discussed. The critical role of information in services and its primary role in creativity suggest that an information-based framework of managing creativity in service organizations may be useful.

Managerial Implications

The fundamental value of new ideas is the basis of the emerging age of creation. Knowledge and information are the building blocks that are used in idea creation. Yet, creativity is of different types (modification, synthesis and creation), which use information differently. All these approaches to generating new ideas are useful in services. Also, all employees should be the "thinkers" of an organization. As competitive advantage increasingly becomes dependent on creativity, it is also becoming increasingly clear that everyone must contribute to the creative capital of an organization. A greater understanding of managing services in this context is critical.

The creativity management framework developed in this paper provides an integrated approach to managing services, all of which are information-intensive. By adopting a systemic approach to organizations and an information-centered approach to creativity, this model provides continuity for managers currently involved in other change initiatives like quality, reengineering and organizational learning efforts. It shows that aspects of improvement such as effective information-sharing, hearing people regardless of position and learning to reflect critically are now prerequisites for an emerging type of organization. The framework helps identify the key information and knowledge-oriented characteristics that influence organizational creativity.

While the pilot survey study was a first step in determining where services are on the road to the age of creation, the results provide managers with an early warning that much needs to be done in all the areas identified. While more comprehensive studies are obviously required, managers can benefit by asking themselves the questions raised in the study.

Research Issues

A number of research issues exist. First and foremost, a larger sample size and suitable analysis is required to evaluate the components of the framework presented in this paper. Further research is also needed to determine the interactiveness of the elements of the model in relationship to the creativity measures. In addition, larger questions that remain to be answered in organizational creativity research (such as the effectiveness of the measures of organizational creativity) also need to be addressed.

The linkages between organizational change initiatives such as quality, organizational learning and efforts in creativity enhancements in services need to be investigated, and the information-based creativity framework provides the vehicle. A possible hypothesis that could be investigated here is that quality management and organizational learning initiatives in organizations have led to reducing organizational and individual inhibitors to creativity.

Finally, attempts at identifying best practices in this domain can be made as other studies are conducted to investigate creativity in services. A step in that direction can be taken by initiating specific case studies in creativity management in services utilizing the framework developed here.

In conclusion, it must be noted that while our immediate attention in business and academia appears to be focused on the competitive benefits of creativity, the real challenge that faces us all is the creation of an environment in which people are gainfully employed to serve and add value to themselves and society. This will be the true test of human creativity in the age of creation.

ACKNOWLEDGMENTS

Expression of oneself in a creative way that has value is deeply satisfying and is one of the most important things that human beings can do. Therefore, it is one of the most important responsibilities that managers can have–to make that process happen well.

—John Kao

This author would like to thank Professor Teresa Swartz and the anonymous reviewers for having admirably fulfilled their responsibilities in guiding this contribution to completion.

REFERENCES

Ackoff, R.L. (1993), "Rethinking Education," *Journal of Management Consulting*, 7 (4), 3-8.

Amabile, T.M. (1990), "Within You, Without You: The Social Psychology of Creativity and Beyond," in *Theories of Creativity*, M.A. Runco and R.S. Albert, eds. Newbury Park, CA: Sage, 61-91.

Anderson, J.V. (1992), "Weirder than Fiction: The Reality and Myths of Creativity," *Academy of Management Executive*, 6 (4), 40-47.

Barron, F.B. and D.M. Harrington (1981), "Creativity, Intelligence, and Personality," *Annual Review of Psychology*, 32, 439-476.

Bart, C.K. (1994), "Gagging on Chaos," *Business Horizons*, 37 (5), 26-37.

Basadur, M. (1992), "Managing Creativity: A Japanese Model," *Academy of Management Executives*, 6 (2), 29-42.

Bell Atlantic (1996), "Bell Atlantic to Lower Rates 15% to 86% for Consumer Access to Cyberspace," *Bell Atlantic* (October 31). http://www.ba.com/nr/96/apr/4-17isdn.htm

BigBook (1996), "Welcome to BigBook—A Whole New Kind of Yellow Pages," *BigBook* (October 31). http://www.bigbook.com

Cavaleri, S. and K. Obloj (1993), *Management Systems: A Global Perspective*. Belmont, CA: Wadsworth Publishing.

Coates, J.F. and J. Jarratt (1994), "Workplace Creativity," *Employment Relations Today*, 21 (1), 11-23.

Cooper, R.G. and U. de Brentani (1991), "New Industrial Financial Services: What Distinguishes the Winners," *The Journal of Product Innovation Management*, 8 (2), 75-90.

De Bono, E. (1992), *Serious Creativity*. New York: HarperCollins.

Disney Institute (1996), "Welcome to a New Kind of Vacation," *Walt Disney World* (October 31). http://www.Disney.com/DisneyWorld/DisneyInstitute/welcome.html

Edvardsson, B., L. Haglund and J. Mattsson (1995), "Analysis, Planning, Improvisation and Control in the Development of New Services," *International Journal of Service Industry Management*, 6 (2), 24-35.

Farnham, A. (1994), "How to Nurture Creative Sparks," *Fortune*, 129 (January 10), 94-99.

FedEx (1996a), "AsiaOne FedEx," *Federal Express* (October 31). http://www.fedex.com/Al
———— (1996b), "FedEx Learning Lab," Federal Express (October 31). http://www.fedex.com/logistics

Gaudin, T. (1993), "The Age of Discontinuity," *Challenging Conventional Thinking for Competitive Advantage*, The Conference Board Report Number 1021, 8-10.

Harker, P.T. (1995), "The Service Quality and Productivity Challenge" in *The Service Productivity and Quality Challenge*, P.T. Harker, ed. Dordrecht, The Netherlands: Kluwer Academic Publishers, 1-10.

Houston Chronicle (1996), "How About a Rain Check?" (May 4), C1.

Iwamura, A. and V.M. Jog (1991), "Innovation, Organization Structure and Management of the Innovation Process in the Securities Industry," *The Journal of Product Innovation Management*, 8 (2), 104-116.

Kanfer, R. (1990), "Motivation Theory and Industrial/Organizational Psychology," in *Handbook of Industrial and Organizational Psychology*, Vol. 1, M.D. Dunnette, ed. Palo Alto, CA: Consulting Psychologists Press, 75-170.

LaBarre, P. (1994), "The Creative Revolution," *Industry Week*, 243 (May 16), 12-18.

Martin, C.R., Jr. and D.A. Horne (1993), "Services Innovation: Successful Versus Unsuccessful Firms," *International Journal of Service Industry Management*, 3, 25-38.

_____ and _____ (1994), "The Congruence of New Product and New Service Development in Management of Services: A Multidisciplinary Approach," paper presented at the Third International Research Seminar in Services Management, Aix-de-Provence, France.

McGowan, J. (1996), "How Disney Keeps Ideas Coming," *Fortune*, 133 (April 1), 131-134.

Moore, M. and J. Eastman (1993), "Disruption in the Marketplace," *Challenging Conventional Thinking for Competitive Advantage*, The Conference Board Report Number 1021, 17-19.

Morris, L. (1993), "Corporate Creativity Defined and Observed," *Training and Development*, 47 (1), 73-76.

Morrison, I. (1993), "The Futures Tool Kit," *Challenging Conventional Thinking for Competitive Advantage*, The Conference Board Report Number 1021, 29-31.

Murakami, T. (1993), "Creating Creativity," *Challenging Conventional Thinking for Competitive Advantage*, The Conference Board Report Number 1021, 20-23.

Nakashima E. and M. Singletary (1996), "Show and Teller," *The Washington Post*, (August 10), D1-D2.

Nonaka, I. (1991), "The Knowledge-Creating Company," in *The Learning Imperative*, R. Howard and R.D. Haas, eds. Boston, MA: Harvard Business School Publishing, 41-56.

Oldham, G.R. and A. Cummings (1996), "Employee Creativity: Personal and Contextual Factors at Work," *Academy of Management Journal*, 39 (3), 607-634.

Quinn, B.J., P. Anderson and S. Finkelstein (1996), "Managing Professional Intellect: Making the Most of the Best," *Harvard Business Review*, 74 (2), 71-80.

_____ and B.R. Guile (1988), "Managing Innovation in Services," in *Managing Innovation: Cases from the Services Industries*, B.R. Guile and J.B. Quinn, eds. Washington, DC: National Academy Press, 1-8.

Sebastian, P. (1996), "Be Creative. Now! Companies Try to Inspire Creativity in a Leaner Workplace," *The Wall Street Journal*, (June 13), A1.

Shalley, C.E. (1991), "Effects of Productivity Goals, Creativity Goals, and Personal Discretion on Individual Creativity," *Journal of Applied Psychology*, 76, 179-185.

_____ (1995), "Effects of Coaction, Expected Evaluation, and Goal Setting on Creativity and Productivity," *Academy of Management Journal*, 38 (2), 483-503.

Simon, H.A. (1985), "What We Know About the Creative Process," in *Frontiers in Creative and Innovative Management*, R.L. Kuhn, ed. Cambridge, MA: Ballinger, 3-20.

Stevens, T. (1995), "Creativity Killers," *Industry Week*, 244 (January 23), 63.

Thackray, J. (1995), "That Vital Spark," *Management Today*, (July), 56-59.

Van Gundy, A.B. (1987), *Creative Problem Solving: A Guide to Trainers and Management*. New York: Quorum Books.

Velthouse, B.A. (1990), "Creativity and Empowerment: A Complementary Relationship," *Review of Business*, 12 (2), 13-18.

Wise, R. (1991), "The Boom in Creativity Training," *Across the Board*, 28 (6), 38-42.

Woodman R.W., J.E. Sawyer and R.W. Griffin (1993), "Towards a Theory of Organizational Creativity," *Academy of Management Review*, 18 (2), 293-321.

ABOUT THE EDITORS

Teresa A. Swartz is a Professor of Marketing at California Polytechnic State University in San Luis Obispo, California. Prior to joining Cal Poly, she was on the faculty of Arizona State University for 11 years and was actively involved with The First Interstate Center for Services Marketing at A.S.U. for 11 years. In addition, she has twice served on the International Board of Directors of the American Marketing Association and was Vice President of the Services Marketing Division. Her research interests focus on various behavioral issues related to the services sector, including: a special emphasis on professional services, identifying ways service principles and concepts can be applied in the public sector and understanding various factors that impact the customer's evaluation of the service experience. She has published numerous articles and her work has appeared in a number of outlets, including the *Journal of Marketing, Journal of the Academy of Marketing Science* and *Journal of Public Policy and Marketing*. Dr. Swartz earned her Ph.D. in Business at The Ohio State University.

David E. Bowen is a Professor of Management at Arizona State University West. From 1983 to 1991, he served on the faculty of the University of Southern California, School of Business, Department of Management and Organization. He received his Ph.D. in Business Administration from Michigan State University. Dr. Bowen's areas of expertise include (1) human resource management (HRM) practices in service organizations; (2) managing customers; (3) service strategy, culture and quality; and (4) international HRM practices. He has consulted with numerous service companies, including Bellcore of AT&T, First Interstate Services Corporation and Kinko's Copies. He is a regular faculty member of the Customer Service Executive programs offered by the University of Southern California and the First Interstate Center for Services Marketing at Arizona State University in Tempe. Dr. Bowen has published more than a dozen articles on services management in recent years in journals such as *Sloan Management Review*, the *Journal of Applied Psychology, Organizational Dynamics* and the *Academy of Management Review*. His most recent book is *Winning the Service Game* (Harvard Business School Press, 1995), and he coauthored *Service Management Effectiveness: Balancing Strategy, Organization and Human Resources, Operations, and Marketing*, published by Jossey-Bass in 1990. He is a member of the editorial review board of the *Academy of Management Review*.

Dawn Iacobucci is a Professor of Marketing in the J.L. Kellogg Graduate School of Management at Northwestern University. She received her Ph.D. in Quantitative Psychology from the University of Illinois in 1987, after which she joined Northwestern. She teaches Services Marketing and Marketing Research to M.B.A. students and Multivariate Statistics to Ph.D. students. Her research on modeling dyadic interactions and social networks has appeared in such journals as *Psychological Bulletin, Psychometrika* and the *Journal of Marketing Research*. Her research on services and customer satisfaction has appeared in *Advances in Services Marketing and Management*, the *Journal of Marketing*, the *Journal of Consumer Psychology*, the *Journal of Retailing* and *Consumer Services*.

ABOUT THE CONTRIBUTORS

Ravi S. Behara is an Associate Professor at George Mason University, Virginia. His primary research interests are in Services Management and currently include issues in design, quality, decision making and systems thinking. He has published articles in the *International Journal of Quality and Reliability Management*, the *International Journal of Purchasing and Materials Management*, the *Journal of Small Business Strategy, Quality Progress* and numerous conference proceedings. He has also published articles related to services management in research-oriented books. Dr. Behara received his Ph.D. from Manchester Metropolitan University, United Kingdom, and a B.E. in Electrical Engineering from the Indian Institute of Science, India. He has taught at the Manchester School of Management, the University of Manchester Institute of Science and Technology, United Kingdom, and Stephen F. Austin State University, Texas. Before moving into academia, Dr. Behara worked in project management in India and Saudi Arabia.

Deborah L. Cowles is an Associate Professor of Marketing in the School of Business at Virginia Commonwealth University, Richmond, Virginia. She has authored numerous articles in the areas of services and relationship marketing which have appeared in a number of publications, including the *Journal of Marketing*, the *Service Industries Journal* and *The International Journal of Service Industries Management*. Her degrees include a Bachelor of Arts in Journalism from Ohio Wesleyan University, Master of Arts in Advertising from The University of Texas at Austin and Ph.D. in Business Administration with a major in Marketing from Arizona State University. Her primary research interests include the dynamics of the service encounter as well as the role of the service encounter in transactional retail settings.

Lawrence F. Cunningham is a Professor of Marketing in the Graduate School of Business at the University of Colorado at Denver, where he is regularly recognized for his outstanding research. He is the author of numerous case studies, textbook chapters and journal articles in the fields of Marketing and Transportation. His most recent articles have addressed the issue of service quality in the airline industry, service dimensions from a domestic and international perspective, and service loyalty. Recently, Dr. Cunningham has served as principal investigator on a large number of major contracts involving service quality and related issues for state and local governments. In addition, he is a sought-after guest lecturer on the topic of services marketing for major computer firms across the United States. He has served as a Visiting Professor of Marketing at the Fuqua School of Business at Duke University, Bond University in Australia and the Helsinki School of Economics.

Ko de Ruyter is an Associate Professor of Marketing and Marketing Research at Maastricht University. His research interests include services marketing, customer information technology, customer complaining behavior, service innovations and relationship marketing. His work has appeared in the *International Journal of Research in Marketing, Advances in Services Marketing and Management*, the *Journal of Marketing Education* and the *Total Quality Management Journal*.

Richard Germain is an Associate Professor in the Department of Marketing, College of Business Administration, Oklahoma State University. He has authored books in marketing history and business logistics, including *Was There a Pepsi Generation Before Pepsi Discovered It? Youth-Based Segmentation in Marketing* (1992) and *Logistical Excellence: It's Not Business as Usual* (1992). His refereed works have appeared in the *Journal of Marketing Research*, the *Journal of the Academy of Marketing Science*, and the *Journal of Business Research*, among others.

Roger Hallowell is a Doctoral Candidate at the Harvard Business School whose research focuses on Service Management. His dissertation examines service firms with dual competitive advantage (organizations having cost leadership while delivering differentiated service). He has served as Research Associate to the Service Management Interest Group at Harvard Business School, in which capacity he researched and wrote case studies on service companies and contributed to several academic and popular books and articles. His work has appeared in *Human Resource Management, Human Resource Planning* and *The International Journal of Service Industry Management*. He holds an M.B.A. and a B.A. from Harvard University and has worked in service industries as diverse as banking and industrial uniform rental.

Moonkyu Lee is an Assistant Professor of Marketing at Yonsei University, Seoul, Korea. He received his M.S.B.A. and Ph.D. degrees from the University of Illinois at Urbana-Champaign. His research interests include consumer information processing and choice, marketing strategy and services marketing. He has published in the *Journal of Business Research*, the *Journal of Services Marketing* and the *Journal of International Marketing*. He has also presented at national and regional conferences, including the Albert Haring Symposium, the Marketing Science Conference and the Association for Consumer Research Conference. Dr. Lee received the 1988 Steven J. Shaw Award for the best student paper, presented by the Southern Marketing Association.

Jos Lemmink is an Associate Professor of Marketing at the Department of Marketing and Marketing Research at Maastricht University, the Netherlands. He received his Ph.D. from the University of Limburg. He has held a visiting professorship in Australia (1995) and published six books on the topic of quality management in services. He has published extensively in marketing and quality journals such as the *European Journal of Marketing*, the *International Journal of Logistics Management* and the *Journal of Reliability and Quality Management*. Dr. Lemmink won the 1995 Hans B. Thorelli Best Paper Award of the *European Journal of Marketing*. His research interests include quality management, service quality, multivariate modeling and dynamic aspects of service encounters.

Sharron J. Lennon is a Professor in Consumer and Textile Sciences, College of Human Ecology, The Ohio State University. She received her Ph.D. in Consumer Sciences and Retailing from Purdue University. Her major areas of publication are concerned with the social perception of clothing characteristics and wholesale and retail delivery systems and their customers. She is an International Textile and Apparel Association Fellow and is a prolific author, publishing in a wide range of journals, including the *Journal of Small Business Research, Semiotics*, the *Family and Consumer Sciences Research Journal*, the *Clothing and Textiles Research Journal*, the *Journal of Law and Inequality* and *Dress*.

Barbara Lutz is Chief Underwriter for Century Life of America, where she began her career in 1980 in the policy service area. She has a B.A. from Luther College and an M.B.A. from Northern Iowa University. She has been active in various professional organizations as a member of both the Iowa Home Office Underwriters Association and the Home Office Life Underwriters Association (HOLUA). She served two years on the board of the Institute of Home Office Underwriters (IHOU). Both the HOLUA and the IHOU are organizations made up of home office Underwriters in North America. Barbara spent the last eight years in various capacities of the Life Underwriting Education Committee.

Gian Luca Marzocchi is an Associate Professor of Marketing in the Faculty of Economics and Business Administration and the Faculty of Statistics at the University of Bologna. Previously, he was an Associate Professor of Marketing Research at the University of Calabria. His teaching fields are marketing management, services marketing and marketing research methodologies. His major area of research is services marketing and management, focusing specifically on the development and testing of service quality models in the retail environment. His research interests also include the role played by information and communication technologies in sustaining and enhancing network relationships among distribution channel members. He has published numerous articles in scholarly journals.

Jan Mattsson has been a Professor of Business Administration in the Department of Social Sciences, Roskilde University, Denmark, since 1996. He received his doctorate (D.B.A.) in International Management from Gothenberg University, Sweden, in 1982 and was appointed Associate Professor in the Department of Business Administration in 1985. He has held several professorships and international visiting professorships, in Norway (1986-1987), New Zealand (1993 and 1996) and Australia (1994-1996). He has published extensively in marketing and services in journals such as *European Journal of Marketing, International Journal of Service Industry Management* and the *Service Industries Journal.* His current research interests focus on the dynamics of the service encounter.

Brian Moores was, until his retirement, a Professor of Operations Management and the Director of the Institute of Services Management at Manchester Business School. Prior to that, he held faculty appointments at the University of Stirling, UWIST and UMIST. Originally qualified as an aeronautical engineer, he pursued postgraduate study in Operations Research at John Hopkins University, where he developed a long-standing interest in the management of health care services. That interest eventually led indirectly to research on a range of quality and customer service issues both within and without that particular health care environment. In 1986, he published *Are They Being Served?*, the first British collection of papers on the theme of customer service. He has published in excess of 100 articles and has contributed chapters to a number of books, including one on Customer Service in the recently published *Financial Times Handbook of Management.* Now an Emeritus Professor of Manchester University, he continues to provide advice to a limited number of organizations.

Michelle C. Paul received her B.A. from Emory University in 1993 and is currently a graduate student at the University of Maryland at College Park. She recently completed her M.A. and is now pursuing her Ph.D. in Industrial/

Organizational Psychology. Her research interests include services management, leadership and organizational climate and culture.

Javier Reynoso is a member of the faculty of the Graduate School of Business Administration and Leadership (EGADE) at The Monterrey Institute of Technology (ITESM) in Monterrey, Mexico. Prior to joining academia, he worked as an internal consultant on total quality management in major Mexican manufacturing industries. He has presented results from his interventions in Mexican industries in the United States, Canada and Japan. He obtained his Ph.D. in operations management and strategy in the service sector at Manchester Business School, University of Manchester, England, where he developed his interest in the service field. He is a leading researcher in services management in Latin America. He has presented papers in major international service conferences in Finland, Sweden, France and the United States. He is coordinator in Mexico of the *Service Research Interest Group* (SERVSIG) and collaborates as referee for the *International Journal of Service Industry Management*. He also conducts research and consultancy projects in service industries in Mexico and South America. He participates as an advisor for the Modernization Program of Public Administration of the Mexican Federal Government. His main interest is in promoting and developing research and teaching activities on services management in Mexico and Latin America. Currently, he is working on the integration of the *Latin American Academy of Services Management*.

Benjamin Schneider, a Professor of Psychology at the University of Maryland, College Park, received his Ph.D. there in Industrial and Social Psychology in 1967. Since then, he has had appointments at Yale University, Michigan State University and, for shorter periods, Bar-Ilan University (Israel, on a Fulbright), Peking University (P.R.C.) and the University of Aix-Marseilles (France). His research interests include organizational climate and culture, personnel selection, person-organization fit and service quality. He has published more than 80 articles and book chapters as well as six books on these topics, his latest book being *Winning The Service Game* (Harvard Business School Press, 1995) with David E. Bowen. He has also been active professionally, having served as President of the Society for Industrial and Organizational Psychology as well as the Organizational Behavior Division of the Academy of Management. He is also a Fellow of several professional societies, including the American Psychological Association and the Academy of Management. He serves on the editorial boards of the *Journal of Applied Psychology, Personnel Psychology*, the *International Journal of Service Industry Management* and the *British Academy of Management Journal*. He has also consulted with many private and public organizations, including, recently, Allstate Research and Planning Center, Prudential Real Estate Affiliates, Inc., the State of Pennsylvania and the State of Alabama.

Susan Schoenberger White received her B.A. from Rice University in 1994 and is currently a graduate student at the University of Maryland at College Park. She recently completed her Master's thesis on the topic of customer commitment and relationship marketing and is now working toward her Ph.D. in Industrial/Organizational Psychology.

Samia M. Siha is an Associate Professor of Operations Management at Kennesaw State University. She received her Ph.D. in Industrial Engineering from Iowa State University. Her research and teaching interests are in the area of operations management. Her recent research has focused primarily on service operation and quality management. She has published in *Advances in Industrial Engineering, Computers and Industrial Engineering*, the *Journal of Operational Research Society*, the *International Journal of Production Research* and the *International Journal of Service Industry Management*. She is a member of A.P.I.C.S., D.S.I. and P.O.M.S.

Nancy F. Stanforth is a member of the Faculty of Design, Housing and Merchandising, the College of Human Environmental Sciences, Oklahoma State University. She received her Ph.D. in Consumer and Textile Sciences from The Ohio State University, and has published in the areas of salesperson service in retail stores. She also has 15 years of experience in retail management and sales.

Tracy L. Tuten is a visiting Assistant Professor at Randolph-Macon College in Ashland, Virginia. She completed her doctoral work at Virginia Commonwealth University in Richmond, Virginia, in 1996. She received her degrees of Bachelor of Science in Business Administration and Master of Business Administration from East Carolina University in Greenville, North Carolina. Her primary research interests include the role of management in services marketing and problem-solving behaviors among employees, including the effects of communication on such behaviors.

Martin Wetzels is a Ph.D. Candidate at the Department of Marketing and Marketing Research at Maastricht University, the Netherlands. His current research interests include the management of service organizations, service marketing, quantitative methods in marketing and marketing channels. The journals in which he has published include the *European Journal of Marketing*, the *Journal of Customer Satisfaction, Dissatisfaction and Complaining Behavior*, the *International Journal of Logistics Management*, the *Journal of Business and Industrial Marketing* and various Dutch managerial journals.

Clifford E. Young is an Associate Professor at the Graduate School of Business, University of Colorado at Denver. His research thrust is in the area of marketing research methodology, survey development and research analysis. He has also conducted personal selling seminars for business and professional groups. He has experience in selling and sales deployment analysis. Dr. Young has published articles in the *Journal of Marketing*, the *Journal of Retailing*, the *Journal of Marketing Research*, the *Journal of Public Policy and Marketing*, the *Journal of Personal Selling and Sales Management* and others. His recent work includes the development of a parallel marketing information system for a health-care company to supplement their process control system.

J A I   P R E S S

Advances in Services Marketing and Management
Research and Practice Series

Edited by **Teresa A. Swartz**, *California Polytechnic State University—San Luis Obispo,* **David E. Bowen**, *Arizona State University-West,* and **Stephen W. Brown**, *Arizona State University*

Volume 5, 1996, 352 pp. $73.25
ISBN 0-7623-0009-4

CONTENTS: A Canonical Model of Consumer Evaluations and Theoretical Bases of Expectations, *Dawn Iacobucci, Amy L. Ostrom, Bridgette M. Braig and Alexa Bezjian-Avery.* Service Quality: The Construct, Its Dimensionality and Its Measuremnet, *Jozée Lapierre.* The Productivity Paradox is False: Information Technology Improves Services Performance, *James Brian Quinn.* Time Perceptions in Service Systems: An Overview of the TPM Framework, *Linda V. Green, Donald R. Lehmann and Bernd H. Schmitt.* Fair Service, *Elizabeth C. Clemmer and Benjamin Schneider.* The Antecedents of Brand Switching, Brand Loyalty and Verbal Responses to Service Failure, *Laurette Dubé and Manfred Maute.* Tight and Loose Comprehensive Customer Contact (3C) Plans, *David A. Collier.* Development of the Service System in a Manual Service Firm: A Case Study of the Danish ISS, *Jon Sundbo.* Cooperation in New Service Development: A Social Dynamic Approach, *Ariane M. von Raesfeld Meijer, Ko de Ruyter and Pépin Cabo.* The Fundamentals of Relationships: An Exploration of the Concept to Guide Marketing Implmentation, *Daphne E. Sheaves and James G. Barnes.* Friendship Over The Counter: How Social Aspects of Service Encounters Influence Consumer Service Loyalty, *Cathy Goodwin and Dwayne D. Gremler.* Critical Incidents in Internal Customer-Supplier Relationships: Results of an Empirical Study, *Patricia Neuhaus.* Service Quality in Professional Business Services: A Relationship Approach, *Aino Halinen.*

Also Available:

Volumes 1-4 (1992-1995) $73.25 each